INDIANTHUSIASM

Indigenous Studies Series

The Indigenous Studies Series builds on the successes of the past and is inspired by recent critical conversations about Indigenous epistemological frameworks. Recognizing the need to encourage burgeoning scholarship, the series welcomes manuscripts drawing upon Indigenous intellectual traditions and philosophies, particularly in discussions situated within the Humanities.

Series Editor

Dr. Deanna Reder (Cree-Métis), Associate Professor, First Nations Studies and English, Simon Fraser University

Advisory Board

Dr. Jo-ann Archibald (Stó:lō), Professor Emeritus, Educational Studies, Faculty of Education, University of British Columbia

Dr. Kristina Bidwell (NunatuKavut), Professor of English, University of Saskatchewan

Dr. Daniel Heath Justice (Cherokee Nation), Professor of First Nations and Indigenous Studies/English and Canada Research Chair in Indigenous Literature and Expressive Culture, University of British Columbia

Dr. Eldon Yellowhorn (Piikani), Associate Professor, First Nations Studies, Simon Fraser University

For more information, please contact:
Dr. Deanna Reder
First Nations Studies and English
Simon Fraser University
Phone 778-782-8192
Fax 778-782-4989
Emai:l dhr@sfu.ca

INDIANTHUSIASM

Indigenous Responses

Hartmut Lutz,
Florentine Strzelczyk,
Renae Watchman,
editors

WILFRID LAURIER UNIVERSITY PRESS

Wilfrid Laurier University Press acknowledges the support of the Canada Council for the Arts for our publishing program. We acknowledge the financial support of the Government of Canada. This work was supported by the Research Support Fund and by the German Association for Canadian Studies, and the University of Calgary's Faculty of Arts.

Library and Archives Canada Cataloguing in Publication

Title: Indianthusiasm : Indigenous responses / Hartmut Lutz, Florentine Strzelczyk, and Renae Watchman, editors.

Names: Lutz, Hartmut, editor. | Strzelczyk, Florentine, editor. | Watchman, Renae, 1974– editor.

Series: Indigenous studies series.

Description: Series statement: Indigenous studies | Includes bibliographical references and index.

Identifiers: Canadiana (print) 20190157941 | Canadiana (ebook) 20190158018 | ISBN 9781771123990 (softcover) | ISBN 9781771124010 (PDF) | ISBN 9781771124003 (EPUB)

Subjects: LCSH: Indigenous peoples—North America—Public opinion. | LCSH: Indigenous peoples—North America—Attitudes. | LCSH: Cross-cultural studies—Germany. | LCSH: Cross-cultural studies—North America. | LCSH: Intercultural communication—Germany. | LCSH: Intercultural communication—North America. | LCSH: Germany—Relations—North America. | LCSH: North America—Relations—Germany.

Classification: LCC E98.P99 I53 2019 | DDC 305.897—dc23

Front-cover image: Detail from *Miss Europe* (2016), by Kent Monkman (acrylic on canvas, entire work 84″ x 132″). Cover design by Martyn Schmoll. Interior design by Angela Booth Malleau.

© 2020 Wilfrid Laurier University Press
Waterloo, Ontario, Canada
www.wlupress.wlu.ca

This book is printed on FSC®-certified paper. It contains recycled materials, and other controlled sources, is processed chlorine free, and is manufactured using biogas energy.

Printed in Canada

IN MEMORIAM

Jo-Ann Episkenew
(1952–2016)

and

Ahmoo Angeconeb
(1955–2017)

CONTENTS

ACKNOWLEDGEMENTS

This volume would have not been possible without the help and support of contributors, students, colleagues, and senior university leaders.

First and foremost, we express our heartfelt gratitude to Indigenous colleagues for their time and interest in discussing Indianthusiasm with us and contributing the bulk of this volume.

We are grateful to the University of Calgary's Killam Grants Committee, which awarded Hartmut Lutz the Killam Visiting Scholar Fellowship that brought him to Calgary in 2012 and allowed us to begin this project. The University of Calgary's Faculty of Arts provided generous research funds to support the project, and additional funding was provided by the *Gesellschaft für Kanada-Studien* (GKS), the German Association for Canadian Studies.

The interviews we recorded required transcription. Many graduate students, both Indigenous and non-Indigenous, from the University of Calgary worked on these transcriptions. Vicki Bouvier, David Gallant, Paulina Maczuga, and Bernadette Raedler provided the very first drafts of the central part of this volume. A postdoctoral fellow at the University of Calgary, Christopher Geissler, provided initial feedback on early drafts of the introduction.

Dianne Hildebrand, experienced editor, strategic communications specialist, and designer of Indigenous teaching resources, supported the editing of the transcribed interviews and the overall format of the volume. Ruth Lutz-Preiskorn is to be credited with generating the index to the volume, increasing its usability for researchers and students.

We want to thank Siobhan McMenemy from Wilfrid Laurier University Press and copy editor Matthew Kudelka for their advice and guidance on bringing this anthology to completion. We are also very grateful for the constructive criticism the anonymous reviewers of our manuscript provided.

We dedicate this book to the memory of our friends Jo-Ann Episkenew (1952–2016) and Ahmoo Angeconeb (1955–2017), who sadly passed away before seeing this anthology in print. We remain immensely grateful for their generosity, their good humour, and the enlightening thoughts they so generously shared with us.

INTRODUCTION

I. FRAMING THE STORY

"Stories remind us of who we are and of our belonging," writes Margaret Kovach (2009, 94). Within Indigenous research frameworks, stories and research share an inseparable relationship in which stories serve as "both method and meaning" and present a "culturally nuanced way of knowing." Some stories are oral, others recall events, personal narratives of place and happening, in order to convey important insights into how to relate to the world (95). We begin this book by invoking a number of stories and events to frame the context in which Indigenous peoples in what is currently Canada position themselves, within a transatlantic network of Canadian and European relationships that are marked by converging and diverging legacies of colonialism.

In 2015, Renae Watchman boarded a non-stop Condor flight from Calgary to Frankfurt, Germany, to commence a year-long sabbatical. Condor took a unique approach to convey its pre-departure safety information. In lieu of a speech by live flight attendants, they had invested in a pre-recorded in-flight video featuring pop cultural icons to convey the safety features of the aircraft. In order to explain that "There is no smoking on our flights," the clip depicts Winnetou and Old Shatterhand, the two most iconic characters from German novelist Karl May's fictions about the North American West. The blood brothers are about to light a peace pipe when a flight attendant instructs them that smoking is not allowed on this aircraft. After twenty years of travel back and forth between North America and Germany, Renae was surprised that she had not confronted this previously. Even before leaving Turtle Island, travellers to Germany were being introduced to Indianthusiasm, the problematic German infatuation with the Indigenous peoples and cultures of North America.

In April 2018, *Segeberger Zeitung*, a northern German newspaper, carried an unusual job advertisement sponsored by a heart clinic.[1] A photograph showed a smiling young *indian*[2] woman with braided hair adorned by three feathers and wearing a bone choker necklace and a fringed top. Bold letters announced that she was "looking for blood-brothers and -sisters" to work in the heart catheter lab and radiology lab of said clinic, located in Bad Segeberg, the site of the annual open-air Karl May festival. The ad self-ironically referenced the city's popular fame as the German capital of re-enactment of Karl May's novels; this annual event draws thousands of German hobbyists, who flock to the city during the summer months (Sieg 2002, 219). Blood brotherhood is a core aspect of male bonding between May's fictitious Apache chief Winnetou and the equally fictitious German superhero Old Shatterhand from Saxony (Gemünden 2002, 248). Thus the heart clinic at Bad Segeberg locates itself consciously within popular German discourses of Indianthusiasm, even while it is oblivious to the cultural appropriation its advertisements condone.

Similarly, in the spring of 2018, an article in the *New York Times* described how European sports teams were blithely continuing to use Indigenous mascots, names, and rituals (Keh). Insulated from discussions on the North American continent about the cultural appropriateness of naming NFL football teams and professional baseball teams in this manner, sports teams from Belgium, Sweden, Great Britain, and the Czech Republic largely reject the arguments of critics who point out that such names and rituals reduce myriad heterogenous and culturally distinct Indigenous peoples to one blundering caricature. For these European teams, the cultural and political contexts of North America are unconnected; they argue that the appropriation of Indigenous symbols is an homage and a mark of respect and that North Americans have a historic debt to pay that simply does not apply to contemporary Europeans (Keh).

The cultural appropriation of Indigenous symbols, the commodification of Indigenous spirituality, and the copying of Indigenous practices and rituals have all been debated for thirty years.[3] The appropriation debate has recently resurged in Canada in the public cultural sphere. Its first iteration appeared in January 1990 with the publication of Lenore Keeshig-Tobias's article "Stop Stealing Native Stories," in the *Globe and Mail*, Canada's newspaper of record. That article sparked a debate regarding the political and cultural power differentials between Indigenous and non-Indigenous people in what is currently Canada. Then in 2017, Hal Niedzviecki, novelist and former editor of *Write Magazine*, published by the Writers' Union of Canada, wrote an editorial for that magazine titled "Winning the Appropriation Prize," in which he argued that he did "not believe in cultural appropriation" in the context of literature and encouraged writers to "write what they don't know." Niedzviecki soon resigned as editor when his editorial sparked outrage among members of Indigenous communities and others over a lack of understanding of the impacts of cultural appropriation. The debate led to a number of high-profile retractions, resignations, and reassignments in the Canadian media landscape, and the discussion over the ongoing commodification of Indigenous cultural production is still far from over. In response to this, Robin Parker (a non-Indigenous attorney) and the Indigenous Literary Studies Association (ILSA) organized and founded the Indigenous Voices Awards (IVA) in 2017 to "support and nurture the work of Indigenous writers in lands claimed by Canada."[4] Appropriation marginalizes and silences the works of art and culture that Indigenous people produce and publish about their ways of being and knowing, and about their lives past and present – including the impact that colonization has had on families and communities. The IVA was overwhelmingly successful in garnering financial support. What began as a goal to raise $10,000 through crowdfunding, resulted in raising $116,565 toward illuminating the diverse works of Indigenous creatives, while rejecting cultural appropriation. The conversations recorded in this book reflect diverse views on cultural appropriation: a number of the discussion partners feel less marginalized and silenced in Europe (where appropriation by hobbyists is so blatant) and often balance their acknowledgement of hobbyism against the earnest interest in their artistic works, while at the same time acknowledging the racism and indifference to their work during the pre-TRC era in Canada.

This book makes space for Indigenous voices in their experiences and exchanges with contemporary Europe, particularly Germany. These transatlantic exchanges and their academic, artistic, and journalistic lenses are framed by a history and ongoing presence of colonization and racism. As Indigenous peoples locate themselves as agents in the context of Canada's national history, the transatlantic perspective elucidates, complicates, and interrogates points of convergence and divergence in European and North American histories of appropriation and misrepresentation.

A number of recent studies[5] have explored and critiqued how since contact, European and North American non-Indigenous researchers, travellers, traders, artists, and writers have turned their gaze toward Indigenous peoples of North America. In the process, through a combination of scholarly and imaginative works, they have constructed the *indian,* whose ostensible positional marginality and inferiority within the imperial-colonial system of power has been cemented through a variety of interlocking institutions, discourses, and processes that have authorized this construction of *indianness* (L. Smith 2012, 1–2). In Germany, a nation that was only very briefly a colonial power and never in the Americas, a particular version of this construction emerged. This was the romanticized representation of Indigenous peoples that had circulated in popular culture since the eighteenth century and has reverberated in folklore, environmentalism, literature, art, theatre, film, and historical re-enactment.

The interviews collected in this volume return the colonial gaze and illuminate how Indigenous artists and intellectuals view this German fascination as well as how they articulate and position contemporary Indigenous identities across spatial, temporal, and cultural divides. Many of the collaborators were guests in Germany, a country that is profoundly implicated in one of the most heinous acts of systematic genocide in history and that to this day is struggling with continued racial discrimination and hatred. At the same time, the Indigenous discussion partners attempt to come to terms with the settler state built on Indigenous territories that is today's Canada, a country that is attempting to publicly atone for this colonial legacy. The Indigenous responses in this book offer a range of perspectives on both German and Canadian positions regarding Indigenous production and thus provide a commentary on a global market that generates a growing demand for Indigenous storytellers, performers, artists, authors, and critics, creating the conditions both for cultural appropriation and for Indigenous agency and intervention.

II. RESPECTING PROTOCOL

"Research," asserts Linda Tuhiwai Smith, "is one of the dirtiest words of the indigenous [sic] world's vocabulary" (2012, 1). It conjures up not just traumatic memories from the past, but also the mistrust of Western researchers and research, which continues today. Western scientific research is incriminated in some of the worst excesses committed against Indigenous people in the name of universal progress and knowledge. Measurements, extractions, recordings, interviews, and collections of Indigenous bodies, knowledges, and practices have served Western science to judge Indigenous peoples as culturally and ethnically inferior, to deny their claims to land and territories, and to refute their right to self-determination (L. Smith 2012, 1–2). Universities, in particular, have been bastions of Western knowledge where these methods and theories have been preserved well into the twenty-first century. Indigenous communities have developed treaties, charters, and declarations whose purpose is to require ethical codes of conduct and to articulate and safeguard intellectual and community property rights. Significant research has been conducted by Indigenous researchers related to ethical research conduct and to respectful research dissemination.[6] Today, research projects with Indigenous peoples require adherence to a set of protocols designed to foreground an Indigenous research agenda that sets out not just how to engage Indigenous communities as partners in the research, but also how to articulate clearly how the research will benefit Indigenous communities and how new knowledge will be shared (L. Smith 2012, 122–24).

Research protocols, argues Margaret Kovach, thus play an important role in decolonizing the research relationship (143). They place the responsibility on the researchers who plan to work with Indigenous peoples (Kovach 2009, 143), compelling them to justify their research interest within a framework that "is less about liability than relational." Building trusting relationships includes following protocols and validating cultural knowledge (147). Indigenous cultural knowledge is contained and communicated in oral systems, while traditions of Western science have privileged the written word.

By locating ourselves within kinship, our family relationships, our backgrounds, we reveal our intent as researchers, our relationship to the project, and our responsibility as researchers who seek to work with Indigenous researchers. It is our starting place, one that promises ethical conduct while also signalling our awareness of the multiple power dynamics at play between Indigenous peoples and Canadians, and Indigenous peoples and Europeans as part of a transatlantic exchange. Revealing our epistemological positioning exposes the interpretive lenses through which we as researchers will be conducting and making meaning of the research (Kovach 2009, 42–46). By validating Indigenous protocols and methods of knowledge transmission and putting these principles into practice, we seek to begin this project in a good way.

Renae Watchman

Yá'át'ééh! Tódich'íi'nii éínishłį dóó Kinya'áanii báshíshchíín. Áádóó Tsalagi éí da shichei dóó Táchii'nii éí da shinálí. Naat'áanii Nééz déé' íiyisí naashá. Dóó Saskatoon, Saskatchewan, Canada di shighaan. Shi éí Renae Watchman yinishyé.

Yá'át'ééh! I am Navajo and my clans are Bitter Water, born for the Towering House people. My maternal grandfather was Cherokee (Bird Clan) from Tahlequah, Oklahoma, and my paternal grandfather was from the Red Running Through the Water people. I am originally from Shiprock, New Mexico, but work in Calgary, Alberta, and live in Saskatoon, Saskatchewan, Canada.

My involvement in this project stems from my unique high school experiences, which I elaborate on in the Afterword. I mostly attended school just off the reservation in a border town, Farmington, New Mexico. I attended Navajo Academy, and during my junior year of high school, I was selected to participate in a year-long foreign exchange. I lived with a host family in Rellingen, Germany. Through this experience, I was introduced to the German fascination with *Indianer,* which further piqued my interest in learning more about the Germans. I additionally wanted to counter their perceptions about Indigenous peoples by educating them about where I was from and who I was as a Diné. My love for my host family, coupled with my scholarly interests, evolved into a lifelong journey of transdisciplinary studies that intersect at Indigenous Studies and German Studies. In university, I continued taking German-language classes, at first out of a desire to never lose contact with my host family, but ultimately my studies led to further training as a Germanist in graduate school. My upbringing, coupled with my education, combined to inform my graduate work, as I attempted to combine Indigenous ways of thinking and scholarship with those of other interdisciplinary topics. I earned my PhD in German Studies jointly with the Graduate Program in Humanities from Stanford University in 2007, and went on to an academic career that took me back to Germany many times to witness, experience, and research the German fascination with *Indianer*.

Florentine Strzelczyk

I was born south of Frankfurt, Germany, of Eastern European and German ancestry. The family on my mother's side were refugees from the East, and my father's family had both Polish and German roots. After the Second World War, my mother's family, which included a number of committed communists who had been in concentration camps during the Third Reich, settled in East Germany. When the Russian victors installed a socialist regime staffed by Moscow-trained German exiles, actively excluding camp survivors, my mother's family moved west. One of my grandfathers co-founded the Liberal Party in one of the West German provinces. As a young teenager, my father had survived the devastating Allied bombing of Dresden during the last days of the Second World War, but he never spoke about this experience until shortly before his death. My teachers in high school belonged to the student movement that, during the 1960s, had questioned German society about former Nazis serving in government, stressing society's refusal to face its responsibility for the atrocities committed under the Third Reich. My family history and my teachers sparked my interest in German history and literature concerned with the German past.

I studied at the Georg-August-Universität Göttingen, and much of my course work focused on the Holocaust and its legacies in relation to minorities in contemporary Germany. In 1990, I moved to Vancouver to attend the University of British Columbia as a PhD student on a one-year exchange, but remained to complete my PhD in German culture at UBC with a dissertation on the exclusionary and xenophobic mechanisms of the concept of *Heimat* in German culture. My focus throughout my academic career has been on the political implications of cultural representations of otherness in literature and film.

Hartmut Lutz

I was born in April 1945 in Rendsburg, a small town in northern Germany, which had by then doubled its numbers due to the influx of refugees from the east, among them my own family. This was three months after the liberation of Auschwitz by Russian troops, and twelve days before the horror of the Second World War ended, along with the Nazi terror that had provoked it. Participation in the student movement and the shameful legacy of being the son of a Nazi led to my lifelong commitment not to let nationalist chauvinism, fascism, and racism prevail again. In my youth, I was exposed to and partook in German *indian* hobbyism. Years later, after receiving a PhD in English literature in 1973, I began researching my post-doctoral habilitation on racial stereotyping in American and German cultural productions, with a focus on the portrayal of *indians* in literature. Over more than forty years of teaching American and Canadian literatures and cultures, I had the great privilege of visiting Turtle Island many times, for research and to teach at Indigenous institutions of higher education. I learned from Indigenous academics, artists, and elders, with whom I have enjoyed lifelong friendships, and have been able to invite Indigenous authors and scholars to Germany. Some of them are interviewed in this book. After decades of studying the ways in which we Germans have constructed our images of *Indianer*, I grew curious about how they, the Indigenous people of North America, saw us. The first-hand experiences of Renae Watchman and John Blackbird and their reflections on the German fascination with *Indianer* opened a new window for me, and I am immensely grateful for the opportunity that brought us all together in Calgary, where the concept for this book developed.

Working Together

Our common project developed gradually. During a visit to Germany, Florentine – at that time a professor of German film and literature at the University of Calgary – explored with Hartmut Lutz – then professor of North American literatures at Greifswald University – an institutional funding opportunity that would bring Hartmut for a longer visit to Calgary. When he was awarded the 2012–13 University of Calgary Killam Visiting Fellowship, Florentine and Hartmut co-taught a class titled "Refractions: German 'Indianthusiasm' – Aboriginal Responses" during the fall term 2012 in Calgary. Students examined the ideologically and politically complex and problematic European – particularly German – fascination with North American Indigenous peoples and examined artistic reactions to this phenomenon by Indigenous writers and visual artists. During Hartmut's stay in Calgary, he introduced Florentine to Renae Watchman, associate professor at Mount

Royal University in Calgary, and their conversations on the topic, along with the responses to the co-taught seminar, encouraged the three of us to put our minds together to see how we might explore this transatlantic exchange in conversation with the authors and thinkers who were our guests during the seminar as well as with others who were connected with Renae Watchman and her scholarly projects.

Like Florentine and Hartmut, Renae had published on the phenomenon of *indian* hobbyism, examining German powwows. Moreover, she had met many other Indigenous people from North America who had visited Germany or lived there permanently. Writer and artist Howie Summers (who works under the pen name John Blackbird), had also been to Germany many times. In Calgary, Howie and Renae shared their German experiences with Florentine and Hartmut. They brought their own first-hand biographical experiences to the project, as well as their contacts with other Indigenous individuals living in Germany. In a series of meetings and discussions, we, the editors, decided to ask Indigenous scholars and artists about their responses to Germany and German *indian* hobbyism. The discussions with these Indigenous conversation partners are captured in this book.

III. Ethical Research Methods

Many major epistemological obstacles have prevented Western scholars from learning from Indigenous knowledge. These include the racist legacy of colonialism, the ontological intolerance toward other *Weltanschauungen* embedded in Christianity, and the Enlightenment's anthropocentrism, as well as the axiological hubris of privileging Western literacy over orality in academia (Lutz 2018). Western research and Western cultures certainly privilege thought as the primary pathway to knowledge, placing feeling, spirit, and experience second or dismissing them outright (Kovach 2009, 41). Concepts, systems, and theories typically employed in Western academia impose a logic that, despite its claims to objectivity, is culturally and racially biased (Buendia 2003, 51). Furthermore, Western research frameworks rely on the written word and "the abstract quality of the written language," whose syllogistic reasoning is not easily able to capture and value the symbolic oral literacy and the values and world views of cultures that are based on oral traditions (Kovach 2009, 41). The result is that such research tends to reproduce and reinforce its own biases. Nevertheless, argues Kovach, Western research structures can be adapted to allow the "entrance of visual, and metaphorical representations of a research design that mitigates the linearity of words alone" (41).

The choice of conceptual frameworks illuminates researchers' standpoints and beliefs about knowledge production. Our choice to opt for the interview format – to conduct, record, and publish the conversations we hosted with Indigenous collaborators – reflects our commitment to oral processes of knowledge transmission. We sought to honour, observe, and follow the ethos of Indigeneity as identified by Jeannette Armstrong in her doctoral dissertation (2009, 320–34). Our book prefers orality as a medium, because oral knowledge transfer rests on immediate and direct personal conversations that foster relationality and that allow for a degree of personal agency, autonomy, and spontaneity written texts cannot convey. The conversations are immediate and directly personal, enabling participants to contextualize their perspectives and sometimes also the robust longevity of the relationship between the discussion partners. Almost all of the Indigenous contributors to this volume were guests at the University of Calgary, and we spent several days with them. The interviews were designed to be more discussions than formal interviews, and were held in Florentine's office, in hotel rooms, in restaurants, at private residences, and over the phone. The locales of the interviews encouraged discussion and supported the relationship between us, the editors, and discussion partners. The questions were initially set to explore the connection between Indigenous peoples and German Indianthusiasm that most of them would have encountered as frequent travellers to Germany for shows, readings, or exhibitions. However, we had also decided to follow our conversation partners into other stories they wanted to share with us, honouring oral tradition, where stories can never be decontextualized from the teller, where stories are agents to give insights into phenomena, and where there is an inseparable relationship between story and knowing (Kovach 2009, 94). We respected their preferences as they reflected on their European experiences with cultural, literary, and political movements and with decolonization and racism here in Canada. In many ways, those stories became the most valuable aspects of the volume. The discussion partners explored the complicated histories of colonization and racism of Germany and Canada, each of them positioning themselves in different ways in this web of connections according to their own paths.

Our overriding concern in our editing of the interviews was to attempt to retain the unique voices and ideas of the discussion partners. For example, changes in grammar or syntax were made only where the original made it difficult to understand the meaning. We retained many of the detours in the conversations for their storytelling value and illumination of personality, identity, and culture; however, we omitted some of the repetitions, hesitations, or the beginnings of ideas, so common in conversation, when they were not followed through. We also significantly reduced many conversational responses, such as "right," "okay," "I see," "um," that are natural in speaking but can be distracting when written, while retaining enough of these responses to indicate the friendly, relaxed, and relational back and forth of the discussion. The underlying principle was always one of respect for each discussion partner, whose on-the-spot thinking and responses proved invaluable, as was their time, which they graciously gave to this project.

Our project underwent ethics approval at the University of Calgary. This required written consent from the interviewees, who not only read and sanctioned the transcriptions but were also encouraged by us to elaborate and to clarify their thoughts during a post-interview phase. These and other legalized protocols are vital for interviewers and publishers within the historical experience of appropriation that has dominated Western research. What Saulteaux storyteller Alexander Wolfe so aptly called a "copyright based on trust," referring to the ethical foundation of research projects with Indigenous peoples, forms the underpinning of this project (Wolfe 1988, xiv; see also Lutz 2002, 113f.).

Indigenous protocol also guided our use of terms referring to ethnicity and national identity. We asked all conversation collaborators to introduce and locate themselves at the outset of each conversation. In our introduction and conclusion, we standardized our terminology to use "Indigenous" when referring to people living in North America, but "*indian*" or "*Indianer*" for the images non-Indigenous people have constructed of the former. Wherever possible, we have also used the proper names in the languages of the First Nations, Inuit, and Métis discussed. Respecting the words of conversation partners, we did not change the terms chosen by the individual interviewees themselves. Gregory Younging's *Elements of Indigenous Style* (2018) has been an indispensable guide for us to produce a manuscript that reflects the Indigenous people we worked with in an appropriate and respectful manner.

IV. German Indianthusiasm

German culture has produced an idealized and romanticized fascination with, and fantasies about, Indigenous peoples of North America that has its roots in the nineteenth-century German colonial imagination. In his attempt to pinpoint this broad and sustained popular enthusiasm, co-editor Hartmut Lutz deployed the term "Deutsche Indianertümelei" for the first time in his German-language study *"Indianer" und "Native Americans"* (1985). He derived the term from the German word "Deutschtümelei," which mocks ethnocentric, exaggerated, and nationalist celebrations of an idealized Germanness. In searching for an English term that would preserve the irony of the original German, Hartmut coined the English neologism "German Indianthusiasm" (Lutz 2003a, 167) and introduced it at the first international conference on German–Indian relations, held at Dartmouth College in 1999:

German 'Indianthusiasm' is racialized, in that it refers to Indian-ness [*Indianertum*] as an essentializing bioracial and concomitantly, cultural ethnic identity that ossified into stereotype. It tends to historicize Indians as figures of the past, and it assumes that anybody "truly Indian" will follow cultural practices and resemble in clothing and physiognomy First Nations people before or during first contact. Relatively seldom does *Indianertümelei* focus on contemporary Native American life.[7]

For over two hundred years Germans have found *Indianer* so fascinating that even today an Indian iconography is used in advertising. The most popular image of the *Indianer* is provided by Karl May's (1842–1912) fictional Apache chief Winnetou ... Indian lore is profitable and marketable, as some Native Americans travelling in Germany may attest ... There is a marked Indian presence in German everyday culture, even down to the linguistic level, where sentences like "ein Indianer weint nicht" (an Indian doesn't cry), "ein Indianer kennt keinen Schmerz" (an Indian braves pain), or figures such as "der letzte Mohikaner" (the Last of the Mohicans) have become part of everyday speech. (2003a, 169)

Different strands of historical experiences, anxieties, and projections have fuelled German Indianthusiasm throughout the twentieth century and continue to do so in the twenty-first. They include imaginings of wide-open landscapes unspoiled by humans that, since the nineteenth century, have been increasingly hard to find in an ever-more-crowded Europe. They conjure up romantic notions of an idealized authentic humanity, rooted in the desire to return to a pre-industrial state in the face of the belated and accelerated Industrial Revolution in Germany in the late 1800s (Klotz). Karl May (1842–1912), who devoured James Fenimore Cooper, produced countless novels of the American West and fabricated and distorted Indigeneity through his Apache hero, Winnetou. Ironically, May did not visit North America until four years before his death, long after his first three Winnetou novels were published, yet his books have been bestsellers for the past 125 years. Winnetou wages a heroic yet tragically ill-fated battle against unscrupulous White people and even helps his White German friend Old Shatterhand to stake the route for a planned railway. The books' juxtaposition of horseback-riding freedom and government corruption, spiced up by a good dose of Christological motifs, made Karl May's Winnetou novels prime candidates for adaptation and dramatization in the mostly open-air festivals that began in the 1940s. The Winnetou novels also became an underground sensation behind the Iron Curtain, further contributing to their enduring popularity today (Gemünden 2002, 250).

To be sure, *Indianer* had been fixed firmly in the German collective consciousness over a time spanning Imperial, Weimar, and Nazi Germany into the Cold War, a divided Germany, and continuing on into the present day (Lutz 1985, 244–444). Indigenous people travelled to Germany as early as the mid-nineteenth century, for example, when the Anishinaabe Methodist minister Kah-ge-ga-ga-bow (George Copway) came there as an official delegate to the Third General World Peace Congress at Frankfurt am Main in August 1850 (Peyer 1997, 224–77; Lutz 2003b, 217; D.B. Smith 2014, 164–211). A few decades later, in the aftermath of the Indian Wars and genocidal policies that were occurring on American and Canadian soil, some Indigenous people chose to leave their sufferings behind and travel with human zoos and *Buffalo Bill's Wild West* show, which offered enormously popular "live" performances, and brought Indigenous performers from North America to the hinterlands of Germany. In 1910, a Lakota man from Pine Ridge, South Dakota, travelled to Germany to work as a live human exhibit at the Hagenbeck Zoo in Hamburg. His name was Edward Two Two (ca. 1851–1914), and around 1913 he returned to Germany to work at the Sarrasani Circus in Dresden, where he is buried.[8] Vine Deloria Jr. has viewed the work of the men and women from the Plains at the human zoos and *Buffalo Bill's Wild West* show in positive terms, foregrounding their agency and self-determination, in that their employment enabled them to be more independent of the US government and its policies, and arguing that Buffalo Bill "treated the Indians [*sic*] as mature adults capable of making intelligent decisions and of contributing to an important enterprise."[9]

German Indianthusiasm also finds it roots in Germany's much desired but never quite materialized transformation into a colonial nation. Recent research has revealed the peculiar extent to which the colonial idea in Germany prospered before Germany even existed as a nation or had entered its short-lived era of colonialism. German "colonialism without colonies" culminated in a distinct cult that took root in the later part of the nineteenth century, a kind of *Handlungsersatz* – that is, a surrogate for action that substituted and compensated for real colonial power. In travel accounts, political pamphlets, and print news, Germans imagined that they would be better, kinder, and more just colonizers than other European nations if they were just granted that opportunity; this premise prepared the ideological ground on which Indianthusiasm and its cultural exploits would grow (Lutz 2003a, 175; Strzelczyk 2014, 347–49; Zantop 1997, 6). Incidentally, at the end of the First World War, Germany was stripped of the very few overseas possessions it had acquired at the end of the nineteenth century, none of them in the Americas. Yet the idea of colonialism continued to play a complicated role in Germany.

Germany's loss of its colonies after the First World War worked much to Hitler's advantage. It allowed him to promise the German people a racial state in which colonial expansionism would return to Germany its status as a world power. German standards of ethnic purity would elevate Germans to "carriers of civilization" (Klotz 2005). Novels and travel accounts from that time were besotted with foreign spaces, including Canada, and showed immigrant Germanness (*Auslandsdeutschtum*) functioning as a civilizing bulwark against the Canadian wilderness while at the same time incorporating romanticized notions of Indigenous life and values as a critique of modernity's ills (Strzelczyk 2014, 349). In these works, Indigenous people are described as noble and dying races suffering under the unjust rule of the English, yet their narratives are subsumed under fascist mythemes of the superiority of German culture (Strzelczyk 2012, 197–220). Curiously, Adolf Hitler kept all of Karl May's books on his bookshelf, and in times of crisis he would read May's works the way others might read the Bible (Lutz 2003a, 178). In May's fictional Apache chief Winnetou, Hitler saw an exemplary military commander (cf. Lutz 1985, 360–61; Haible 1998, 83–86; Penny 2014, 169–205), just as other Nazi contemporaries turned Indigenous peoples into icons of ferocious nationalism and nobility (Haible 1998; Usbeck 2015).

During the post–Second World War era, when occupation authorities insisted that the Holocaust be remembered, the Wild West emerged as a site of misplaced racial imagination, where the roles of victim, avenger, and perpetrator of genocide could be redistributed (Sieg 2002). The desire to delve into a distant, vaguely defined past where it was "the others," and not Germans, who were the perpetrators, or where resistance against a socialist East German regime could be indirectly tested, motivated these fantasies and identifications during the postwar years. The traditions established by May resulted in many post-1945 cultural manifestations of Indianthusiasm that have been well documented: the West German *Winnetou* films from the 1960s and the East German *Indianerfilme* from the 1960s and 1970s (Gemünden 2002, 244; Lischke and McNab 2005, 1); the continued popularity of the annual open-air Karl May Festival; German hobbyism or Indianism (Reagin 2012;[10] Sieg 2002); the phenomenon of German powwow dancing (Watchman 2005), and increased interest in Indigenous art, and in Indigenous spirituality in the context of the German New Age (Briese 2005), all attest to the currency of this discourse (Lutz 2003b, 217–45).

There have been plenty of studies about the relationship between Europeans and Indigenous peoples from European perspectives by non-Native scholars,[11] but only recently have Indigenous scholars been critically examining the same phenomenon. In 2005, David T. McNab and the German

Canadian scholar Ute Lischke edited a collection of essays titled *Walking a Tightrope: Aboriginal People and Their Representations*, in which Indigenous and non-Indigenous scholars address silencing and (mis)representations of First Nations and Métis people in public discourses. Co-editor Renae Watchman's pioneering essay on powwow culture in Germany draws attention to the wealth of transatlantic contacts between Germans and Indigenous people from North America. The contributors to the present volume draw a complex picture of how the lives and works of contemporary Indigenous people from what is currently Canada have been influenced, questioned, enriched, and changed by engaging with Germans and Germany. The interviewees, through their work in or about Germany, are likely to alter the self-referential German debates about Indigenous authenticity located in a distant past, and bring the contemporary concerns of Indigenous people to the forefront of these debates.

V. HOBBYISM

Indianer hobbyism – a popular aspect of German Indianthusiasm – is a veritable industry in contemporary Germany and other European nations. Western and so-called *indian* theme parks (including Pullman City in Bavaria and El Dorado in Templin/Berlin) enjoy steady popularity, and the German hobbyist scene attracts people of all social backgrounds and ages to camps and clubs that practise beading, powwow dancing, and (pre-reservation) Indigenous lifestyles. By the early twentieth century, hobbyist clubs were sprouting all over Germany; one of the oldest was the Cowboy Club of Munich, founded in 1913. Hobbyist clubs were organized throughout the twentieth century, attracting members from all over Germany.[12] A multitude of influences have shaped hobbyist practices and preferences, including English-language fiction, Karl May's bestselling books, and movies based on May's novels produced on both sides of the German border (Gemünden 2002, 243–56). Penny estimates there are between 40,000 and 100,000 Germans who participate in *Indianer* hobbyist clubs. "Shared by men and women alike, this fascination cuts across political, confessional, social, and generational boundaries. It is also much more than a current, postmodern enchantment with 'the primitive'" (2014, 169). Describing her hobbyist activities, an *Indianer* club member explains:

> Our camp is always in summer, in July for two weeks. During this time, we live in tipis, we wear only Indian clothes. We don't use technology, and we try to follow Indian traditions. We have those [pretending to be] Lakota, Oglala, Blackfoot Blood, Siksika, Pawnee … and we go on

warpath against each other day and night, anytime at all. In two weeks, every tribe can fight each other. We don't know when somebody will attack or when they will come to steal our horses. And the battles are always exciting, too. I really enjoy them. (Holley 2007, 189)

According to Penny, German hobbyism, or surrogate Indigeneity as he calls it, is directed toward a romanticized pre-reservation past and is obsessed with performing presumed authentic[13] Indigeneity – which is, however, thoroughly mediated and shaped by German historical and political experiences, anxieties, and projections.

German and European Indianthusiasm and hobbyism have been debated for decades by journalists, scholars, museum curators, and filmmakers. As early as 1966, an article in a Cologne newspaper, "When Papa becomes a Sioux," showed West Germans defending their hobbyist activities as legitimate and serious because they were really an ethnological association (Penny 2014, 172). Additionally, there are two early documentaries: one made in 1995 by John Paskievich titled *If Only I Were an Indian*, about Czech Indianists, and another titled *Seeking the Spirit: Plains Indians in Russia*, directed in 1999 by Lakota anthropologist Bea Medicine. John Blackbird's documentary *Indianer* (2007) has also contributed to understanding German hobbyism. Colin Calloway's, Gerd Gemünden's and the late Susanne Zantop's aforementioned book, *Germans and Indians: Fantasies, Encounters, Projections* (2002), is still considered pioneering, and most recently H. Glenn Penny's 2013 book *Kindred by Choice: Germans and American Indians since 1800,* has added to the scholarship. Penny cites *Kansas City Star* reporter Daniel Rubin, who interviewed a hobbyist, Jörg Diecke, and described him as "neither a social misfit nor insane. His wife was a dentist, and his compatriots included doctors, engineers, cooks, and scholars."[14] Co-editor Renae Watchman was invited to Diecke's home in Grimma, replete with a small bison herd and a garden with plants from North America. Diecke, an active elder and leader in the organization "Friends of the Crow," was respectful, humble, and knowledgeable.

Indianer hobbyism bears resemblance to, but is also markedly different from, the hobbyism that has become a pervasive "cherished American tradition" and a means of defining American identity and narrativizing American history, a phenomenon that Shari M. Huhndorf has described as "going native" (2001, 2). The Woodcraft Indian and Boy Scout movements that began at the end of the nineteenth century, and the conservationist movement from the early twentieth century, as well as present-day Indigenous-inspired communes and the New Age consumption of *indian* cultural objects, artistic designs, and spiritual traditions, have imagined Indigenous peoples as idealized versions of themselves and as an embodiment of values and virtues lost in a consumer-dominated world of technological progress.

While these forms of hobbyism or going native frequently entail benevolent gestures toward Indigenous peoples or mount a cultural critique of Western civilization, they ultimately subsume Indigenous histories under the progress-driven project of colonization, besides reaffirming White dominance and racial hierarchies by making a sanitized, depoliticized, and romanticized version of Indigenous life subservient to the national narrative of the dominant culture (Huhndorf 2001, 5–6). The instances of hobbyists going native described by Huhndorf all involve adopting a mythical version of Indigenous life and practices in ways that regenerate White American identity, naturalize the bloody and violent conquest of the Americas, and reinscribe the racial hierarchies that define American society.

As an example, the American Boy Scout and Woodcraft Indian movements appropriated Indigenous practices: they established tribes, camped in tipis, practised archery, symbolically scalped each other, and smoked peace pipes, all in an attempt to build boys into true American men – principled and physically fit. Yet in doing so, they were subsuming a fictitious Indigeneity under an all-American identity (Turner Strong 2008; Turner Strong and Posner 2010). Parallel developments occurred in Canada (Francis 1992). Similarly, the modern conservationist movement of the 1960s and 70s idealized North America's Indigenous peoples as the first ecologists, whose wisdom would provide an alternative to the mechanistic exploitation of the environment. Yet even while these groups began to adopt what they believed to be Indigenous values and teachings from an already distant mythical past, broad segments of the public were turning against treaty rights and portraying Indigenous peoples as exploiters of the land, exemplified by the Washington fishing dispute from the early 1970s (Cornell 1985, 104). As Huhndorf (2001) shows in her study, these competing projections and imaginations – that Indigenous peoples were to be both pacified and emulated – became embedded in the North American cultural imagination and central to a sense of national identity.

German *Indianer* hobbyism also lives off the truncated, compressed, and depoliticized version of a mythical Indigenous past that Huhndorf describes. Some of the contributors to our volume describe their encounters with German hobbyists who claim to be the rightful custodians and heirs of a past yet authentic Indigeneity that contemporary Indigenous peoples have in fact abandoned. Claims like theirs disavow European colonial history as well as German colonial desire. During the post–Second World War era, German hobbyism took on new meanings as a nation of perpetrators looked to refashion itself into a nation of victims – a phenomenon well described in Alexander and Margarete Mitscherlich's famous book *The Inability to Mourn* (1967).

The interviews collected in this volume do not privilege an academic discourse per se. Nor are they united on how to evaluate this phenomenon. The opinions expressed by the contributors range from condemnation and rejection of hobbyism as appropriation, to understanding and even sympathy in the context of Indigenous history and experiences as well as of German experiences of fascism that have contaminated German tradition and ethnic practice as a whole.

VI. Indianthusiasm and Academia

Western academia is one of the most influential spaces where colonial epistemologies and knowledges have been produced, maintained, and circulated. Post-secondary research institutions and their century-old archives of knowledge, data, methodologies, and concepts that validate one another, perpetuating colonial ideologies, have been slow to open themselves to Indigenous frameworks and methodologies. Academia consists of tight networks of scholars: they evaluate one another's grants and publications, dominate hiring and graduate supervisory committees, and thus regulate entrance into academia. This relatively closed system has made it difficult for Indigenous scholars to permeate academia and for Indigenous knowledge systems to challenge Western knowledge (Kovach 2009, 83). At the same time, as Margaret Kovach notes, Western academia today has been marked by an increasingly non-homogeneous environment "evoking new theoretical discourses of inclusiveness engaging the once invisible and excluded" (156). The release of the final report of the Truth and Reconciliation Commission's (TRC) *94 Calls to Action* has tasked Canadian post-secondary institutions with critically re-examining the ways in which they have been teaching and researching. Those who are committed to decolonizing and Indigenizing the academy will have to scrutinize the long-standing colonial practices that have profoundly affected Indigenous peoples, acknowledging their truths, and understanding how these practices have come to be so deeply embedded in our educational systems. This work has begun in the academy, and it will "test every aspect of the 'tried and true' aspects of institutional knowledge centres" (156).

Universities have narrativized their own process of knowledge generation as neutral and objective. In response to the TRC's calls to action, post-secondary institutions have now set themselves the goal of transforming themselves to include Indigenous knowledges alongside Western ones by bringing the historical struggle for Indigenous rights into the academy, connecting Indigenous rights and cultural survival with the mission of post-secondary education, and bringing Indigenous knowledge and Indigenous researchers into the academy (158). One example of the systemic underrepresentation of Indigenous peoples in the academy is the small number of Indigenous faculty and the ways in which Indigenous peoples' scholarly contributions to knowledge have been left out of the larger disciplinary conversations.

German Indianthusiasm has had a number of transcultural effects on academia that can help elucidate the complexities and challenges involved for those Indigenous researchers who are now entering and transforming the culture and structure of the academy. In the 1970s, American and Canadian Studies programs grew and expanded at German universities, many of them with a pronounced emphasis on Indigenous Studies, including Indigenous politics, rights, language, literature, and art. Today, the Association for Canadian Studies in German-Speaking Countries (GKS) is the third-largest Canadian Studies association worldwide. There are twenty-three Canadian Studies centres in Austria, Switzerland, and Germany, as well as programs for Indigenous and Native Studies such as the Center for Comparative Native and Indigenous Studies, founded at the University of Mainz in 2011. The academic focus in these programs on Indigenous peoples and their present-day struggle for rights and recognition – a struggle necessitated by colonialism – has often furthered the critical examination of German Indianthusiasm as a popular and ideologically problematic phenomenon.

These programs have attracted a number of Indigenous scholars, who decided to complete their graduate degrees in Germany rather than Canada or the United States. At the University of Greifswald, two Indigenous scholars have earned their PhDs within the last decade. The late Jo-Ann Episkenew, professor of English literature and director of the Indigenous Peoples' Health Research Centre (IPHRC) at the University of Regina, to whose memory our volume is dedicated, defended a thesis on Indigenous literature in 2006, which was later published in Canada as the award-winning book *Taking Back Our Spirits: Indigenous Literature, Public Policy, and Healing* (2009). In 2009, Jeannette Armstrong, now a Canada Research Chair in Okanagan Indigenous Knowledge and Philosophy, carried Indigenous knowledge right into the heart of Western academia by submitting and defending her thesis, *Constructing Indigeneity: Syilx Okanagan Oraliture and tmix*ʷ*centrism*, also at the University of Greifswald.

In their interviews for this volume, both Armstrong and Episkenew speak about their motives for entering PhD programs in Germany, their experiences in and with German academia, and their roles as knowledge brokers who taught their teachers as much as they learned from them. Episkenew was a mature student and a single mother at the time she entered the PhD program in Germany. The fact that German PhDs focus solely on producing original research and do not require course work at all allowed Episkenew to remain in Canada in her hometown, where she connected regularly with Hartmut, her German supervisor, visiting the Greifswald campus at intervals. The program allowed for flexibility, and focused as it was on original research, it proved to be more receptive to Indigenous knowledges and systems of thought. Episkenew had to battle perceptions of her German PhD at home in Canada, where both academics and non-academics would make assumptions about the rigour of academic work in the context of German Indianthusiasm. In Episkenew's case, the problematic legacy of German Indianthusiasm had fuelled not just an earnest engagement with contemporary Indigenous peoples in German academia, but also a certain openness toward Indigenous research methodologies.

Jo-Ann Episkenew was the first Métis woman to earn a PhD in Germany; and Jeannette Armstrong the first First Nations (Syilx Okanagan) woman we know of to do so. Armstrong's thoughts on German academia and her PhD studies at Greifswald pick up much the same themes as those emphasized by Jo-Ann Episkenew in her interview. German academia was attractive to Armstrong because of its strong commitment to the study and protection of the environment – a commitment that reverberates through German public discourse and culture. Armstrong recalls how the relationship with her co-supervisor Konrad Ott evolved, beginning with his insistence on forming a set of arguments around a thesis and her rebuttal that her process was grounded in Indigenous ways of gathering all information and illuminating an issue from all angles before forming a thesis or argument or making a decision. Armstrong recounts how the dialogue with Ott evolved over the five years she worked on her PhD, from a teacher/student hierarchical relationship into a much more equal relationship where each learned from the other and grew stronger as a result of challenging the other's methodologies and approaches. Ott's research expertise and focus on environmental ethics complemented her interest in Okanagan Indigenous oral literature and world view.

Both Armstrong and Episkenew were attracted to pursuing a PhD in Germany because of their previous strong relationship with Hartmut Lutz. In their interviews, they speak about his extensive engagement with Indigenous peoples across North America and about the trust they had in him and his work. At the same time, their separate decisions to pursue a PhD in Germany despite having had other options in Canada also speak to the status and system of Indigenous graduate research at Canadian universities.

It is in graduate education that a new generation of Indigenous researchers is practising and honing Indigenous research methodologies and frameworks. At the same time, this is the area in the academy where Indigenous researchers require the strong support of senior Indigenous and non-Indigenous faculty in order to challenge Western scientific narratives of objectivity and introduce Indigenous research frameworks and knowledge into the academy. Both Indigenous and non-Indigenous supervisory committee members need to understand the importance of community relationships as the basis for Indigenous research; they also need to appreciate the values of holistic, relational learning and support the curiosity that new Indigenous researchers bring to their topics (Kovach 2009, 164–65). To encourage Indigenous graduate researchers at Canadian universities, Kovach urges current faculty to know and be empathetic to new Indigenous researchers and their short history in and often negative experiences with Western academia and its codified research practices. Faculties need to offer a non-prescribed space in which Indigenous epistemologies can grow, to redefine the hierarchical roles within the competitive research landscape, and to fully engage Indigenous communities in the trajectory and outcome of Indigenous research (169–73). It seems that for both Jo-Ann Episkenew and Jeannette Armstrong, the presence of these conditions in Germany helped motivate them to pursue their graduate degrees there at the time.

Indigenous graduate research in North America presents only one aspect of the work universities are presently engaging in. In December 2015, the Truth and Reconciliation Commission of Canada issued its Calls to Action, which placed education at the centre of the reconciliation process. The TRC's *94 Calls to Action* ask Canadians to eliminate educational and employment gaps between Indigenous and non-Indigenous Canadians, address the backlog of Indigenous students seeking a post-secondary education, and incorporate Indigenous education into existing programming. Many universities are embracing the recommendations. They have hired Indigenous senior administrators tasked with leading Indigenization initiatives that include building Indigenous strategies designed to increase and retain Indigenous student populations and faculty members, setting up scholarships and bursaries, changing tenure requirements for Indigenous scholars, rethinking thesis requirements for Indigenous graduate students, creating elders' councils, and designing spaces for Indigenous engagement. As this work accelerates, many universities continue to ponder the question of how foundational these changes should be. How is the academy to transform itself to become truly inclusive of Indigenous practices, methodologies, and pedagogies, and how is it going to build relationships with multiple peoples and communities? Simply adding Indigenous peoples to increase representation or adding more courses with Indigenous content does not address the core structures of post-secondary institutions, whose systems – from the values and methods in teaching, learning, and research all the way to financial and human resources – have made them inhospitable and inequitable places for Indigenous people and for the incorporation of Indigenous perspectives and knowledges. Scholars Adam Gaudry and Danielle Lorenz's article "Indigenization as Inclusion, Reconciliation, and Decolonization: Navigating the Different Visions for Indigenizing the Canadian Academy" (2018) offers critical insights into these challenges, and more. For many Indigenous scholars in the academy, shifting the framework of all university programs is central to the reconciliation process, which is about recognizing truths that include Indigenous perspectives and ways of knowing, being, doing, and connecting. In a 2018 article "Doing Indigenous Work: Decolonizing and Transforming the Academy," Maori scholars Graham Hingangaroa and Linda Tuhiwai Smith advocate for deeper engagement. For Canadian institutions, this will be a very long process.

Indigenizing the academy in Germany and other European countries has been less an institution-wide endeavour than one that involves the disciplines of American, Canadian, and Indigenous Studies. The engagement of European scholars and students with Indigenous rights, politics, justice, literature, and arts takes place in a cultural context of continued broad and unreflected popular fascination with North American Indigenous cultures of the past. Their engagement is in part an attempt to expose those romanticized notions and replace them with a community-focused approach that is respectful of Indigenous knowledges. In Europe, the attempts to bring Indigenous knowledge and methodologies into European academia and apply them alongside Western knowledge have also created ripples, with a marked German Canadianist contribution: the entire 2014 annual conference of the GKS was focused on the topic "Indigenous Knowledge and Academic Discourses"; this was followed in 2016 by an international conference, "Postcolonial Knowledges," convened by postcolonial scholar Kerstin Knopf at the University of Bremen.[15] Scholars took up the discussion of Indigenous knowledges and Western academia. They advocated listening with respect and exploring the challenges that Indigenous epistemologies, axiology, and methodologies entail for Western scholars and academic institutions.[16]

Based on Armstrong's thesis, non-Indigenous readings on relationality in natural sciences,[17] and the pioneering interventions by Indigenous scholars cited below, Hartmut Lutz has identified some of the major obstacles that have prevented Western scholars from learning from Indigenous knowledges, among them the racist legacy of colonialism, the ontological intolerance toward other world views entailed in Christianity and other monotheistic religions, the Enlightenment's anthropocentrism and "hyper-separation" from nature (Kuokkanen 2007, 6), as well as the axiological hubris of literacy over orality in academia (Lutz 2018). Engaging the works of Indigenous scholars,[18] Hartmut (2018, 74–80) recently argued that the ethics of relationality, accountability, and land-embedded Indigeneity appear as foundational in all the Indigenous knowledges and are entailed in an ethos, which Armstrong described as "Indigeneity" (Armstrong 2009, 309–10, 320–23, 332–34). Our decision to base this book on recorded oral interviews, rather than asking the interviewees to submit written essays, is contingent on respecting and honouring this ethos of Indigenous traditional knowledge.

VII. Contributors and Their Work

Indigenous artists, authors, performers, researchers, and intellectuals have increasingly asserted their voices over the past several decades, telling their own stories, developing Indigenous methodologies and approaches, and actively shaping the socio-political context surrounding them. Using English as their lingua franca, employing canvas and acrylics, theatre stages, film cameras and performing arts, scholarly publishing and the internet, the individuals assembled in this volume adopt a diversity of methods and approaches to respond to German Indianthusiasm and reflect on contemporary Indigeneity and its construction both past and present. Some expose, reflect, and deconstruct the assumptions Germans have held about them in the sense of "writing back" (Ashcroft, Griffiths, and Tiffin 1989); others create spaces to reflect on the complexity of a place and a people that have produced consistently petrified representations of Indigeneity fixed in an imagined and romanticized past, even while committing themselves to environmentalism and manifesting ongoing support for Indigenous cultural production, resulting in new opportunities for transatlantic and transnational exchange. Still others utilize their position of spatial distance from Canada as observers and guests in Germany to critically reflect on the converging and diverging colonial and genocidal histories of both countries and the legacies of these, which reverberate in the present. In fact, the parts of the interviews where the discussion partners employ their connections with Germany to frame such diverse topics as Indigenous literary theory, the meaning of racist hierarchies in both countries, the many faces of connections to the land, and the appropriation of Indigenous culture and spirituality, belong to the most insightful aspects of this volume. Many authors we interviewed have been visiting artists at German or Austrian universities; others have lived and worked in Germany. All of them position themselves as critical interlocutors and agents shaping a transatlantic dialogue that began centuries earlier.

For decades, Indigenous visual artists have been engaging with Western art. Canadian artists like the late Inuit novelist, poet, and cartoonist Alootook Ipellie (1951–2007), the late Métis painter Bob Boyer (1948–2004), and the recently deceased Anishnaabe[19] visual artist Ahmoo Allen Angeconeb (1955–2017), whose voice we are honoured to preserve in this volume, and to whose memory this book is co-dedicated, have employed their art to critically engage German and European heritage.

The "Anishnaabe print maker," as Angeconeb modestly called himself, went to Europe in the 1980s looking for opportunities to exhibit his work in Switzerland and Germany (Angeconeb 1987; 2001). He soon realized that Germans were mainly interested in Plains cultures of the past, rather than Woodland First Nations or contemporary Indigenous peoples; at the same time, he experienced their genuine interest in traditional Anishinaabe philosophy, which he saw as compatible with German ecological concerns. His interest in European pre-Christian mythologies and medieval heraldic and Stone Age cave paintings led to a number of hybrid works that drew on Anishinaabe iconography as well as on European tribal and modern influences. He employed a variety of styles and art forms to interact with European art, mythology, and popular culture, simultaneously drawing from Indigenous traditions and approaches. In his works, contemporary urbanity and Woodland cultures' storied beings converse with European heraldry and fauna. The Pomeranian gryphon is said to have nested in the town centre of Greifswald before he was driven away in the early twelfth century by monks, who felled the trees to build their monastery and convert the Pomeranian tribes to Christianity. After one of Angeconeb's repeated visits, he created a large linocut featuring the Pomeranian gryphon in conversation with the Anishinaabe Thunderbird, an image used for Canadian Studies at the two Pomeranian universities, Greifswald, Germany, and Szczecin, Poland.

In our interview with Angeconeb, he remembered the irony of having exhibited "pagan paintings" in a Cologne chapel, which reminded him of the chapel at the residential school he attended. He saw himself as a cultural ambassador, both in the arts and in traditional spirituality, and having been endorsed by his elders to share his gifts, he felt free to do so with those Germans who were as deeply concerned about the earth and its environment as he was. Thus, he supported the perspective and works of German artist Joseph Beuys, who believed that "shamanism will help save the world" (Gasyuk 2016).

Jeannette Armstrong's connection with Germans and German culture draws on personal relationships, professional experiences, and her position as an Indigenous writer, activist, and scholar who pursued a PhD at a German university. She finds German interest in Indigenous cultures and politics to be often well informed – especially regarding Native American and First Nations resistance to treaty violations and settler intrusion – and generally respectful, and she attributes this to Germans' self-critical acknowledgement of their history and to the academic environment in which she spent much of her time. Among the reasons for pursuing an interdisciplinary PhD in Germany, she includes a perceived greater readiness in Germany than in Canada at the time to listen to and accept Indigenous knowledges and methodologies. She gives as an example the Syilx Okanagan Nation's *Enowk-inwix^w* process of discovering facts communally and drawing conclusions only after listening to everyone with an open heart and mind. In Germany, she was permitted to take this approach and thereby opt out of the traditional Western structure for writing a doctoral thesis. In German academia, she encountered openness to the traditional orality of knowledge transmission in Indigenous cultures. She also feels that German environmentalism, which often incorporates a sense of a relationship to nature and connectedness with the land, differs from that of European settlers in Canada. Currently a Canada Research Chair at UBC Okanagan, she has perceived an increasingly greater interest in Indigenous knowledge among her students.

John Blackbird (Howie Summers), Cree, originally from Waterhen Lake, Saskatchewan, considers Germany his second homeland. He lived in Germany on and off for twelve years from 1997 to 2009. He earned his film degree and made two documentaries, *Indianer* and *Powwow,* now available on YouTube. He experienced that it could be economically beneficial to be *Indianer* in Germany, as he was recruited to talk about his people and his culture to German audiences. Meanwhile, he raised two daughters between Canada and Germany, where they eventually settled. He preferred to have his daughters grow up among the cobblestone streets of a small German town, rather than on the reserve in Saskatchewan. Blackbird had grown up on a farm in rural Saskatchewan, where racism against First Nations remains visceral. In Germany, he attests that his daughters were free to take long hikes, play safely with friends in the neighbourhood, and travel with ease. Blackbird shares that while he was growing up in Canada, he did not take advantage of the cultural teachings passed on through family members. It was in Germany, where he saw the value of elders' stories and histories, that he began to appreciate his culture more. While he experienced racism in Saskatchewan, the more passive racism in Germany propelled him into educating, public speaking, filmmaking, writing poetry and prose, and writing for online magazines about the German hobbyists, some of whom he had befriended.

Warren Cariou, of Métis, German, and Norwegian ancestry, is the Canada Research Chair for Creative Writing at the University of Manitoba. He visited Germany in the early 2000s as part of a lecture tour and a full-term guest professorship in connection with Canadian and Indigenous Studies programs in Germany. His first-hand experience of German Indianthusiasm prompted him to reflect on how literature and culture can be considered from very close and within, but also from a cultural distance, resulting in important new insights. His experience abroad strengthened his view that Indigenous literatures are both resilient and important enough to deserve to be read and understood from many perspectives. Cariou's encounter with European colonial legacies such as the display of Indigenous people in the eighteenth and nineteenth centuries, and his observation of how European nations are working to confront the shameful parts of their histories, led to his reassessment of Canadian identity – of how it fundamentally assumed its own goodness while conveniently disregarding the colonialism on which the country was built. Canadian society could, asserts Cariou, reflect more self-critically on its past and its colonial relationship with Indigenous people, and writers can and should support these efforts to confront a shameful national history. Cariou reflects on why Indigenous peoples receive positive attention in Germany compared to other minorities, drawing on Slavoj Žižek's account of the fantasmic organization of enjoyment, which provides a compelling explanation for ethnic nationalism. Žižek argues that enjoyment is what holds a community together, that enjoyment amounts to more than a collection of features, specific traditions, foods, and myths, and is in fact the added value that results from these practices (Žižek 1993). In that respect, argues Cariou, Indigenous people circulating to and from Germany will never pose the same perceived threat to Germans as other minorities do. Although he does not have first-hand experiences with German hobbyist communities, Cariou assumes their intent is not disrespectful – indeed, in East Germany hobbyism served as a point of resistance and was motivated by an idealism not intended to diminish the identity of Indigenous peoples.

Asked about her "tribal identity," Jo-Ann Episkenew identified "many tribes," such as "educated Native women with PhDs," "mothers, grandmothers, and great-grandmothers," "Métis Nation of Manitoba, now transplanted to Saskatchewan," and "trashy paranormal romance readers." Her first contact with Germany came in 1990–91, when, as a mature student, she served as teaching assistant to Hartmut Lutz, who was then a guest professor at SIFC (Saskatchewan Indian Federated College, now First Nations University of Canada), and who many years later became her supervisor when she earned her PhD at the University of Greifswald in 2006. She also supervised German exchange students pursuing Indigenous literary studies in Regina, and witnessed interracial romances between German and Indigenous students. When visiting Germany, she was initially intimidated by the level of knowledge some German students had of Indigenous literature. Born in 1952 and raised on war movies, she had expected a monolithic German culture, so she was struck by the regional cultural diversity in Germany and the mutual stereotyping between "Prussian" northerners and "Bavarian" southerners, and especially between "Wessies" and "Ossies," with the latter feeling colonized by the West. Episkenew brought ironic allusions into her academic interactions but found that they did not transfer easily to European audiences. For her, German Indianthusiasm is a complex issue with many perspectives, ranging from encounters with self-proclaimed German experts on authentic Indigeneity, and commentary about her physical appearance that did not conform to German expectations about Indigeneity, to an acknowledgement that Indigeneity was so attractive to Germans because their complicated history made it difficult for them to embrace their own traditions, which had been tainted by their Nazi past.

Audrey Huntley's father (Scottish and Anishinaabe) was a Canadian soldier stationed in Germany, where he married her mother. Between the age of three and five she grew up in her mother's village in Westphalia. She returned to Europe as a teenager, travelled in Mediterranean countries, came to Marburg in 1986, graduated with an MA in social sciences, became a political leftist activist, and did not return to Canada until 1998. While a student, she struggled to deconstruct German stereotypes about *Indianer* and to combat cultural appropriation. Initially appalled by hobbyists dressing up as Indigenous people and running sweat lodges, Huntley has become more lenient toward Indianthusiasm, especially where serious attempts are being made to learn from Indigenous spirituality. The Oka crisis was a consciousness-raiser for her. She helped stage a demonstration at Frankfurt airport, which placed the Oka crisis on the agenda of German media. Her German experiences influenced her profoundly, and she has a high regard for German political radical thought. Her involvement with the Palestinian struggle taught her about the complexity of the German history of antisemitism since the Holocaust. Through her work with non-White Germans and immigrants, she has experienced how much racism remains in Germany. While she felt at the time that Canada was more progressive regarding literature by writers of colour, she has witnessed in Germany a gradual opening toward minority writers such as Audre Lorde. Huntley observed that Germans interested in Indigenous cultures have not yet fully grasped the importance of the land for Indigenous identity. She strongly believes that Germans and Europeans have much to learn from Indigenous people in terms of understanding race, land, and the environment.

The writer Thomas King has, in his creative works, repeatedly made humorous reference to German Indianthusiasm, addressing satirically (without ever having been to Germany) the German fascination with Indigenous peoples in his 1999 novel *Truth and Bright Water*. In this novel, a Blackfoot youth, dressed up in a self-made stereotypical Bavarian costume, and playing a tuba, marches through throngs of German tourists visiting the Blackfoot reserve during the annual Indian Days celebrations. He founds a one-man German Club on the Blackfoot Reserve. King's experience with German Indianthusiasm has been in North America rather than Germany; he has encountered Germans at powwows or other gatherings. King has witnessed the peculiar desire to "be more *indian*" than the Indigenous people in attendance, to express a self-proclaimed expertness and ownership over "all things *indian*," and to "master the art of Indigeneity." Germans come to Canada and the United States to perfect their powwowthusiasm, and they relish performing a historical Indigeneity that is steeped in a romanticized fictionalized past, but that they assume is authentic. In King's words, the art of "being a dead Indian" necessarily leads to disappointment when Germans meet contemporary Indigenous people. King discusses the stereotypes ingrained in German Indianthusiast conceptions of Indigeneity as well as the complex realities that Indigenous people face when having to decide whether to "sell" their own cultures to such enthusiasts – to feed their families by feeding the appetites of tourists.

In our interview with David T. McNab, he calls for an "unlearning" of our collective complacent historical assumptions before we can begin to learn about those aspects of history that have been marginalized, hidden, or silenced. He sheds light on the complexities of racial discrimination as well as interracial marriage, offering his own marriage to the German scholar and immigrant Ute Lischke McNab as an example of a respectful and successful German–Indigenous connection. He explains that tolerance and mutual respect between different nations and cultures are reflected in the Two Row Wampum and then focuses on the "heart" of Indigenous and German relations by sharing the history of his own ancestry on the Six Nations territory of the Haldimand Grant and "Berlin," now Waterloo, Ontario. His attitude toward German Indianthusiasts is tolerant and predominantly positive, because their interest, argues McNab, however stereotypical it may be, provides a basis for further learning and communication, a basis he finds largely absent among non-Indigenous Canadians. McNab believes that many Germans are hungry for spirituality after the trauma of two world wars, and they identify with Indigenous people in an attempt to move past their own nation's atrocious history. He often uses his experiences with Germans and the photographs he collected in Germany to encourage students to engage with Indigenous people.

Waubgeshig Rice, Anishinaabe from Wasauksing First Nation in central Ontario, and author, journalist, and documentary filmmaker, identifies himself as a "mythbuster" who challenges the preconceived notions Germans have about Indigenous peoples. As a high school student, Rice went to Germany for an entire year, and the encounter with Germans in Germany sparked his interest in writing and journalism. He realized quickly that German interest in Indigenous peoples was focused on the past rather than the present. He was challenged by Germans who did not consider him to be an authentic *Indianer* because his clothes did not match their ideas, shaped by Karl May's novels, of the appropriate attire North American Indigenous persons should wear. He began speaking publicly at events to educate Germans about issues Indigenous people face in North America today, in doing so busting the often condescendingly romanticized myths of Indigenous past ways of life that Germans had so lovingly petrified in their cultural memory. Germans were genuinely interested in his Indigenous background, but at the same time, Rice witnessed their harsh treatment of Turkish immigrants. Rice grew to appreciate that displays of German national pride were understated as a result of a guilt-ridden history, in stark contrast to what he perceives as uncritical Canadian displays of national identity. He also explored the problematic historical legacies that lie at the root of the German fascination with Indigenous cultures. Rice credits the complexity of his German experience with his desire to become a journalist. Experiencing his own culture through the eyes of another sharpened his view of Indigenous culture and of the role of Indigenous people in Canada.

Short fiction writer, playwright, humourist, and essayist Drew Hayden Taylor, Anishinaabe from Curve Lake First Nation, travelled and lectured in Germany more than a dozen times before he began writing about Indianthusiasm. Taylor is, in fact, the most prolific author on the topic. In his 2010 novel *Motorcycles and Sweetgrass* (2011), he explicitly refers to the "hero worship of First Nations. One academic had even coined the term 'Indianthusiasm'" (123).[20] But until the release of his documentary *Searching for Winnetou* in 2018,[21] it was in his play *The Berlin Blues* (2007) that he addressed the topic of German Indianthusiasm most substantially.[22] Its hilarious plot follows the complications and conflicts that occur in the small Otter Lake First Nation reserve when it is economically invaded by a German multi-million-dollar investment company determined to build "Ojibway World," an "*indian*" theme park, the "biggest and best in the World" (2007, 18).

The two German characters in the play, Reinhart and Birgit, are enthusiastic about Native cultures, and in many aspects, they are keenly interested and well informed about Indigenous history and culture, but they are less perceptive when it comes to contemporary realities. While shifting between multiple layers of mutual stereotyping, Taylor does not fall back on the most prevalent stereotype of Germans as Nazis.[23]

Setting aside the long-embedded association of Germans with Hitler and the Holocaust, Birgit's and Reinhart's identities seem to be constituted more through their knowledge of Karl May, their modern fascination with Indigenous people in North America, and, most importantly, their professional interests as entrepreneurs. This willingness to look past stereotypes to see Germans as contemporaries is also evident in numerous works by other Indigenous writers and artists from what is currently Canada. All of Taylor's works have been positively received in Germany and continue to be taught at German high schools and universities. Taylor's work in Native theatre has transcended North American borders, and he collaborates with the University of Lüneburg annually. Like other interviewees in this volume, Taylor notes the value of writing about German stereotypes through an Indigenous lens. His satire neither discriminates nor privileges when it comes to poking fun at stereotypes and preconceptions, and his works have opened up difficult conversations for audiences worldwide.

Emma Lee Warrior, the Piikani author and poet from southern Alberta, is the very first Indigenous writer to deal specifically with the phenomenon of Indianthusiasm. She did not visit Germany until two decades after her first works on this topic had appeared. The characters in her short stories "Compatriots" (1987) and "The Powwow Committee" (2003) are informed by transcultural individuals who have taken on Indigenous lifestyles and identities. Warrior's short stories examine not just how German tourists to Canada appropriate Indigenous traditions, from wearing traditional attire to powwow dancing, but also how their expectations of Indigenous cultures are shaped by romanticized representations of the past, often resulting in a refusal to acknowledge contemporary Indigenous people. She also wonders about the many ways in which Indigenous people find their way over to Germany and make a living there, capitalizing on the century-old fascination with Indigenous people from North America and commercializing Indigenous cultures. She acknowledges Germans' interest in Indigenous spirituality as a search for authentic fulfillment and meaning, but she also points out that many Indigenous traditions and rituals, after decades of colonial suppression, are only slowly returning to the reserves, with one nation borrowing traditions from another and adapting them to their own nation's culture. Warrior, often reluctantly, touches on such complex questions as the essential elements of Indigenous culture, how they change over time and because of the expectations that others bring to them, and how self and other clash in today's interethnic and transnational encounters.

The conversation partners assembled in this volume bring their particular affiliations, identities, stories, and experiences to critically reflect the ways in which German Indianthusiasm in all of its manifestations has shaped and is shaping their transnational and transcultural connections and perspectives, ranging from the personal to the professional, and from the cultural to the commercial. The volume's focus on the experiences of contemporary Indigenous people, and on the real effects and consequences of Indianthusiasm, prioritizes a respectful understanding of Indigenous peoples' languages, knowledges, cultures, histories, politics, arts, intellectual traditions, and research methodologies. It bridges the multidisciplinary field of Indigenous Studies with those of other Western scholarly discourses that are preoccupied with historical, Eurocentric representations of Indigeneity. The discussion partners speak as knowledgeable agents determined to challenge the concepts and the effects of Indianthusiasm in the context of ever-evolving transatlantic relationships between Indigenous and non-Indigenous peoples.

INTERVIEWS

AHMOO ANGECONEB

I thought to myself: "Well, I'll appropriate from the people who appropriated from us."

Phone interview by Florentine Strzelczyk and Hartmut Lutz, 1 December 2012, from Calgary, AB, to Lac Seul, ON

Hartmut: The project we are working on is about the phenomenon of Indianthusiasm in Europe and Germany, and about artistic, literary, and personal reactions to that phenomenon. We are asking you because you have travelled the world, and have been over to Switzerland and Germany several times. We'd like to start by asking you to introduce yourself, and then say something about how you came into contact with Germany.

Ahmoo: My name is Ahmoo Angeconeb, and I come from Lac Seul First Nation, Ontario. And I am actually an Anishnaabe, an Ojibway, from Lac Seul First Nation. Years ago, in 1982, I was looking for more markets to sell my artwork, and somebody recommended that I should go to Germany, and also to the German-speaking part of Switzerland. So, in 1982 I travelled through Germany with my former wife and our oldest son, Terry. We drove around to various places. We flew into Frankfurt, and we started from there. Before we left Canada, I asked the Ontario government, the Ontario Office of Culture and Tourism, for names and addresses of galleries in Europe that might be interested in my art. So, I got a list of about four or five galleries, and so we started from there. Much before our trip, I wrote to the galleries and sent them some materials, a CV, and then asked them if they might be interested in my artwork, carrying and selling my artwork for me.

Hartmut: Why, do you think, people recommended the German and the German-speaking market?

Ahmoo: Well, I heard that there was an interest in First Nations peoples, from Germany and also from the German-speaking part of Switzerland. Yeah, I heard that there were the so-called *indian* clubs of Germany. [chuckles]

Hartmut: You were laughing when you were saying that. Can you explain that a little more?

Ahmoo: There are these clubs, I guess, that I heard about, that admired First Nations cultures. And then, also, they "played *indian*." [chuckles] They dressed up like *indians*, they lived, they spend weekends in so-called "*indian* camps," and have these so-called "*indian* activities."

Hartmut: Have you been to any of those camps or to meetings of such groups in Switzerland or Germany?

Ahmoo: No, I've never been invited, actually! [much laughter] Actually, there was one club that I saw when I was in Bern, Switzerland. They set up a tipi and then they had pony rides. [laughs] And they sat around.

Hartmut: So you could not display your "Anishnaabe horsemanship," eh?

Ahmoo: Actually, most of these *indian* clubs were interested in Plains Indians. So when they found out I was Ojibway, they had no idea who the Ojibway were. We weren't Plains Indians, so therefore we weren't "real *indians*."

Hartmut: But you could have told them that your people whipped the Sioux![1]

Ahmoo: Yeah, but they probably wouldn't want to hear that we whipped their favourite First Nation group. But again, it is funny they never did invite me to these meetings or *indian* activities.

Hartmut: Do you have any idea why?

Ahmoo: I guess I was from a different culture, a different *indian* culture. And then, they seem to have this romantic view that they didn't want to have altered. I was too "real" an *indian* for them. [laughter] They wanted to keep their romantic view; they didn't want to hear about the modern way of living for Ojibway people here. That we lived in wooden-structure homes, that we drove cars. [laughs]

Hartmut: And that you came to market contemporary Native art, right? That didn't fit.

Ahmoo: Yeah, yeah.

Hartmut: How did Germans and people in Switzerland react to you?

Ahmoo: Well, actually it's interesting. There were two reactions. One was that they got turned off because I wasn't [from a] Plains [culture], that I was a so-called modern *indian*. But the other side of the reaction was that some people were very interested in the traditional world view and the traditional philosophy of the Ojibway. They were intellectuals who were interested and curious about our world view and the philosophy.

Hartmut: Have you thought about why you would find so much interest in Ojibway and probably also other Aboriginal traditions and world views in Europe?

Ahmoo: I think in Europe, generally, there is no more so-called "wilderness," and that the land has been so-called "tamed." There are no more so-called "wild" animals. So, I think the German view is that they have to look for ways of maintaining a sort of conservation world view. There is no more wilderness, so they have to find ways. For example, the recycling and all that. It's a good idea that things should be recycled and that things should be reused. They can only take so much from nature in Europe.

Hartmut: How did people react to your artwork?

Ahmoo: Well, again, some people wanted to see the romantic view. They wanted to see the paintings of guys on horseback. [laughing all]

Hartmut: Remington, eh? Or Bierstadt.

Ahmoo: Yeah, Remington. I actually got a copy of *Winnetou*. In German! But I haven't read it yet. [laughter]

Hartmut: You know, there is an English version. We read that here in class. It's shortened, and it's a little less racist than the original, I would say, and politically, it's cleansed.[2]

Ahmoo: Actually, I got the original book, [at] a book dealer in Basel, Switzerland, in German.

Hartmut: Ahmoo, if you want to learn about "real *Indianer*," you have to read it.

Ahmoo: Yes. Getting back to my artwork. There were artists and intellectuals in Europe who looked at my artwork and said, "Oh, this work is fascinating. We have never seen anything like it." And so, I had interesting exhibitions, like Cologne, and also in Basel, Switzerland, and also in Berlin. People were curious about it, and in the visual art world people are generally always looking for something new they haven't seen before. So, there was this reaction of intellectuals and historians, saying "Wow, this stuff is really fascinating."

Hartmut: Has your travel in Europe, in Germany, Switzerland, and other countries impacted your art?

Ahmoo: Yes, it has. I got interested in hearing and reading about some of the traditional legends and stories of the European cultures. And I also got interested in the prehistoric designs of European cultures. I got interested in looking at some of the art books on the cave paintings in, let's say, France. And then also designs of other cultures, for example the German-speaking part of Switzerland, or learning about the *Greif*, or the "Wild Man."

Florentine: Yeah!

Hartmut: Thank you for the "Wild Man!"[3]

Ahmoo: And, what is it, the Lion? And for northern Germany I got interested in the images and the stories about the *Greif*, as well. And so, I incorporated some of these images into my artwork. I put them alongside Anishnaabe, or Ojibway, designs, sort of saying, "Here's the meeting of the two so-called ancient cultures," and also the meeting of the different spirits of the cultures. What I did was, I stole from the European cultures. [chuckles]

Hartmut: And we are so-o-o-o upset about appropriation! [laughter]

Ahmoo: By the way, I thought to myself: "Well, I'll appropriate from the people who appropriated from us."

Florentine: [still laughing]: Very good, I like that, actually! So, the galleries and exhibitions which accepted your work, how did they market you? As an Aboriginal artist? Or as a Canadian artist? How did they go about that?

Ahmoo: As Canadian Indian art. Art from the "wilds of Canada." [chuckles]

Hartmut: How did you feel about that?

Ahmoo: Oh, I felt okay about it, I guess. They've never even used the word "Ojibway" because I guess a lot of Germans never heard about the Ojibway. [laughs]

Hartmut: But remember, when you came with Roy Thomas and Blake Debassige,[4] we advertised the whole thing "Anishnabe Art."

Ahmoo: Yeah, yeah.

Hartmut: And so, I think that with your artwork you probably did a lot to spread the term "Anishnabe."

Ahmoo: Yes. Yeah. I was trying to use "Anishnaabe."

Hartmut: The first time you travelled to Germany, you had it all very well planned and laid out. You had addresses, and you knew what you wanted to see, and so on. But what were your original ideas or images that you had about Germany?

Ahmoo: Well, I had this idea that Germany was, you know, one of the most industrialized countries in Europe [chuckles], and, again, not so much so-called "wilderness" there … land, and lots of industry, and lots of so-called "development" in terms of cities and towns.

Hartmut: When you came to Germany, did you find your expectations about urbanization confirmed? Or did they change?

Ahmoo: I did find them confirmed. Yes.

Hartmut: How did you experience German racism?

Ahmoo: Yeah, I've experienced some German racism. Times I was going to stores, and being the last one served there. They knew I was a foreigner, and for some strange reason some people thought that I was from Asia. [laughs] And I also experienced racism in Switzerland, as well.

Hartmut: Is that any different from racism that you experience in Canada?

Ahmoo: Not much difference. No.

Hartmut: It's the same old song everywhere.

Ahmoo: Yes. But when I tell people that I am an *Indianer* [chuckles], they become curious.

Hartmut: Can you cash in on being *Indianer*?

Ahmoo: Yes. I do. Yeah. That's one of the ways I got my foot in the door when I taught galleries about my artwork.

Hartmut: Some of your work engages with German Indianthusiasm?

Ahmoo: No, my artwork doesn't engage with that issue, no.

Hartmut: Well, isn't the "Wild Man of the Woods" that you gave us, the drawing for the book, also an ironic play with that?

Ahmoo: No. Not really. It's just an old First Nations North American design. And I haven't done the interpretation of the European Wild Man of the Woods with this. I don't know what he wears.

Hartmut: Fur and long hair. He's furry.

Ahmoo: I heard that he wore some kind of evergreen boughs or something.

Hartmut: Sometimes, yes, and long hair, long beard. So that's why the first depictions, the first woodcuts that illustrated Columbus's letters they have bearded Aboriginal people, you know, because the Europeans thought, "They live in the woods, so they must be wild men of the woods."

Ahmoo: Oh, I see. [laughs]

Hartmut: That's where the terms *Waldmensch* in Germany, person of the wood, [comes from], and in Latin – I think we talked about that – *silvaticus*, the dweller of the woods. Out of that came the French *sauvage* and the English "savage," you know. It really means "wood dweller."

Ahmoo: That's ironic, actually, because we call Europeans in the Ojibway language "Antegooshiak" – people-who-live-in-wood – because traditional Anishnaabe people lived in wigwams, sort of a tipi-shaped thing, made out of bark or hides. And then, when the Europeans came into our country, they built wooden houses, so we called them "People-of-Wood." [all laugh]

Florentine: Wood dwellers. Full circle!

Ahmoo: Full circle, [laughs] yes!

Hartmut: You also did a lot of presentations at schools and universities. You talked about Anishnaabe art, art in general, but also about your culture. And you have also done ceremonies with some people, selected people. I was wondering about the reactions of those German audiences to your presentations – and even the ceremonies.

Ahmoo: They were received enthusiastically. They found that the presentations were informative and gave a good view of Anishnaabe culture and Anishnaabe world view.

Hartmut: Did the European or the German audiences react in any way differently from audiences that you have addressed here or elsewhere?

Ahmoo: No, no. Most of my presentations and lectures have always been … The reaction has been enthusiastic. Therefore, I am a good teacher. [laughter]

Hartmut: When you think of your many trips to Europe, showing your artwork and sharing your knowledge with people, do you see yourself as a kind of ambassador?

Ahmoo: Yes, I do, yeah. And then, also, I like to think of myself as a spiritual messenger also, when I do my ceremonies.

Hartmut: How do people in your community support that?

Ahmoo: Yeah, they do, actually. Most of them do that. They think it's a good thing that somebody has gone out and shared our culture with other people.

Hartmut: And also the spiritual side?

Ahmoo: Also the spiritual side, yeah. I find it ironic that I do these spiritual ceremonies. It's sort of a reversed role. Here, we have the missionaries that came to us to convert us to Christianity. And here I am in Europe, in Switzerland, doing ceremonies, and we are having Europeans participate in the so-called "pagan" ceremonies. [chuckles]

Hartmut: Yeah! Apart from the irony in that situation, do you think it goes beyond that? Do you think there is a need for this in Europe?

Ahmoo: Yes, I think there is a need for that. I was talking to some German artists in Cologne, and they told me that, you know, some of them have got fed up with that Christianity, and that Christianity outdid itself in Europe. Some Europeans are looking for some alternative.

Hartmut: And do Anishnaabe elders whom you talk to, or yourself being an elder – are you ready to help people along and fill that gap or that yearning?

Ahmoo: Yes. I was told that I was given these gifts, and that I should try to help people.

Hartmut: And you do!

Ahmoo: Yeah. Tell you another ironic story. Roy Thomas and I had an exhibition in Cologne, and we had it in a little chapel. And then the gallery owner told us, "I would like you to hang your painting, your artwork in the little chapel." And I had a print called "Super Thunderbird" that the gallery owner wanted me to hang where the altar was. [chuckles] And so, I thought to myself, "Here, we both, Roy Thomas and I, went to residential school, where they convert us to Christianity. And here, years later, we're hanging our so-called 'pagan paintings' in a chapel." [laughter]

Hartmut: Yeah! Maybe there's justice after all! [laughter] So, how do you feel about that?

Ahmoo: The chapel in Cologne reminds me for some strange reason of the little chapel that used to be at the residential school that I went to.

Hartmut: So, it was a déjà vu?

Ahmoo [chuckles]: A déjà vu, yeah.

Hartmut: I think from our side we've asked the questions we would like to ask, but is there something you would like to add to this from your side? When you think of this romantic stereotypical fascination with *indians*? Or anything else that comes to your mind?

Ahmoo: Hmm. Yeah, I think it's great that there is Indianthusiasm in Germany and in the German-speaking part of Switzerland. I think it is a good thing that there is an interest in the cultures, the world view, and sometimes in the religions of these cultures of North America, because I really, really think that we have to save the earth. And then I think that the traditional world views of First Nations cultures matter, you know? There is the idea of trying to save the earth.

Hartmut: You know Jeannette Armstrong – or you know of her, right?

Ahmoo: Yeah, I remember.

Hartmut: She did her PhD in Greifswald, and there she looks at the oral traditions of the Syilx Okanagan people and how they entail all the knowledge that people need to know to survive well on the land they are given to. It's a very complex thesis. It's a wonderful book, and the result is that people need to "re-Indigenize" – and re-Indigenize not in a racial sense, but in the sense of learning from and about the land, so that we can survive. And I think this is confirmed by what you say.

Ahmoo: I admire the German artist Joseph Beuys, and his attitude, and his artwork. And I think at one time he said that shamanism will help save the world.

Hartmut: Yeah, and some people in Germany thought that he was crazy, but I think he was the greatest or the most influential artist in Germany after the war.

Ahmoo: Yeah.

Hartmut: Anything else, Ahmoo?

Ahmoo: No, nothing that I can think of now.

Florentine and **Hartmut:** Thank you!

JEANNETTE C. ARMSTRONG

Most people can't be informed, because of the way they are being informed.

Live interview by Florentine Strzelczyk and Hartmut Lutz in Florentine's office, University of Calgary

Florentine: You're the first Aboriginal woman who earned a PhD from a German university. How was it studying and visiting Germany?

Jeannette: I really enjoyed it. I wasn't prepared because I had not really studied anything about the people in Germany, or their contemporary society or anything. I just knew Hartmut and a few other German scholars who had visited in Canada and taken the time to come and talk with me.[5] And then I also had been invited by a number of scholars to come to western Germany, and then we went out to Osnabrück to do a number of talks. I did get to see it in a kind of touristy sort of way, because I was travelling with Greg Enright and Paul St. Pierre and others on a CBC authors tour. It was seeing with their eyes as well.

And I was quite fascinated when we went out to Osnabrück at that time. So, I got to know Ruth and Hartmut, and their children, and I really liked it. My impression was that they were more like my family back home than other non-Aboriginal people that I encounter pretty normally here in Canada. I also felt that I didn't feel the sort of hidden deep prejudices that are prevalent all over in Canada toward Aboriginal people.

Florentine: You didn't feel that at all?

Jeannette: I didn't feel that in Germany. And I don't feel it in a lot of European countries when I'm there. And obviously because they're not here, and they're not colonizing, and they're not on the defensive about it. And so, not being on the defensive, you know, sort of puts you at ease. I liked it, and I really enjoyed my time at my studies, when I went there for the colloquia and when I went to meet Konrad[6] for the first time. It was wonderful. I really enjoyed it, and I really like the people, and I feel at home there. It is something that I don't feel even outside of the reserve in the city of Penticton, in the community that belongs to me. [laughs]

Florentine: Right. Did people react in a specific way? Because you have an Indigenous background and Germans have had that long infatuation, and fascination, and obsession with North American Aboriginal people.

Jeannette: I think that there was that, but it wasn't blatant, and it wasn't disrespectful. It wasn't coming from Konrad or from Hartmut, my professors, you know, or just normally others that I encountered, but it was there.

Florentine: Students?

Jeannette: Students, yeah, mainly. But it was very nice, actually. It was inquisitive more than disrespectful, [un]like putting a person on a pedestal and having expectations of them. It wasn't any of that.

Florentine: So, you perceived it as positive?

Jeannette: I did. I felt it as positive. But of course, I've never been exposed to the *Indianistik* kind of enthusiasm that's there in western Germany. And it just wasn't there in East[ern] Germany.

Florentine: Hmm, interesting. Why? When you think about, I mean, Germany still has many issues with racism today.

Jeannette: Sure!

Florentine: For example, we've had Turkish people for generations living in Germany now, not being considered German at all. So, there are a huge number of issues still with cultural others ...

Jeannette: That's the same in Canada. There is this rhetoric, you know, about multiculturalism and all the acceptance of immigrants, but [the acceptance isn't there]. Very clearly, there is a division. I see it happening every day, say in Penticton, or Oliver, or *indian* communities in Vancouver, whatever. There's the attitude, you know? Clerks, waitresses, bankers, teachers, whatever! They just have really a low tolerance for anyone of different cultural background. And it may not even have anything to do with the way people dress, but simply the way they look, which is racism, based on physical attributes. And so, it's not surprising that that's there as well in Germany. And any other country I have visited. It's there. But I found that there is – just from my perspective, my husband's perspective – that there was a real clear difference between the people who are aware about the past history, and problems, and the people who are sort of pushing the idea of racism. The body language was really clear. There is a clear division, and I would say that I felt it and saw it only in a small percentage that I encountered on the train, or, you know, in the *Hauptbahnhof*, or any other places like that.

Florentine: And you went on a lecture tour? How did the German audience react to what you were presenting and reading? What aspects did they pick up on, do you remember?

Jeannette: Well, I think the responses were really scholarly. There were a lot of good questions from the scholarly perspective about Aboriginal writing in Canada, and marginalization, and those issues. More questions about resistance actions. They were very informed about things like that, you know … Oka[7] and Gustafsen Lake,[8] and Wounded Knee,[9] and other things like that. And they were very informed about the oppressive policies that are pretty much still the tactics of this government, and the use of the legal doorway to oppress. They were very knowledgeable about that and very astute in regards to what the government was up to, and what they were doing. So, I found that really refreshing.

That's not the case in Canada when I do readings across the country. [Canadians] believe Canada's rhetoric, for instance, about the Treaty Commission in British Columbia and the fact that Aboriginal people are in agreement with this and that, or whatever. And most Canadian people have blinders on about it, because of the way the rhetoric and the media portray Canada's actions, or inactions in some cases – mostly inaction in a lot of cases!

So, that was very different. It allowed me to speak more comfortably about some of the issues and to provide further information that might not have been there. The response was really, I think, surprising.

Florentine: And were those university audiences?

Jeannette: Yeah.

Florentine: And even at the university, this would be different here, you think?

Jeannette: Right. That's most very true. [laughs]

Florentine: Have you in your creative work ever written about anything in relation to Germany?

Jeannette: No. I really don't feel compelled to. I think, maybe, in creative writing I would go back to having some time to be able to do that.

The non-fiction writing, the writing for activism or the research writing, for me is really focused. And I haven't done any research, of course, in Germany. I would like to do some in the future. And I'm very fascinated, for instance, with the work that's going on in conservation; from an Aboriginal perspective, I think [that] would be really interesting – and the parallels, to re-Indigenize in areas.

Florentine: The environmentalist side?

Jeannette: Yeah, I would be interested in writing about that. But I really need time to allow the side of my consciousness that works with the creative to have more time to absorb what the people are about and more time to be able to put that into words in some way. And I haven't. I don't feel that I've had that time because I've been concentrating on the work, that PhD work, and whenever I was there, I never really allowed my consciousness to examine anything other than continuously thinking about my research.

Florentine: Right. Right. Right.

Jeannette: And my professors' opinions, of course. [laughter all]

Florentine: I thought it was interesting when you said yesterday during the talk that you weren't aware that there is this other side to Hartmut's research, too.[10] He is an Americanist, and a Canadian literature specialist, but he's also worked on the German fascination with, and stereotyping of, North American Aboriginal peoples. Do you think that other side, that you weren't so aware of, influences and has influenced your working relationship?

Jeannette: No, I don't think so. I've actually put that off to the side, because I really, really feel that the work that Hartmut has done in regards to Indigenous literatures, and the listening, and the facilitation of that, was not only informative, but really necessary for me to hear more clearly: the different Aboriginal Indigenous voices in North America. So, for me that was really an essential aspect.

And the other part of it, I think, was the understanding about the orality, and the literature that's contained in the orality, that Hartmut has. That's just not there in any other academic writing that I could find. There are a few people writing about Indigenous stories and storytelling, and attempts to look at the structure position, and examining it against maybe other forms of European storytelling, but not a real understanding that is coming from a whole different ... Well, Hartmut didn't do a lot of writing about that. I knew he understood that. And I think that, combined with the other professor, Konrad Ott's understanding about what environmental ethics should be, or what it could be, not what it is, and all the theories that have surfaced around it –

I think those two things for me were really, really core and essential. And that's the reason that I made the decision to go that direction. And I'd been aware that I could get criticism, you know, and be criticized, in many different ways.

Florentine: For doing the thesis the way you did?

Jeannette: No.

Florentine: For doing it there?

Jeannette: For doing it in Germany, yeah. Not so much with Hartmut, because anyone who knows Hartmut's work is highly respectful of the work that he has done on Aboriginal and Indigenous Native American writing. To the point, for example, when we first opened the program in the writing school,[11] they were aware of his work at the University of Victoria and I said, why don't you try hiring Hartmut at the Writing School, because we were at the time looking for, you know, some higher-profile names to come there to teach the courses, [to] get established.

Florentine: And you could have done the PhD at UBC [University of British Columbia]?

Jeannette: I could have. Yeah.

Florentine: Or Victoria?

Jeannette: Yeah. Or Victoria. Victoria offered me a very prestigious position if I would do my PhD there. And it was really a temptation. [Hartmut laughs, Jeannette laughs] No, so it wasn't that I was choiceless. And it wasn't that it was easier to do it in Germany.

Florentine: So, it was really the Hartmut connection?

Jeannette: It was a Hartmut connection, yeah.

Hartmut: I'm glad that you say all that, because I think sometimes when I hear remarks, people think, "Oh yeah, they do it over in Germany. It's easy there." I don't think it is! It's different. And if – as you said earlier – you weren't aware of the work that I did with regards to *indian* stereotyping, I think for me that was very, very important. When I came to Native Studies, I came to it studying racism in Germany. I mean, I'd been an Indianthusiast as a kid, and that fascination, or love, or whatever you call it, was always there.

Jeannette: And we talked about that.

Hartmut: Yeah, I had to analyze the stereotypical structures first. And that's what I also tried to do with my students back home, that they're aware of the perceptional frame that we imbibe, and that we have to dismantle that, and understand it, so that we can actually communicate.

Florentine: So, would you say then, or agree, that maybe being a German and knowing our history of racism made you more aware, or more ready to listen? Because that's what Jeannette highlighted.

Hartmut: I think so. I think I sometimes also utilized that. I remember there was a time when I was invited to *Volkshochschulen* [literally 'people's high schools'; equivalent to "open university" evening classes] to talk about Native Americans. And people would come. Because they are so fascinated. And then I would turn around at one point and say, "Okay, what about Gypsies in this country?" And then all of a sudden, the shutters went down. And sometimes – by looking at a situation that seems to be further away from you, you can – learn something, and then you turn around and say, "Okay, let's look at our own." So sometimes I also functionalize that fascination or that positive attitude.

Florentine: Because we're less emotionally entangled with Indigenous people on Turtle Island.

Hartmut: Yes. And it's far away. But the prejudices, the racism against Gypsies, is so blatant. And against other groups, of course.

Jeannette: That's exactly right. That's exactly the way I saw, how you thought about it, you know, deep thinking about what was happening here, and the oppression of voice, and culture, and existence in a way. And wishing, you know, that we would just somehow – Aboriginal people – be more like everybody else in Canada. And that I have felt all my life, from my teachers in school to people that I do business with, and so on.

I have to prepare myself to go out in that world, every day. And I am a person who was brought up in the twentieth century, and I liked certain things when I was a teenager, you know? The pop music and so on. I liked Bob Dylan, all of those things! I was fascinated with the late sixties and early seventies. All the things that the Civil Rights Movement [represented] ... I really believed in it and really believed in the women's liberation, and so on. I felt very much the connection between those things and my Aboriginalness. And in a sense, I always continue to feel that, and Marlowe feels this as well. He says, "It's really nice to go to one of the European countries." 'Cause we felt the same in Ireland, and in Britain ... and when we visited Germany together. He says, "We should just go there, so we can relax." 'Cause you can't relax here. Even when you are on vacation! There's no place that you can go, that you can ...

Florentine: Escape?

Jeannette: Yeah. You can't escape it, so.

Hartmut: I remember once when you picked me up from the airport, and you had to get a prescription from the drugstore, for your mom.

Jeannette: Yeah.

Hartmut: And this assistant there, a young girl, she talked to you like to a child, and she said: "You tell your mom, don't eat it all at the same time. Don't use it all at once!" It was all her reaction to your being Aboriginal. And I was so angry! I didn't say anything, 'cause it wasn't my business, but I could have strangled that young lady there.

Jeannette: But you could strangle someone pretty much every day [here] … [laughs]

Hartmut: Yeah. Exactly. And I felt like saying "Do you know who you are talking to?" It's amazing.

Florentine: So, in a way then, going to Europe gives you that space that's not marked and defined …

Jeannette: Yeah. Exactly. It's so prevalent and it's so accepted that all Aboriginals are uneducated, or unscrewed, and should be treated like less than, or like children, or like pagans, or some ways. And it's so accepted. For me … the smaller percentage of people are mainly in the universities that don't think that way or act that way. But there's still this undercurrent of not knowing the truth and the reality, and not knowing the situation for Aboriginal peoples there because of this Canadian rhetoric and this media rhetoric. So, most people can't be informed, because of the way they are being informed.

And so it's a difficult thing, right? But for universities that have made Native Studies, Indigenous Studies, and so on, I think they're really necessary. And I think they're really important in academic institutions, to open those doors. And that, I think, is making some changes. I know that the courses at UBC Okanagan, for instance, really draw a wide variety of students from various disciplines. And when they do come to the courses, they walk away changed. And they have a different understanding when they go. And I think that can influence and change a lot of other circles, because they're going to be out there, doing things. The change is slow but it's much more prevalent today than it was twenty years ago, or fifteen years ago, even five years ago.

Florentine: Right. Yeah.

Hartmut [to Florentine]: You're part of that, too.

Florentine: Now I am part of that?

Hartmut: Otherwise we wouldn't be doing this.

Jeannette: We wouldn't be doing this. Yeah.

Hartmut: Whether you know it or not, but you are.

Florentine: And I am listening, too. I'm trying to, anyway. At one point, I wanted to come back to – I mean that seems to be such an important part of your thinking – how students in your classes have to learn to listen. I was going to ask a little bit more what the role of listening takes in your work in general. That seems to be really fascinating and important to me, that aspect of your work where listening is facilitated or encouraged, and the role it plays.

Jeannette: Well, it's the foundation of the process we call *Enowkinwix*ʷ, which is for the Okanagan a very critical and important element of how we should be as human beings, because of our intelligence, and because of the way that we understand and know things.

   And the way that we understand and know things about anything, any subject, according to the Okanagan, is based on what data, or what information, you have at hand. And so, if you have a limited amount of information and data, your mind will still make a decision about what it knows, regardless of how you think about it. And so, one of our concepts is that, unless you have as much data as is available to everyone else that's present about a subject, you're not informed. And so, if you're not informed, you shouldn't trust your assumptions. You shouldn't trust your own analysis. You should listen to all the data, and allow that to accumulate, and then you will form a new assumption, and a new understanding therefore. That's what the *Enowkinwix*ʷ was based on.

   So, the very first step in the process, and it's a staged process, the requirement is for everyone to agree that the reason we're all going to sit together is that we're simply going to listen to what each person has to offer on this subject. We're not going to debate, we're not going to argue. Even if we think or feel that the other person is somehow missing some information, that doesn't matter. At this point it doesn't matter. Later on, it might matter, but at this point, what we're there to do is to listen to what they have to say, and why they're saying it. Why they're offering the information that they have, and where they received that thinking from. And so, in other words, we're there to listen without judging, or without trying to make judgments about what we're hearing. We're there to hear it and understand why they're saying it. So, the onus is on us, to hear what they're saying and to try to understand why they're saying it.

And the onus for the person speaking is to try to clarify why, where they got the information from, and how they came to that information in the way that they present it. So, their clarification is really important, because it might add something that you don't have. So that whole area of listening and clarifications is really an intellectual exercise that is maybe, kind of, like the scientific method.

Hartmut: Exactly.

Jeannette: We just absolutely will not accept someone's opinion or someone's thinking or our own thinking as valid or in any way important unless that process has taken place, where the deep listening has occurred and the deep clarification has occurred, and then we can say, after hearing all of this and putting all of this together, then maybe this is how we should think about it. How we should collaborate and rethink what has been happening. So that really is foundational to the way we do things.

So, it's immensely frustrating to policy-makers, Indian Agents, and so on that come: "What's your opinion on this?" Like: "Make your decision, we wanna know," you know? "Vote!" Right? And Okanagan people are sitting and saying, "Well, we haven't talked about it, we didn't have a dialogue about it." And a dialogue may take, you know, whatever time it takes for everyone. If it's a really important and critical issue, then it's going to take some time to get everybody's clarifications, and everybody's input, 'til we understand where everybody's coming from. And then we can collaboratively be comfortable with how we think about it.

So, it's very collaborative and very community-oriented, but it's also very, very respectful of differences in the way people come to what they think, and what they think they know. And so, in a lot of ways, for me, that listening is the only thing you can rely on when you're soliciting opinion.

And I find that in the Canadian society, it's the talking that people rely on, and they don't listen. It's like: "This is what I think, and I'm gonna argue with you until you agree with me." Or, "We're going to put forward my argument, and I don't need to hear your argument. I'm just opposed to it. I'm in opposition to what you're thinking. I don't agree with what you think." We would never have an Okanagan person traditionally say, "I don't agree with you," or say no in that way. They're saying, "Well, here is how I think about it," and, "Here is how I think about it, and what's in your mind, and what's in your heart about it?" And then we can decide which way we're going to go. And if we decide we'll go separate ways, that's still the way it has to be for now.

So, it creates a very non-conflict, non-adversary desire in the consciousness of the Okanagan person. So, in a lot of ways, conflict is hard to come by in the Okanagan. You have a hard time arguing with someone. [laughs]

Hartmut: Sometimes that's hard for us, you know. People [are] so used to getting an answer: "Oh, I don't agree with you" or "This is it." And I think as somebody with our background, you expect people to state their opinion. And if they don't, you think, "Oh, they agree." And if they then afterwards do something totally different from what you expected, you as an outsider almost feel betrayed, because you misread that protocol.

But what you said, you know, when you were talking about *Enowkin-wix*ʷ, in a way that is very similar in structure to sort of the best traditional philological research. If you work on an issue or an author, you do your bibliography. And if you're good, you read everything.

Jeannette: That's right, yeah.

Hartmut: You try to get a hold of everything you can find. And you may disagree with that, but you have to know it in order to get an opinion. And I think that is changing in academia. You know, when we did research for dissertations or so, you spent months, and sometimes years, just doing bibliographies and reading. And things are getting faster, and I think that is less so today.

Jeannette: The good example is with Konrad. Do you remember when I did that talk first, and he said "Well, where is your argument?" You know: "I didn't hear an argument." Remember that?

Hartmut: Yeah.

Jeannette: So, I didn't answer him then, but then we went behind closed doors, and I talked with him for maybe three hours at that time. And I explained my process to him, and I said, "I can't form an argument. What I'm doing at this time is laying out what I know and clarifying what I know about this subject." I'm not saying that it argues with you, or for you, or against you. All I'm saying is "Here is what I know about the Okanagan, and that's what I hope to expand information on. So, I need from you what you know and understand about that, so I can then examine it and incorporate it in my thinking. I have no argument." He says, "Well, how can you start a dissertation without an argument, without a thesis?" And he was very concerned that I wasn't going to be able to do the research, because I didn't have an argument, and I didn't have a thesis. Like, what was I arguing against?

Florentine: Did he listen to you?

Jeannette: Oh, he did.

Hartmut: He had to learn; oh well, he learned a lot.

Jeannette: And he's a *strong* scholar. So, he was very tough, you know, to explain my process to. But I think he was skeptical as well, all the way through. Which was good, because he was challenging me and saying: "No. Read this!" [laughs] "Read that." And then slowly starting to say, "Well, that really makes a lot of sense!" And "What do you mean by this, and by that?" And then the dialogue with him changed over the five years.

At the end, when we met for the last time, he said, "What I'd like you to do is, I would like you to take these four areas of environmental ethics, these four separate areas, and I'd like you to look at what they're saying. How does it compare to what the Okanagan are saying?" And so I said, "That makes a lot of sense in the process to me. So then I can come up with the difference. I can come up and say, 'This is what we're arguing.'" And then my thesis was clear. But it was not until the fourth year. And so that's a very different methodology. And I insisted on the *Enowkinwix*ᵂ methodology.

I teach methodology now,[12] as a research methodology, as an *Enowkinwix*ᵂ method. And it's very uncomfortable to some of the PhD students that come in to look at that methodology, and back away from it. And some of them say, "Well, this makes a tremendous amount of sense. And I'm gonna use it." But it's very frustrating to those who have been trained in the opposite: you make an argument, and then you defend that argument all the way through.

And so, the methodology is really interesting – the one that I do at the UBC. A really interesting mix of people come into the course to examine the methodology, and then, at the end of their course, they apply it to the area of focus that they're in, and then decide whether they're going to use it or not. It is really an interesting, highly animated process.

Hartmut: I think it was for us – I mean, Konrad and myself – it was very exciting to witness that process. And I'm glad that our system is more flexible still, and can accommodate that. And I think the most exciting thing about having doctoral students, or people doing research, is that you, as the supposed "Doktorvater," you're learning all the time, and you're in a dialogue, in this case interdisciplinary, interacting with Konrad, learning from him, learning from Jeannette. It was just amazing, and I'm very happy about that.

As I said yesterday, I felt that when Jeannette, as the *first* First Nations woman (as far as I know) in history, to do her PhD in Germany, it was really a historical moment. I mean for five centuries we've been talking to "them," about "them," down to "them." And all of a sudden there is somebody from the group [among us] – from the group that has been subalterned and has been forced to listen all the time, whether they wanted to or not, whether they knew or not. Often they knew better but still, we were talking "to" them."

And that's also how I see Native Studies and Aboriginal Studies. The initiative originally came from Aboriginal people. Now academia is reshuffling, and anthropology seems to be taking over again. So, some people who say they do Native Studies – I've heard this in Europe – they say, "We are studying them." Yeah, that's the old! That's the old attitude, you know? "We, as the academic masters, studying them."

But this was not a reversal. The way I saw it, it was a dialogue. So, you did some pioneering work. [Jeannette, Florentine laugh]

Jeannette: Which I didn't know I was doing. [laughs]

Hartmut: Yeah.

Jeannette: I was just doing it the way we do things.

Hartmut [to Florentine]: Jeannette is not the first Aboriginal person. That was Jo-Ann Episkenew, who is Métis.[13]

Jeannette: Yes.

Hartmut: Who also did her PhD, but Jeannette is the *first* First Nations woman.

Florentine: If you had to sum up what the essence, or in a few sentences, what the German connection really is with your work, what would you say?

Jeannette: Well, there were two things, I think, that struck me. One was that listening, the ability of listening from the outside, without the sort of accepted ingrained assumptions, that was really necessary for me.

The other thing, I think, was on the environmental side, that it wasn't just rhetoric. It's a very deep consciousness in … at least in the part of Germany that Konrad and Hartmut [live], and hopefully it's that way anywhere else in Germany. But the very first time I went, when I was introduced to Konrad, he said, "We'll take you out to the country to see some of the work that's happening." And we went out to the country, we went out to the land. And his boys were littler at the time, and we went out to the Baltic and they swam. They took their clothes off and swam. [chuckles] And then we went walking in this conservation area, and you could see the depth of connection that he had with the land, and with the environment and with … with nature! That wasn't just academic. And I feel that all the time with Ruth and Hartmut in the same way.

You don't feel that here in Canada. Even with the conservationists! It's about the management of the place, or it's about the species, and the care about finding ways to reintroduce them. But you don't feel that, I would say ... You know, I'm hesitant to use the word, but a spiritual connection. The depth of that was there. And I felt that very clearly, and very much in terms of the humankind way, that you can feel what nature really is, in terms of its aliveness and its life. And I felt that with Konrad, and I felt that with Hartmut. And I knew that with Hartmut it wasn't just intellectual, you know, just that it was there. And it's there with Aboriginal and Indigenous people.

There isn't any need really to talk about it, or analyze it, or explain it. You know? It's there. And that was the other thing, I think, that connection. For me, I found other human beings that could feel the way that I felt, as an Indigenous person, toward nature. I know that that sounds, sort of, maybe romantic, or romanticized, or whatever, but that was the other thing that I required in my mind, and that I couldn't find very easily ... other than with a few people in various capacities in the US, in environmental capacities, and David Suzuki, for instance, and his children ... They have that feeling, and there isn't any need to talk about it or question it. And very few others as well.

But that was necessary, I think, for me to have that comfort zone and to be able to rely on that. And that it isn't something that I have to try to figure out, whether they really feel that or not. And for me in academics, you know, that is as important for me, that there's that truth there, that human truth that is foundational. That sometimes isn't done in words, or analysis, or academics, but it's a foundation to the academics. And I really felt that with Konrad. He's a deeply spiritual person. You know, immensely spiritual person.

Hartmut: And a sharp intellectual!

Jeannette: And a scientist. [laughs]

Hartmut: Absolutely.

Jeannette: So that's an amazing combination, you know?

Florentine: That was really my last question. Thank you for the interview.

Hartmut: Is there something you want to add?

Jeannette: No. I just wanted to add that I think the series that you're launching here,[14] I think is really the way to go and should be done by all these different departments.

Florentine: I'm trying. [laughs]

Jeannette: Yeah. And I'm just so pleased that it's here in Alberta, actually. You know, Alberta is a tough province [Hartmut and Jeannette laughing] because those ingrained biases, they are much, much more prevalent than in maybe some of the other provinces. So, I'm really grateful to have come here and to be interviewed in this way, and, you know, have this series going on.

Florentine: We are grateful that you have made the time to come and see us and agreed to be interviewed. Thank you.

Jeannette: Thank you.

Hartmut: Thank you.

JOHN BLACKBIRD

Germany is my other Heimat now.

Live interview with Hartmut Lutz, Renae Watchman, and
Florentine Strzelczyk, recorded at a private home in Calgary

Hartmut: John, can you start by introducing yourself?

John: Okay. I'll start with a traditional greeting: *"Hi*, how *are* you? *Hi*, how
are you?"[15] My name's John … that's my pen name. Anyway, so I work as a
filmmaker, made a couple of films of my own, one about the powwow, called
Powwow. I travelled with a powwow group in the past to powwows across
Saskatchewan, and some were in Alberta, and I made interviews with them.
Powwow you can find for sale under Moving Images distribution.

I made one called *Indianer*[16] when I lived in Germany, and that was
about hobby Indians: Germans' attempt to be *indians* on the weekend.

Hartmut: Coming to Germany – can you start by saying how you came in
contact with Germany, what brought you there, and what your connection
with Germany is?

John: I think it was '96, I met some Germans who came to my reservation,
and I was the communication coordinator at the time on my reserve. My
boss, the director of education, said, "Hey, there are some Germans here,
would you like to be their host? [laughs] Be their contact here?" And I said
okay. And I met some Germans, and one of them was a German girl, and we
stayed in touch, and then we got married in '97 in Germany.

I went to Germany in May '97, got my diploma in film. And so, while I
was in Germany, she took me to a conference or some kind of day workshop
[laughs], and she was talking about plights of Native people and took me
along, and we got four hundred D-Marks for it. And that kind of opened my
eyes. I was kind of like, "Oh, why would they be interested in Native people?"

Because, you know, in Canada, I came from a culture that didn't really care about *indians*. In Canada, *indians* had a bad image, and they followed me around stores – security guards – and stuff like that, so that I wouldn't shoplift [laughs]. I didn't notice any of that stuff. Some of my Canadian friends were like, "Hey man, did you see that security guard following you around?" You know, I didn't really notice things like that because it just wasn't a part of my mentality. I wasn't this kind of a person to be followed around in a store.

Hartmut: Did any of that happen in Germany too?

John: I don't think so. No, it wasn't a part of my mentality, and I think if it was a negative experience, then it might be in my mentality, but it was never there. In Germany one time there was a little kid crying, and there was a crowd and it was Christmas. We're walking down the street there and I overheard the mother say to her little kid, "Hahh, guck mal, ein *Indianer.*" ["Ooh, look, an *indian.*"] That stopped the little kid from crying. [Hartmut laughs] And I thought: "Oh, that's me!"

Hartmut: [laughs] How could she tell that you were Aboriginal?

John: I guess I had a long braid. And I wore bone beads on my braid, you know, beads tied with a leather strap.

Hartmut: So how did Germans in general react to you while you were in Germany?

John: Well, I figured out that there was an interest, and I started to connect with those other groups, like environmental youth organizations or Native support groups. I found them online. I wrote them letters and I said, "I'm interested, so if you guys are interested, I'd like to come to speak about something, about *indian* people." And so, because of that I had to do research about people, about issues, and some of our concerns, some of our history and interaction with the government. You know, United States and Canada, locally in Saskatchewan and my own tribal council, the Meadow Lake Tribal Council. I worked there, and that kind of helped out, too, because part of my job was to interview elders and to get traditional stories and also some of the history.

Hartmut: So, you had all that knowledge.

John: Yeah, so I had a lot of knowledge but I never tapped into it.

Hartmut: How did people back home react when you told them what you were doing in Germany – that you were sharing some of that knowledge with people over there?

John: Well, one of them – my mom – took me aside. She told me about another guy from home who was travelling around and doing sweats over there and touring. She was, you know, curious about if I was doing the same thing. I said, "No. I'm not." [She said] "That's *good!*" [said with great emphasis, then laughs]

Hartmut: And did you try to talk with – besides your mom – other elders about what you were doing? And did they sanction that?

John: No, not really. I mean, I spoke to my uncle, and he thought it was all right. Their knowledge, and getting it out there, and speaking and stuff. Even my auntie took me aside, too, and said, "I hear you're doing medicine wheel workshops." And I said, "Well [laughs], based on my *Powwow* documentary and what I learned. For the medicine wheel, I did some research and reading about it, and there's a lot of published Cree stories out there, and based on what I learned from the elders on my *Powwow* doc, [that's what] I told.

Hartmut: So, you were careful to draw a line between what you could share and what was better left?

John: Yeah. I didn't pretend to be like what *indians* or Native people are always assumed to be [laughs]: medicine men or chiefs. I didn't pretend to be a chief or descendant of chiefs or medicine men, but I just said, "Well, I like stories, I work on stories. I'm a storyteller." The funny thing was, in Germany, storytellers do not have such a great reputation. [laughs] And so people found that this new concept was interesting somehow, so I found, somehow, a little niche right there.

Hartmut: How – if you tell stories here – how were the reactions in Germany different from reactions here? Or what was your experience there with audiences?

John: I've only met a few audiences here. The audiences that I've met so far here in Canada were international students.

So, I showed my film *Indianer* in a class at MRU [Mount Royal University] and one was at U of C [University of Calgary]. They're interested.

Hartmut: I want to go back to the time before you went to Germany. You must have had, probably, some ideas about Germany or about Germans in your head, however vague or rudimentary. With what expectations did you come, and how were they confirmed, or disappointed, or changed over time? How was that?

John: Well, I didn't really have much of an idea about Germany. But I grew up with Germans, and they said, "Well, we'll teach you German." And I said,

"No, I don't want to learn German. What do I need German for?" [Hartmut laughs] Germany is my other *Heimat* now.

Hartmut: Yeah?

John: Yes. So, I think that one of my problems at the time was … I guess I was the first student [laughs], a young person that said: "Go." And I didn't really do my research. I just thought "okay." I didn't even consider that I should learn the language. They asked me, "What are the things you noticed?" I said, "Wow, one of the things I noticed, it's very basic, but I noticed where White people come from." [both laugh] Somehow, being in Germany, I got tasked to know my own identity as a Canadian. Who are Canadians? You know, other Canadians and stuff, and people here in Canada. Some of my friends, their mothers wouldn't call us, or say, "*indians*"; they would say "early Canadians" or "original Canadians." And I got to feeling: Yeah, we are. [laughs]

So, I kind of felt a little good about that. I learned a little bit more about our relationship with the Crown, and the Treaty, and all of these certain things that are always going on, these round tables.

Hartmut: So, you grew more aware of being who you are and the politics involved?

John: True. Yeah.

Hartmut: I think that's amazing, but that always happens. You go abroad and essentially you learn about yourself, and where you come from.

John: Yup. And that was one thing I learned, too, during the filming or making of *Indianer*, that the people are interested. They're looking for an identity. And while they're looking for an identity within a Native circle/context, as a Native person I found my own identity, while searching for theirs.

The Natives that German people have in their minds are in the past. They [today's Indigenous peoples] have reached a potential, gone past that potential. Look at the "old time *indians*" and their relationship to the world. They had this romantic image [of] *indians* a long time ago … the "old time *indians*" on horseback. That's quite the only *indian* that they had an image of. But they had the idea that *indians* were somehow really connected. But at the same time just because of living your life and being a human being, I think there were also idiot *indians*, too, a long time ago.

Hartmut: Yeah. Sure, sure.

John [joking]: Old time *indians* that were kind of clueless and made lots of mistakes, you know, and had bad luck hunting buffalo.

One thing I guess I learned a lot about: how to grow up living in Germany. Because in Canada, you know, I went straight from the farm, the ranch, from herding cattle on horseback, driving a pickup truck, driving a tractor, to going to film school and learning to write then. I mean, if I hadn't left for Germany … I didn't take any time in between to live a little or to learn something about life before I went. I did it in a foreign country, so I had a really steep learning curve.

Hartmut: Sure. And where did you go to film school?

John: I studied two years in one. It was in northern Saskatchewan, in La Ronge.

So, in the end, I'd studied single camera for video, television. Then I came to Calgary for two years and attended SAIT [Southern Alberta Institute of Technology] and I got a film diploma.

Hartmut: That's quite a change, you know, from La Ronge via Meadow Lake to Calgary.

John: Yeah. [laughs] And my next move was to be Los Angeles.

Hartmut: Wow. So, you were looking for a Hollywood career?

John: Yeah. I was looking for a Hollywood career. In the meantime, I took some workshops on producing and writing and stuff like that. And [at] one of them, I met a documentary filmmaker and I said, "Wow, you're really good at this." And he said, "Yeah, when you do it long enough, you know, storytelling, you learn about story and such."

Hartmut: So, you find film the right medium today to continue the storytelling tradition?

John: For me, as long as I can pull a reader in, or a viewer, and try to set myself apart somehow, because I feel I have set myself apart by taking an alternative route in life, going to Germany, I think. And mostly people, even North Americans, weren't considering doing that.

Hartmut: No. No. You must have been confronted also with German racism, or racism in Germany. How did that work out?

John: I didn't know it was racism. [laughs] On one hand, I kind of grew up nice and sheltered on a farm: I was taken away from an environment where I had no parents, basically, until I was nine years old. And one day I had enough and walked away [from the dysfunction to the farm]. So, I kind of grew up in this White family, and suddenly I felt my status elevated.

Hartmut: Aha.

John: And so, the racism, it wasn't about racism growing up anymore when I changed homes. It was about status: who you know, and who you're connected with somehow. That was kind of the idea. But Germany ... I never really experienced any racism. I was familiar with racists: some of the movements over there, like the skinheads.

Hartmut: You are also – or you were – in contact with other Indigenous people from Canada who were in Germany, who lived there, had family there, or who travelled there. So, can you say something about your meetings with them? Or what are your experiences? Different from theirs?

John: I think we kind of came along and met the same people, on the one hand. Like one Native person I met. He talked about a certain group of people, and later on I met the same people, too. It was like they all knew the Natives that came to Germany.

Hartmut: So it's almost a closed circle, huh?

John: Yeah. It was a circle there. And the Native person that I did meet, he was not really so interested in hanging out with the hobby *indian* or the powwow or the weekend *indians*, the wanna-bes.

Hartmut: Who did you hang out with while you were there?

John: Mostly I hung out with German people. German friends and such. I liked it that people weren't interested in me, [as a] Native person, but were just kind of showing me how to act, react and hang out with society. Not that I needed help but it was ... I don't know it's the part of life when you live over there and you get to know people.

Hartmut: Did it occur to you – or happen to you – that you had the feeling people were just seeing the *indian* in you, and that John Blackbird got lost behind that, and you had to break down that perception? Or did people just react to you on a sort of person-to-person level regardless of whether you were Indigenous or not?

John: My friends were all right like that

Hartmut: Another question: Does your work – you paint, you sing, you write, you make films – does any of your work engage with German Indianthusiasm, or hobbyists or your experiences in Germany?

John: No. No, they're not my audience.

Hartmut: No. I mean, do you react to that, or you paint that, or write about that?

John: Oh yeah, I mean, I have made the film about them.

Hartmut: Yeah.

John: I started working with a magazine.[17] And I started writing about my interactions with them, about some of the hobby events. And about some of the hobby people that I'd met, and I was writing for a magazine called *Nativevue*, which doesn't exist anymore.

Hartmut: And do you still have those texts that you wrote for *Nativevue* about your experiences there?

John: Yeah. I still have those texts. There is one poem I'd like to share with you: "Groan": that was kind of my feeling near the end of 2009. I left Germany for a bit. I thought I'm going to quit for a while and take a break. Because I was doing medicine wheel workshops and people were, you know, starting to throw more problems at me. More weight and more heavy energy.

Hartmut: So, did they sort of try to make you their guru?

John: They tried to make me their guru, kind of leader, their spiritual person. To be their spiritual person ... [laughs]

Hartmut: Have you thought about that? Why is there that craving, or this need for spiritual guidance, or the readiness to follow a guru, and say, "Okay, you guide me now, you enlighten me." Have you found that in other parts of the world, too, that you know? Or have you thought about if it happens in Germany quite a bit?

John: I only thought of Germany, and I thought the people that I met in Germany or some of the gatherings that I went to – well, there is a real spiritual hunger here [laughs], and a lot of it has to do ... I don't know, they just somehow, they seem very open people, open enough to Native spirituality, but they're also very, very closed, on one hand. [laughs] Vanity/humanism, or Catholicism, or Protestantism, or whatever, and I thought: Wow, that's funny. Because a lot of Native people are Catholic. And they mixed their traditional beliefs with ... the so-called White man's religion.

Hartmut: Have you thought about why there is [this] spiritual hunger?

John: I think a lot of people don't want to do the work that's involved. Or they don't want to place the trust that is needed. And it's easier sometimes to have faith in something that you can see. And I thought, wow, maybe that's why.

I studied the Bible back in the day – maybe that's what Jesus meant about having faith. And people didn't have, or don't have, faith. There was a lot of questioning about Native spirituality: their ideas that Native spirituality kind of conflicted with some of the traditional ideas that I was picking up through prayer or interviewing elders. So, I thought, "Oh, that doesn't work for me."

Hartmut: You had a feeling that this spiritual hunger ... They were looking for patent solutions or shortcuts, and not to do the work themselves.

John: Yeah. Looking for shortcuts. So, this person came to me and said, "Oh, you spoke about the bear."

Hartmut: So, you also tapped into – or you were in contact with – a whole sort of the subculture of ... what? New Age and vision, spiritual ...

John: ... manic.
   And I didn't really think that was something I want to be involved with. I could've, and then if I did that, then I'd have to go the whole nine yards and do some, you know, reading up on being a medicine man. But I was told: "You can do these things if it's given to you." It was never given to me.
   But to be a storyteller, that was given to me. So, then I thought, okay, well, then I never really learned all of these old stories but you don't have to learn these old stories. You can be a modern storyteller, convey the same old morals and beliefs.

Hartmut: You obviously have met German hobbyists, and you also mentioned people who are on spiritual quests or so. If you look at the whole ... what you have experienced in Germany, how would you classify the different groups that you met? This is a real question for me because I haven't really thought about that. I seem to have lumped together people who are emulating Aboriginal lifestyles as hobbyists or Indianthusiasts, and I learn from you and from Renae how there are different groups. And some of them competing, some of them cooperating, so how would you classify them from your experience?

John: As a spider web. [laughs] Somehow, they're kind of a web. And they're somehow all together like a Native web, and they criss-cross one another: the hobbyists and the powwow enthusiasts, the people who are looking for shamanic quests. They all kind of gather and collect what they need and what they like.

Hartmut: Does this *"indianness"* or this *indian* that they are attracted to have anything to do with Aboriginal people in North America, and does that affect them in any way?

John: Well, individually it can affect them. For example, maybe you could lose your identity. You say, "Oh, I'm a Cree," but no, you're just an *indian* person [to them], you know.

[You] have your own beliefs, your own ideas, and teachings … and they lack respect towards you, truly to you. They promote their own events, perhaps, but I think it can be harmful a little bit for a Native person. You can get too involved somehow.

Hartmut: In the web?

John: In the web, yeah. Because you lose your identity and what it is that you do, and you start doing sweat lodges …

Hartmut: And you give them what they want, right?

John: Exactly: what they want. [Sarcastically] Of course, for an agreed-upon fee.

Hartmut: I think I told you, a friend of mine did his doctoral dissertation on the marketing of Lakota spirituality. This is Marco Briese.[18] He is from Ostfriesland and he found … I mean he researched this for several years and went to some contacts at some of these shamanistic groups or so. It's a whole industry, and there's a lot of money. I mean, a lot of money changing hands, let's put it that way.

John: I met someone from Berlin who said she went to a sweat lodge weekend ceremony with some Native person from over here [and] she paid 250 euros for the weekend. She enjoyed it.

She is a therapist, a psychologist. And for her it was a good thing. She said she feels like people who have a strong base like she does, as a psychologist, doctor, that they should be able to enjoy it. But other people, maybe they don't have the ability to separate, you know?

Hartmut: Yeah. And there's also the question whether the person who conducts the sweat should be charging money for it or not.

John: Yeah, like, back home here, we don't.

Hartmut: No. I know.

John: But in Germany …

Hartmut: But then, I think the people over here who are invited to a sweat or do a sweat, they see to it that the person conducting that hopefully has no needs, you know? And they might give … bring some food or bring along gifts, not to pay but to see that the person conducting the sweat – the medicine person or whoever he or she is – is looked after.

And that protocol, of course, doesn't exist in Germany. Right?

John: Oh no. Like, I understand some things where they need to exchange money at a sweat lodge in Germany. It costs money to pay for the fire, they have to buy the rocks, to rent the place, the rental of land, the weekend, or that night. Okay, well, people should give them a little bit of money, you know. Germany is so small, you have to buy everything, even have to pay for the stones, you know.

Hartmut: Is there anything else you'd like to say in regards to this project about reactions to German Indianthusiasm by Indigenous scholars and artists and people who have been to Germany? Anything you'd like to add from your side?

John: I think what I've learned is that the hobby movements or that group of the spider web [laughs] is not my audience. The Native people should remember, too, that these people aren't your audience. And they might help you out for a little bit, you know, but you started out maybe as a touch.

Hartmut: How do you feel about this: there are Indigenous people who in the past, in the recent past, got degrees in Germany, studying there. There are also German students who come over to Canada and study here, study Indigenous Studies, or Native Studies, whatever they're called. How do you feel about that? These academic connections or exchanges?

John: I think that's fine, you know. I think that seems very sincere, like helping one another, learning about each other's culture – the whole basis [is] academic.

Hartmut: In what areas do you think should, or could, Indigenous scholars and knowledge keepers teach in Germany or in Europe? And, vice versa, what could people from Germany teach here that could be meaningful?

John: Look, I think about language right now. While I was there, I still remember learning German sayings and I think that's something that could be shared between two cultures – is communication, how they communicate [among] themselves.

Hartmut: When you say German sayings, do you mean *Sprichwörter* [sayings or proverbs]?

John: *Sprichwörter*, you know like "*Schall und Rauch*." [hollow words]

Hartmut: Ah, *ja*. Okay.

John: You know ... how the different people group-think [laughs].

Hartmut: [You can understand] different mentalities, too, through the language.

John: That and how they feel about something. And I think it's like any relationship then. You know, we're around each other, and you know what to say, what not to say, and you can bring up a topic because you know them. I think they can teach Native literature over there: there's history, and there's Native storytelling, there's oral tradition, a lot of oral traditions. That's all in book form and something that could be taught over there, too. And the same thing can go over this way. Not just history, not just Native literature. Literature. And I mean we do that already of course, a lot of that, going on in universities.

Hartmut: And how do you feel if I say there's a class in Canada where Native literature is taught. Should it be taught by Indigenous people, or can it also be taught by non-Aboriginals?

John: I think it can be taught by the person who is most qualified to teach. And you know, I spoke once with Tomson Highway. I asked him: "Can a non-Native person play a Native role?"

Hartmut: Oh yeah, I know his position on that.

John: Of course.

Hartmut: Yeah, that's an issue. He sometimes gets flogged for that position. From Aboriginal people. But I think he is right.

John: Yeah. I think about that, for example, in a play form, a stage play ... because then, you know, when you go to that stage play that this person, Hartmut Lutz, is going to play Chief Dan George, you know?

Hartmut: Okay. Sure. [laughs]

John: 'Cause we know that.

Hartmut: Yeah, it's a play. Sure.

John: Yeah. And if it's a movie with a lawyer, you know, or a police officer, I'd like to see a Native person up there. 'Cause [Native] representation in theatre, in film [is lacking]. That's a sore point.

Hartmut: Yeah.

John: 'Cause a lot of Native people have not been cast.

Hartmut: No. They always get Native roles, right?

John: Yeah, they get Native roles. But if there's an *indian* person, he's played by a coloured [red-faced] White guy, you know?

Hartmut: Okay. Either that, or maybe a Native person, but not as a lawyer or priest or politician.

John: Or the person is not even a Native person but he's Iron Eyes, for example.

Hartmut: Iron Eyes Cody.

John: Yeah, exactly. [laughs] An Italian.

Hartmut: Okay. Anything else you want to add?

John: Ahh … what else, let me see. I think what I would like to do, I would like to go back to Germany to make another film, to tell a Native story. I'd like to kind of reclaim the Native identity for Native people in German filmmaking.

Hartmut: Oh yeah?

John: That's what I'd be interested in, that the Native person is not a bad guy, or a mean old *indian*, or someone crazy who lives in the bush. My mom lives in the bush but she is not crazy. [laughs]

Hartmut: No.

John: She loves it there: she has a nice cabin. So, it's just something like that that I'd like to do. To tell a Native story, and, for example, my Native kids, my half-Natives, live there. They're learning the German *Sprichwort* [saying] in life and in school, so … It's fun how one day they'll be able to tell a story, [laughs] with this German thought in their head, also Native understanding, too.

Hartmut: Yeah, they can become mediators, huh?

John: Mediators, and even more than I could ever be. But, that's kind of something I would be looking into.

Hartmut: Did you feel when you were in Germany, that you were in a way an ambassador? I don't mean sanctioned by the state of Canada, but a representative or a cultural, yeah, an ambassador for your culture.

John: I think I was a cliché breaker in one way. People have these ideas about Native people, and go, like, "I didn't know *indians* could grow facial hair."

Hartmut: Ahh, yeah. Okay.

John: Gotta go teach. I could have said, "Well, I'm part White, but I can't prove it." [both laughing] But no, I think that was one thing [I did was] break a stereotype.

Hartmut: So, you realized you had a teaching role in a way?

John: Yeah. My favourite thing to do was to go travel to kids' schools because they were easy for me to book as well. [laughs]

I could go there and do a week and just talk about Native people and culture and teach the language, like how to say hello. Maybe where we live, where we come from, the old ways and the old days and stuff like that. So, it's kind of fun on that hand to just talk to the young kids – I don't know, Grade 4, or something. So that is where I did most of my storytelling. I also did it in *Volkshochschulen*.[19] And I went there and I presented my films and gave a talk there in different parts of Germany, *VHSs*.

Hartmut: Yeah, I did that too. Quite a while ago but I did that, too. And what I noticed was if I talked about, say, Native American history or so, people came in droves, but when I wanted to talk about Gypsies or Roma, they didn't want to hear.

John [laughs]: Yeah. I didn't really tap into it very well or very earnestly. I did it once in a while at the university, showed my film and gave a talk about it. So that was interesting, how they were interested. I would talk about dispelling stereotypes.

The poem I wrote, "GROAN" was kind of like my last try. I was interviewed by NDR 1 to talk about stereotypes. You know, the radio DJ asked me, *after* dispelling stereotypes: "Can you do something today, to me? Can you paint my face with war paint?" [imitating the radio host]. And, I was like: *GROAN!*

Well, technically you're not allowed to paint your face. You have to ask the warriors first. You have to have – I don't know – you have to pray. You have to have ceremony, with a pipe. Well, he said: "Some craziness always has to be on the show."

Hartmut: Oh, yeah.

John: He didn't have that interest, you know? If he was really interested in me as a guest on his show ... I don't know, like, "Oh, today we have real *indians*, oh yeah."

Hartmut: That's what I meant when I say, did people see you as John Blackbird, or did they see you as the *indian*, and you had a hard time sort of getting through to them as an individual being.

John: Yeah, I guess that would be one of those moments, you know, that I think ...

Hartmut: It's very offensive and disrespectful.

John: Yeah, weird. You know, those guys, they annoyed me right at the end, and I wrote about them.

Hartmut: Yeah? Good. [laughs]

John: And then the guy said ... at the end, the radio DJ said something like: "HOWGH, HOWGH."

Hartmut: Ahrrrrr, you know, I was once interviewed – this was WDR 1 – about *indian* stereotyping and about racism in Germany, and blah, blah, blah, and *indian*. And I told them what I found in my research and all that, you know, and the interviewer, he was okay. And then after the end of the interview, when they broadcast it, they did "Huhuhuhuhu." I was so pissed off. [John laughs] I felt, my god, here you are, five or ten minutes talking about that type of thing, and then they do it.

John: Yeah.

Hartmut: Okay. Well, John, thank you very much. Miigwetch.

John: Hey, you're welcome.

> **GROAN** [German version appears on pp. 72–73]
> Let's begin here: there was a pause with the Radio DJ of NDR1 he had just
> asked me if the Indianer costumes were authentic
> i wanted to say no, they promoted racism
> GROAN: is the sound of burden
> don't let them get to you, i was once warned
> after awhile, they will say one thing too much
> like today
> i heard it said
> we try to live in the old indian ways
> GROAN
> when i saw the hobbyist walk up
> i hoped against hope
> that he was one of the parents with kinder
> on this children's day spectacle
> I told the NDR1 Radio DJ
> that face painting was a daily thing in the past

but, I also told him that you couldn't paint your face today,
unless you asked the warriors.
he said, something always happens to him, on the show
GROAN
pow waaa, said the hobbyist
he tried to say pow wow
i corrected him
he shrugged, nodded
and said pow waaa again
i almost corrected him
and then it clicked
GROAN
he's a pow waaa man
he wants to organize a pow waaa man
with his circle of Hobby Indianer
and to live in the old ways
and it clicked
as he asked about the Cree
GROAN
in the tipi
where I sat with the children
the Hobbyist laughed the loudest
wore fake cowboy shoes
made in Turkey
he interrupted the kinder's questions
was rude
and was out of place
taking too much space
GROAN
he reminded me of the Hobby Indianer prerequisites:
travel to america or canada
egal where, but visit a rez
at least three weeks
and learn to laugh like they do
be-friend
become a friend of Indians
GROAN
the NDR1 Radio DJ,

said today is about breaking cliche and stereotype
i said, gut
then he signed off saying
ich habe gesprochen, uff, uff
bis nächstes mal
this is all so unreal.
and unfortunately real
groan

ÄCHZ[20]

fangen wir hier mal an: der DJ vom NDR1 machte 'ne Pause
er hatte mich gefragt, ob die Indianerfaschingskostüme echt wären,
ich sagte, eigentlich nicht, und wollte hinzufügen, sie fördern Rassismus
ÄCHZ: der Klang von Last
lass sie nicht an dich ran, ich war gewarnt
irgendwann gehen sie zu weit
wie heute
sie sagten
wir wollten leben nach alt-indianischem Brauch
ÄCHZ
Ich sagte dem NDR1 DJ
Gesichtsbemalung war früher Alltag
aber auch, dass man das heute nicht tun darf
es sei denn, du fragst die Krieger
er sagte, irgendwas geht ihm immer schief während der Sendung
ÄCHZ
Pau Wah, sagte der Hobbytyp
er wollte Pow Wow sagen
ich korrigierte ihn
er zuckte mit den Schultern, jaja
und sagte wieder Pau Wah
ich hätt es ihm fast wieder gesagt
da machte es Klick
ÄCHZ
Er ist ein PauWah Mann
will Pau-Wah-Mann-Sache organisieren
zusammen mit seinen Pau-Wah-Hobbyindianerfreunden
leben nach altem Indianerbrauch

und es machte Klick
und er fragte mich nach den Cree
ÄCHZ
Im Tipi
wo ich mit den Kindern saß
lachte der Hobbyindianer am lautesten
trug Cowboystiefelimitate
aus der Türkei
unterbrach die Fragen der Kinder
war rüde
und fehl am Platz
machte sich breit
ÄCHZ
Dem Hobbyindianer ein Muß, daran erinnerte er mich:
Amerikareise [oder auch Kanada]
wherever - aber: Besuch eines Reservats
drei Wochen Minimum
und lachen lernen wie sie
Freunde werden
Indianerfreund werden
ÄCHZ
Der NDR1 DJ meinte
aufräumen mit Klischees und Stereotypen!
Ich sagte: Gut.
Er verabschiedete sich vom Mikro mit
"ich haben gesprochen Uff, Uff -
bis zum nächsten Mal"
Unwirklich
aber wahr.
ächz

WARREN CARIOU

The past has to be continually remembered.

Live interview recorded in Florentine Strzelczyk's office at the Department of Linguistics, Languages and Cultures, University of Calgary. In attendance: Florentine, Paulina Maczuga (MA student in German, 2010–12), Warren, and Hartmut

Hartmut: First of all, thank you, and we have a number of questions. I think we'll all help each other.

Warren: Sure.

Hartmut: We have one question that we have from Renae Watchman. She always starts asking people for what she calls their tribal affiliation.[21]

Warren: [chuckles] Sure. That's a complicated one for me, as you know. My father was Métis, and my mother is German and Norwegian ancestry, and both of them grew up in Canada. So, my affiliation is "Métis Plus," I guess [laughs]. But I try to give people the understanding that Métis identity is a complex thing, and that of course all Métis people have a complicated story when you ask them.

Hartmut: Since this is a series about the German connection, can you say a little about your German connection?

Warren: Sure. Yes! As I mentioned, my mom's father was from Germany, and he moved to Canwood, Saskatchewan, in – I can't remember the exact year now – it was in the early 1920s, I believe, as a young man. And two of his brothers also moved there. So, it was a kind of a family enclave there. And there was a fairly large German community in the area. And Canwood is about a hundred miles from my own town of Meadow Lake. So we would go there quite often when I was growing up, and my grandfather spoke German in the household, and my mom understood and spoke German as well. So, when we would go there, we would hear German, and we would see my grandfather reading German, but they didn't speak it to us. They didn't teach us the language.

Also, my grandmother was [of] Norwegian ancestry. She had actually grown up in Minnesota but grew up speaking Norwegian. So we had also our Norwegian uncles in the area, as well.

So at my grandpa's house [we heard] German spoken a lot, and some Norwegian as well. It was the same in my father's side of the family, in a way, because my grandmother spoke French and Cree, and that was not spoken to us either. [laughs] So we didn't really think of it as strange, you know, but we heard these languages around us, a few words here and there, but it wasn't like we were being inculcated into those linguistic worlds really.

Hartmut: And your first connection to Germany – you've been to Germany how often?

Warren: I think five times now. And, as you well know, my wife Alison and I came to Germany the first time, I guess it was 2005, to be visiting professors at the University of Greifswald. And, yeah, that was an amazing and wonderful experience. And that was our first introduction to the reality of Germany, as opposed to what sort of fictions we may have had in our minds.

Hartmut: What fictions did you have in mind?

Warren: Well, I had those stereotypical notions of what Germany was like, even though [I'd] grown up with a grandfather who was German and spoke the language. But yeah, this ... I'm really embarrassed about it in a sense.

Florentine: No. It's okay. [all laughing]

Hartmut: We are talking about stereotypes.

Florentine: We are.

Warren: Absolutely. So, certainly my own work on Aboriginal identities is very much about stereotypes. But I think there is something interesting about examining how stereotypes have a power, you know, even if they are totally inaccurate. On the one hand, I had the idea Germany was a place where serious thinking happened, you know? The great ... the big philosophers.

Hartmut: That is true! [laughs]

Florentine: The nation of "poets and thinkers." [laughs]

Warren: So that was one element, and of course the, you know, the pop-cultural references to beer and enjoyment and that side of it, which is quite different from the very serious German philosophers.

Hartmut: But that's what stereotypes are!

Warren: Exactly. And then, of course, what you absorb growing up in the latter half of the twentieth century is the history of the Holocaust and Nazism. And all of that was very much there in the background of our minds when we went to Germany. At the same time, another sort of very different image we had about Germany was related to environmentalism. We had this idea: this is a place where environmentalism is very important. With the Nazi history, of course, there is this sense where people who are not German will say, "Well, we didn't do that," that we can feel superior, morally, in a way. I think there is a long history of that happening since the Holocaust. But I think with environmentalism there is this other sense. At least what I felt was that "I'm going to a place where everyone is hypersensitive about this – and they're morally superior to us in that regard." So I felt …

Hartmut [laughing]: That's a new one! [all laughing]

Warren: So, I felt, "Okay, we're going to this place, there's going to be the impact of environmental action – not just thought, but action!" So, Alison and I, we were both worried about recycling. In fact, one of our guidebooks said in Germany you're required to recycle everything in different ways. And so, they said: "If you have tea, you'll have a teabag, and you recycle the tea in one place, and then the bag in another place, and then the staple in another place." [laughs] I have no idea if that's [true] anywhere. We never found that to be true, but this is what we were expecting, at least a hypervigilance around recycling and doing it the proper way.

And also, I think, in relation to my Aboriginal ancestry, I have a sense also of coming there, feeling like, "I don't want to let anyone down," like I was not the proper "ecological *indian*." [all laughing] You know, I really felt self-conscious. We didn't mention this to you guys at the time. So anyway, we would decide, "Okay, how are we gonna do our recycling?" And as time went on, it built up in our apartment. We had bottles from juices and water and whatever, we didn't know where to put them, and they were piling up. And we kept wondering, "What are we gonna do?" And Alison and I would go and search on the internet, in German, which we didn't speak, to try and find that …

Hartmut: Why didn't you ask?

Warren: I don't know. That's very strange. We felt, like, this is something we should know or something. I think we may have asked someone at the guest house there and didn't get a very good answer or something.

Anyway, we finally found the place where the recycling was and were so happy. And Alison and I, we took all our stuff, and, of course, there were all these different bins to put things. And we didn't speak the language, so we were trying to gather ... "Okay, there is where the glass goes," and we saw other people going and stuffing white garbage bags into this other bin. So, we went, "Okay that's great, we'll put our garbage there, too!" So for the next few weeks we felt very proud of ourselves; we thought, "Oh we didn't have to ask Hartmut, this is great." [Hartmut laughs] And we've learned to be good environmental citizens in Germany.

But it was toward the end of our stay that first summer – Alison's German was getting better and better than mine – and then she recognized the words suddenly. She says, "Oh my god!" once she'd seen this word, and she knew what it meant.

And I said, "What's wrong?"

She said, "Well, I just realized the word 'Kleider,' what that means."

And I said, "What does it mean?"

She said, "Clothing."

"And so? What's the point of that?"

She said, "Well that's the sign that was on the bin where we thought it was for garbage."

So we had been putting our garbage in this bin where everyone else had been putting clothes for recycling. [all laughing] Our environmentalism went way down. So anyway, a long story, but this was our attempt to fit into what we thought the expectations were, environmentally speaking.

And then, of course, we were learning other things, especially because we were in former East Germany. Seeing that their nuclear power plant had been decommissioned, seeing that our ideas about environmentalism in Germany were not applicable, you know, certainly not all over Germany anyway, and seeing that in former East Germany, there is an ethical movement toward a lot more recycling and environmental sensitivity, but it may be different than what we had been led to believe.

So I think that was something that really surprised us in the sense of the cultural differences that remained between East and West. We spent most of our time in the East, but I think our stereotypes came from the West. That was an interesting kind of difference for us.

Hartmut: You know that there are increasing numbers of people in Germany who get PhDs in Native Studies, and you also have German PhDs given to Native scholars.

Warren: Right.

Hartmut: And there's quite a bit of academic exchange. Do you have any comments on that?

Warren: Well, I guess that sort of goes back to another of my preconceptions that I had before I went to Germany. It was that I had heard about what is now called Indianthusiasm, and I had heard that Aboriginal writers in particular were very popular in Germany. So when we went, already that wave of new Canadian Aboriginal fiction writers had hit the scene. For instance, people like Eden Robinson, Drew Hayden Taylor, a number of really well-established writers had gone, I think. I don't know if Eden had actually travelled to Germany, but I know that *Monkey Beach*[22] was published there, and there was a real interest.

So, I had a sense that there was an interest that was fairly knowledgeable but also another, or maybe separate, level of interest that was fairly superficial. But I did have a sense that there were both, 'cause I think having known your work, Hartmut, and having seen some of Wolfgang Klooss's[23] work as well, and others, and having been part of the University of Manitoba, where there's been a lot of exchange with Germany already. So, we had a sense that there was serious, really important work being done on Aboriginal culture there, as well as this popular phenomenon.

Hartmut: Do you think that this research that's done outside of North America, does that have a function, or does that have repercussions here? Is it different from what is being done here? Of course, it's done at a distance, but if it has a function, where would you see that?

Warren: I think it's really important to consider cultures from very close, from within, in a way, but also it's also extremely important to consider them from a cultural distance. And a distance that is mapped out and recognized.

Right now, you know, in literary studies, in Aboriginal literature, there is a real movement toward literary separatism or literary nationalism. These movements are about reading the work from a particular language group or community, from within the storytelling traditions, the tribal community.

Hartmut: Tribal specific?

Warren: Not only tribal specific, but you know, there is an implication that it's important for Aboriginal scholars from within those communities to write about their own work, their own communities' work. I think that is very important. There is no doubt about that. And I think that's a reaction to the anthropological approach, in which there was a false kind of distance, or a very particular kind of distance, in which the scholar assumed a sense of neutrality, of objectivity, right? So I think the reaction against that was very important.

But I think at the same time, you can overdo the reading from the inside; if you only value interpretations that are very close culturally to the material that you are studying, then you're missing out on some other possibilities of what that work could possibly mean. So I think it's really, really important to have traditions of reading that are obviously and clearly separate and outside of the Aboriginal communities. I think there are ways those kinds of perspectives can show different kinds of things in the work. So it maybe makes different kinds of comparisons, and just allows readers to think that they can approach a text even if it's very different culturally from their own.

This is something I have come up against a little bit in my teaching in the last few years, when I teach Aboriginal literature at the University of Manitoba. We have, as you know, a fair number of Aboriginal students there, and there is a fair interest in Aboriginal culture generally in Manitoba. But what I find is, in some of my classes, that the students who are not Aboriginal, especially when we started reading those literary separatist texts, that they start to feel: "Can I say anything?" You know: "What is my position here?" And so, some of them just go silent, or just think, "I'm gonna work on something else."

Hartmut: There's also politics involved.

Warren: Exactly, yeah. I think it's a shame if a student or just an interested reader says, "I'm not gonna read that. I'm not gonna interact with that, because it's for Aboriginal people. It's for them to explore, and I'm just gonna think of something else." I think that's a mistake.

Hartmut: Why do you think those students think that?

Warren: Well, I think partly because they need to examine their own position critically, if they are to find a place to make a contribution. And sometimes they don't want to do that. They have to think about their own place in the colonial history of Canada. And sometimes that's very difficult. I've certainly seen students have very difficult emotional reactions to it.

Hartmut: I think that's where critics or scholars from outside have a privilege, because they're not sitting on Indigenous land. They come from outside.

And also, I found that it helped me – often in the beginning, when I was working in the US – not to be an anthropologist.

Warren: Yes. Right.

Hartmut: Because then very often the shutters went down.

Warren: Yes. I'm sure. So I think that's very true, and I certainly make it a point to teach work by scholars who are from outside of Aboriginal communities, first because it's excellent scholarship, but also just because I think it's important, the recognition that these texts, these stories, are resilient enough to be read from all kinds of perspectives.

Hartmut: I think it could boost their nationalist pride, saying, "This is read the world over."

Warren: Absolutely. And I thought, I guess their resilience is one thing, but also the stories are rich enough. It shouldn't be that you can only read a Cree story, or a Cree poem, by a Cree writer, through a Cree narrative. It's important that you know if there is a reference to a Cree traditional story within a work of literature, for sure – I think we need to do more work in that regard – but to think you could only do that, that you couldn't do a Marxist reading of it, or you couldn't do some other kind of reading of it: I think that is mistaken.

Because this literature is much richer than any single theoretical perspective can show us, even one that is based within the writer's culture. This literature interacts with the broader world too. I think there sometimes is a problem of trying to read a writer only in terms of an individual tradition, when many Aboriginal writers have experience with more than one Aboriginal tradition or language. And, of course many have interests in things beyond their own cultural heritage as well.

Hartmut: You used the term "beyond." And sometimes when I'm talking to students, I would say: "First there was 'writing back,' and then 'writing home,' and now it's really 'writing beyond.'" A lot of writers are writing beyond and reaching out to everybody.[24]

Warren: Definitely. I really think that's true. I mean you can see in a lot of works that there is very clearly a kind of "double audience," or maybe more than double – multiple audiences. A lot of Aboriginal writers are very clearly writing to their communities on one level, but I think there are very few who are *only* writing to their communities. I think many are really wanting to address the larger world as well.

Earlier in the history of Aboriginal literature in Canada, the writers were almost always writing to a White Canadian audience. They were not really writing to their own people, because they didn't imagine that their own people would read those books. So I think it's very interesting how that has shifted – the question of what the audience for the literature is. And now, I think – as you say – it's maybe multiple, and containing this broadness as an attempt to engage with the world, as well as with the whole community.

Hartmut: Coming back to Germany: How did people in Germany react to you?

Warren: [laughs] I think how people react to me in general as someone ... They maybe heard that I'm a Métis writer, and then they see me, and they see my appearance and I have, as [far as] I can tell, no visible Aboriginal look. So that is sometimes an occasion that raises questions.

Hartmut: A disappointment?

Warren: I think. I haven't seen that so much in Germany, per se. But I think there is that element sometimes.

Hartmut: Where have you encountered that?

Warren: Actually, more in other parts of Europe, to be honest.

Hartmut: Aha.

Warren: I think it may just have been the context in which we were introduced to audiences when we were in Greifswald. Those were audiences of students who had already been introduced to the idea that an Aboriginal person could not necessarily have one particular kind of look.

So, really, I think there is sometimes that element. I certainly saw that in other parts of Europe, at conferences. In France, especially, where people seemed ... who expected me to be performing a certain kind of identity, and were maybe a bit disappointed. [all laugh] And also, what I have experienced in Canada, more so than in Europe, is that people will say racist things about Aboriginal people because they assume ...

Hartmut: Yes, because you don't look Indigenous.

Warren: Yeah, so they assume I am, you know, going to agree.

Hartmut: Be on their side?

Warren: Yeah. So that's again something I think a number of Aboriginal writers have written about. Drew Hayden Taylor has written about that. So I found in Germany that the audiences that we read for, or people that we met, were already fairly knowledgeable. So I didn't feel like I was on display, you know? [laughs] I didn't feel that I was found lacking because I did not perform a particular visual identity. So that was something that I really appreciated.

Hartmut: There is a question – I think you have answered that in a way already: Has scholarly work by Germans on Indianthusiasm influenced your own work?

Warren: I guess the work on Indianthusiasm in particular hasn't been a big part of my own work. I've been aware of it and read certainly something about your work and other articles. That's it. I think it's a fascinating phenomenon, but ...

Hartmut: But you are working on people in zoos and stuff.

Warren: Yeah. I guess the sense of spectacularization of the Aboriginal identity. I guess my definition in my own head of Indianthusiasm was "European people pretending to be Aboriginal." But maybe that's only one side of it?

Hartmut: That's part of it, "Indianistik" or hobbyism, I think.

Warren: Okay. But the other side, of course, is very much the fascination with Aboriginal identities in Europe, going back a long way. So I'm very interested in the histories around from the 1880s into the 1920s and '30s, as a lot of your work, and certainly your book on Abraham[25] indicated. What really got me started on that was when I read the translation of Abraham's narrative. I'm very interested in the ways in which Aboriginal people have been turned into a kind of spectacle, mostly in the European setting, although that did happen in the US as well, in some of those World Fairs in the 1890s, generally.

Hartmut: Not in Canada?

Warren: I haven't found any specific examples of an "ethnographic village" in Canada, but there may well be and I just don't know about it.

Hartmut: I think at the Stampede they have them.

Warren: That's true. I mean there is certainly the Wild Bill and the Wild West shows, where they were constructed [under] a slightly different sort of rubric, I guess. But that's very true, so there were cases, those travelling Wild West shows came through a number of places in the west, including Winnipeg. I'm really interested in how Aboriginal people were displayed in those zoos, in those other kinds of anthropological, proto-anthropological contexts and also how that way of seeing Aboriginal people as museum exhibits, which seems so shocking to us now, is actually still practised in some ways. Ways in which our institutions, especially museums, display artifacts and, of course, still harbour some actual human remains of Aboriginal people. So I think it's easy for us to think about how shocking that is in the past ...

Hartmut: But it's right there at the front.

Warren: Exactly, as is so often the case in our contemporary world.

Hartmut: But it's nice that it happened over in Europe.

Warren: Yeah.

Hartmut: So you can point and say, "Look what *they* did."

Warren: Yes, exactly. Even that sort of presentism: "Look what they did, back there." Canadians often do this in relation to their own past, telling themselves, "In Canada we did some bad things, but that was a long time ago. We wouldn't do them now." And that's really a perennial problem. In Canada we like to believe that we are fundamentally good, and we are inculcated into that ideology. And so to be able to think someone else did something bad makes us feel better.

Hartmut: It may have to do with being so close to the US.

Warren: Yeah.

Hartmut: "Find a different role" [with which to distinguish ourselves]?

Warren: That's very true, yeah. I think so. And of course [it is evident in] the way in which the history of treatment of Aboriginal people in the US as opposed to Aboriginal people in Canada played out. That history in the nineteenth century and early twentieth century is ...You know, Americans were more bloody. It's pretty obvious. But that doesn't mean that what the Canadians did was good. I think there is that sense that national imaginaries and national mythologies were comparative. "Okay, maybe we did some bad things, but they were worse." So, therefore our nation gained maybe a sense of pride or a sense of moral value from the fact that you didn't do something as egregious as another nation did. But I think you are right: The proximity of the US is a big factor there.

Hartmut: I already asked: How did you perceive Germans and Germany? Did your perception of Germany change when you went there?

Warren: [laughs] Yes. Yes, very much. I think this always happens when you travel, but especially when you go to a place and stay in one place for a relatively long time, as we did in Greifswald, a lot of the stereotypes went out the window fairly quickly. Our sense of also just the complexity of Germany in itself ... we were of course aware of the Cold War and aware of this division in Germany, but that became much more visible to us when we were in former East Germany and we could see the architecture and we could see how that was different from one side of Berlin to the other, for example. Seeing the variety was very interesting. And also travelling to some of the neighbouring countries as well, and seeing their relationship to Germany, whether that was long ago, hundreds of years ago, or whether that's more recent in the twentieth century and the shifting borders and all of that, it was a much more complex picture that we got. Our notion of what Germany is – it was a very complicated thing.

Hartmut: *Tja.*

Warren: Some of this complexity is reflected in my own family history. I had been told that my grandfather grew up in a small town in Poland, near the German border, although he was German and spoke German. But when we got to Germany, I realized something.

Florentine: Back then it was Germany.

Warren: Back then his home town was part of Germany, yeah. That was surprising to me, because I had no idea that we had this actual connection to what is now Poland, and what was Poland before as well.

And then I remember telling Hartmut that we had some other relatives in a place called Hoyerswerda, and when he heard this, he told us that place was infamous for neo-Nazis! I guess we weren't as aware of the potential resurgence of neo-Nazism especially in East Germany. And so we would see young people wearing particular garments. We couldn't interpret what it was, whether they were anarchists or neo-Nazis, or what, but we had a sense that there was something going on that we were not aware of, you know, that we were not really able to understand. So that was there, but we didn't really see much first hand, I would say.

Florentine: Can I chime in? Because racism is of course one of my interests. And there is this interesting racist hierarchy that obviously Indigenous people are positively stereotyped in many ways and overtly so and compared to other cultural ethnic groups in one way, but then we have all sorts of issues with Turkish people and so on. They're extremely negatively stereotyped right? So there is this hierarchy on how ... All of them are racist, but what's considered "good racism" [laughs] and not-so-good racism? Any thoughts on that?

Warren: That is fascinating. We spent some time in Berlin, and [had] the sense of the Turkish people there being somewhat, you know, marked, I guess. I have a very vague recollection that some of the graffiti had the word "Turkish" in it.

Hartmut: "Türken raus," ["Turks out"] or something?

Warren: Yeah, yeah. Or something with "Türken" anyway. And I think, being in Berlin and going into some of the neighbourhoods that were largely Turkish, that was very interesting.

Hartmut: Berlin is the largest Turkish urban environment outside Istanbul.[26]

Warren: Oh, that's truly amazing. So it was very interesting for us to see, what we then recognized as a multicultural aspect of Berlin, which was something that we hadn't really expected to that extent. That you would have a whole market that was entirely a Turkish market. But I just can't think of some specific examples. My sort of speculation about that is that Aboriginal people are not going to be a threat in terms of immigration, right? Slavoj Žižek writes about the idea of theft of enjoyment, and he's such an amazing theorist on national relationships. The idea that someone's going to come and steal your national good, your national thing. Well, there is no danger that Aboriginal people are going to come to Germany and take whatever the national thing in Germany is, whereas when there is a big influx of immigration from somewhere, then that's a threat that comes up, and that happens in all kinds of multicultural nations or nations where there is immigration. And their sense is: they're going to change who we are. And I think Aboriginal people are not going to change who Germany is. There is not enough potential immigration [laughs] to be happening. So that's part of it, I think. So maybe that's why, you know, it's easier to idealize Aboriginal people, because they represent certain ideology, I guess, in Germany, but they're never going to be a threat to come and transform a nation.

Hartmut: Well, I think the attractiveness of Aboriginal people for Germans or *Indianer* ... I mean the Karl May image is: they love Germans. Winnetou loves Germans, and Germans are not very used to being loved. And I think that is a message, "they like us," it's okay.

Warren: That's a really good point.

Hartmut: I don't know. [laughs] You have readers – you did readings in Germany, and did you notice anything, criticism or so? Is the reception of your work any different in Germany – or your readings – from, say, North America or here?

Warren: Well, as you know, much of my writing is about place,[27] about a very specific place, that of course no one in Germany, or very few people in

Germany, would have ever visited. So that the sense of its exoticism is maybe played up a little bit there. But I actually found the same thing in Canada to a large degree – when I did a reading in Ontario or in Vancouver – there is not a general sense that people know the landscape, you know. I actually think that was something of a discovery for me when I was writing, especially writing *Lake of the Prairies*, was that these stories that I grew up with, the landscape I grew up with, were actually a gift to me as a writer because no one else really had explored that in the same way that I was able to. People found these exotic. People found these interesting. So without even going outside the boundaries of Saskatchewan, maybe, there's that same element [of exoticism] to a certain degree.

Hartmut: I see.

Warren: One of the things about giving readings at home in Saskatchewan, or Manitoba, or maybe in Alberta as well, is that the local politics are much more present in the room. And that's natural, and when you give a reading, you probably have Aboriginal people in the room, you probably have people who are relatives of someone you may be talking about or writing about. That's a different feeling. When I read in Meadow Lake the first time – and my book *Lake of the Prairies* was about racism in that town – and so, I could read on the far side of the world about that and not be very nervous about it, but when I was reading in Meadow Lake, I was worried. The first time I was really wondering: "What are these people gonna say?" Because I'm holding up this town as a model, you know, of racial tension. A model [of how] things are not working well in the colonial apparatus.

Florentine: Right.

Hartmut: And how did people react?

Warren: Well, I was very fortunate. I think it was something I didn't actually allow myself to think about until I was about to read. And then I was terrified, and I was wondering, you know? It was kind of a huge, relatively big crowd, maybe eighty people in the Meadow Lake library, but they were very generous, actually. A place like that is so complicated as a community – and I knew the complications because I grew up there. So there were members of the Aboriginal community there, and there were people from various other ethnic communities in Meadow Lake that were there. And I started ... As I read every sentence, I would think, "How is that group gonna interpret that? And how is *that* group gonna interpret that?" But I think I was really lucky that the audience in that area recognized that I wrote this book with a spirit of love for the place. I was not trying to just take it apart.

Hartmut: I think it could also be a liberation. I think to put it out there, and people will think, yeah, it is there. You know, let somebody say it, and then we can change it.

Warren: I think that's a really good point, too. The work has come out now, and people have written me from there and said, "We're glad you said that." And now when I go back and do readings, it's always different, you know. It's a different group, but I feel that there is more openness to understanding, or maybe examining some of these questions now. I think they're actually – the town has made some steps toward coming to terms with its past. Not that my book is responsible for that, but I think the community has now just recognized that.

Hartmut: That is responsible for that.

Warren: Well, maybe in a very, very small way.

Hartmut: This is not on our agenda, but did you have that sort of in mind, that you want to effect social change, or change, with your writing?

Warren: Absolutely, yeah. I talked about different audiences for Aboriginal writers – certainly one of my main audiences for my work is back home – trying to speak to those people, you know, who were so important to me when I was growing up and who gave me their stories. And it's the same with my film,[28] that's also directed toward Meadow Lake in a large way, because it's about the oil sands operations that are coming there, and what might change, what might happen there in the future. So I wanted it to be something that the people there could watch and maybe make some decisions based on that. Or at least to ask some more questions. That's, I guess, the main thing, 'cause I don't want to give people the answer, but if at least I can make them ask more questions.

Florentine: I want to drag you back to Germany just for a minute. One of the big markers for Germans is obviously the Third Reich and the Holocaust, and the approach to the past matters to Germans. How Germans are judged today matters. It's measured by how they approach the past and that's where they stand. So it's a yardstick of how far they have come – or not, or what that means. The Holocaust and the Third Reich, in other words, loom large, and the approach to the past really matters to Germans. It says something about them, kind of like for other people, it may be "What food you like," but for Germans, where, how you stand [with regard to the Holocaust] is a question that really matters. And I was wondering if that kind of approach to the past, with all its problematic aspects, while you were there, does that influence somehow, or has that influenced some of your writing or thinking, and how people here approach the past?

Warren: Sure. That's a really good question. Again, it is a very limited experience I had in Germany, really. I can't analyze it hugely. But I found that the state level, that level of the memorials that we saw, were something that were, you know ... Kind of like Prora, for example. So this enormous edifice that had been preserved, partly because it was hard to destroy, [laughs] but also as a memorial to one aspect of the Nazi past.[29] That was something that I knew nothing about. I had heard of some of the other memorials of the Holocaust: the Holocaust memorial in Berlin, which was just opened when we were there, and we went to Auschwitz.[30] The people at the University in Greifswald really took it seriously; that was something that was important for their identities, I think. This was my impression, that it was not something that could just be said, "Okay, that's in the past." I never encountered that. And maybe there, I am sure there are people in Germany who maybe have that, but my sense among the people that I met from Germany was that the past has to be continually remembered. And that there is a responsibility in being a German citizen. And so I saw that reflected at the state level, as I said, but also in terms of individuals. And that really struck me: the focus on remembering, and maybe the sense also that the international community is watching, to see whether Germans continue to remember. I think there may be also a sort of superego thing at work here, where their sense is it's not only their responsibility, but they must also perform that responsibility publicly in order to expiate a bad conscience.

And then, you know, that is so different from Canada – for me. Canada, in my academic expertise, is basically a history of colonialism and the racism against Aboriginal people and many human rights abuses that were perpetrated and that continue to be perpetrated against Aboriginal people here. But some of the things that come up again and again in my writing and in my teaching, is that Canadians don't want to think about that. They really do not want to come to terms with [this]. I think some of them are able to recognize what has happened in the past. Maybe [even] a majority now, with people becoming more aware of the history of the residential schools in the last ten years, for example. Even ten or fifteen or twenty years ago, that was not something that would have been generally discussed. And it is something that only very recently I could take for granted [that my students] knew a little bit about it. So for me, one of the things that I really absorbed from my time in Germany, was to find ways of making these negative sides of Canada's history visible to us in the contemporary world. So I have this essay called "Going to Canada," and it's about when we were at Auschwitz, and we saw on the map of Birkenau, there was a place called Canada, and that was such a strange thing, 'cause I was going [with] all my preconceptions about the Holocaust, and it's so overwhelming, obviously, emotionally, and then to see my country there was so strange. And that haunted me for a long time, and so I went and looked at the place. And so that idea, going there, which I thought was ... again, going to that place which has nothing to do with Canada, this is the shame of Germany that I'm going to see here, right? And somehow I had this weird ... it rebounded on me in terms of the shame of my own nation. And that's, you know, totally different – you don't want to draw any comparisons between the Holocaust and any other atrocity, because I think each atrocity has its own story, and the victims deserve their own ...

Florentine: You can't compare suffering.

Warren: No. That's right. I think it made me think back to: What is not being remembered in Canada? Where are the places that we should be going to remember? What has happened in Canada that I don't know of in Canadian history? And there are probably many other things that I don't know about. But I think that Canadians are not encouraged to remember the negative things about our past, generally. And I do think that the contemporary attempts to deal with and come to terms with the legacy of the residential schools is a different thing for Canada, because it really challenges our idealistic notion of who we are as Canadians. For me that really does come back to my time in Germany, where I thought, "Here is a nation that is very conscientious and has very strong reasons to be conscientious about not forgetting." So I think that is something that Canadians need to learn from because we have a lot of our own very, very difficult histories that are ongoing, that don't go away. That's the thing. As you mentioned, Hartmut, in relation to the rise of neo-Nazis, these things are not finished in a way. And if you try to just not think about them, then it's much more difficult to deal with them when they do resurface. So, I'm not sure what's the next thing. I could probably talk more about that.

Paulina: I'm curious: what is your opinion about powwows that are organized by people in Germany? Do you think it's to express that they socialize with Aboriginal people? Is their intention to show respect for the culture?

Warren: That's a really good question. I have never been to one of the powwows in Germany. I've only seen some film footage of them and read a little bit about them. It's a very interesting phenomenon to see a cultural group replicated – or cultural practices replicated – in a certain way by people who are obviously not from that cultural community. And there is a huge number of examples in the international media of people appropriating images of

Aboriginality. There are many cases – on my Facebook almost every week someone is pointing one out. And it's still happening where, you know, a singer will wear a headdress inappropriately ... So things, people are using this iconography without understanding that there's a history to it and there are stories behind it, and that there are sacred practices potentially behind these. I think that is a problem in our contemporary world. In our media-saturated world, where images can be recirculated without context, without the proper understanding of where they come from and what they mean in their original context.

And I've talked to Jeannette Armstrong a little bit about this, too. She has spent some time in at least one of these powwow communities in Europe, and I was really struck by what she said: I don't see them as being – I'm paraphrasing here, maybe she can correct me – but my impression of what she said was that she takes it as a gesture of respect. And that she understood that they may be mistaken in a lot of things that they're doing in terms of their understanding of the meanings behind these practices, but that they're not intending to defame or destroy the original intent of these practices. So I think in [the case of the powwows] – it's a little different [from] someone ... [like] a clothing company using an icon or a band wearing Aboriginal regalia without having any connection to our understanding. I think there is some deeper kind of practice at work there [at the German powwows] which is maybe more related to our relationship to the environment.

Hartmut: Maybe it's also a difference whether these hobbyists spend money for their outfits or so, but it's not really a commercial venture.

Warren: Right, that's interesting.

Hartmut: It's a hobby, whereas when the singer wears a headdress, it is for marketing. And I think that is maybe an important element when marketing comes into play.

Warren: That is a really good point because it is the commodification of Indigenous identity which is an enormous, enormous problem. Which has been a problem, you know, for at least a hundred and fifty years. And this is something Hartmut has written about quite a lot as well. So the co-optation of Indigenous identity into a capitalist system that has already stolen every-thing else from Indigenous people – it's just the final insult. But I think it is a kind of evolving tradition, I guess, in my understanding in Europe. There it is not being done for profit, as you say, so maybe there's a difference.

Florentine: You know, for East Germans, as far as I've understood, Indian-thusiasm created a point of resistance, almost, to a different regime. So yes, appropriation, but it took on a different shape, right?

Warren: I see.

Florentine: That this could be a point of resistance toward the totalitarian.

Hartmut: On the one hand, they were encouraged to be anti-American, but then, some of them went to the US Embassy and asked for material. Of course they were surveilled. Nobody goes to the US Embassy. So it was always, on the one hand, pushing them on to revolutionize them against America, on the other hand contain them. It was a very, very interesting political situation they had. And it was certainly not a commercial thing. They took great pride in doing everything themselves. And not having the chance, which West German groups had, of maybe going to North America, buying things here.[31]

Warren: Right. Well, I think there are really interesting parallels, in a way, when you look back, even, I mean, Marx writes about this, the notion of Aboriginal people as living a kind of ideal communism.[32]

Hartmut: Oh *ja*.

Florentine: That's right.

Warren: So there may be some sense of which what they're practising is in a way more about ...

Hartmut: It's a primordial form of communism.

Warren: Yeah.

Hartmut: A pre-industrial communism. That's what Engels wrote about and he's, "Oh, it's so wonderful," and then all of a sudden he stops and his theory kicks in and he says, "Yeah, but of course, it's pre-industrial and it's not the right kind of communism." It's crazy. He's caught in his own ideology.

Warren: Right. But I think that's maybe part of it. There is a kind of idealism there for the East German side of it. But yeah, I think it is a practice that is involving its own history and involving its own kind of respect for a tradition, even though people don't necessarily understand the traditions very well. There is a place to at least acknowledge that it's maybe flawed, but at least it's not intended to be stealing. It's not intended to be taking away from the identity of Aboriginal people. I think intention is important for a lot of Aboriginal people. The intention with which one approaches Aboriginal culture generally. If someone is approaching an Aboriginal community, for example, to do some kind of work – and I see this with researchers, who say, "We'll come and help you because you have bad health, and we're gonna go and do this," and very often Aboriginal communities say, "No, we don't want that.

You haven't asked us what we want and you haven't been humble." Humility is an important feature in Aboriginal communities. If you're coming and just telling people what you're going to do, they are very resistant to that. So I think the intent is so important. I haven't seen any of these powwows [as Indianistic events], but just from seeing film footage and hearing about the *Indianistik* movement, it seems that their intent is not to appropriate in a negative way. It would be interesting to see if more Aboriginal people could go and actually talk with them, and maybe talk to them more about what those traditions really are, what the stories behind them really are.

Hartmut: There are quite a number of Aboriginal people living in Germany.

Warren: Right.

Hartmut: Going to powwows and being part of that.

Warren: Okay. Great. So I think if people want to learn about another culture, and learn from another culture, that's wonderful. And I do think also in the contemporary world that – especially with the environmental problems that we are facing – there's a lot to be learned from Indigenous ways of understanding, how we live on the Earth. And there are ways we can just stereotype the environmental *indian*, but I think, looking more closely at the Cree and Anishinaabe and Métis stories that I know, they tell us actually different ways that we can be on the Earth. They give us an alternative to the system of commodification and consumption that has overtaken pretty much most of the world. So I think that's really important. We need to spend more time thinking about that. So from whatever perspective, wherever someone is in the world, I think, we can learn from those, and I hope people continue to do that. Whether they put on a headdress, you know, and do that is another question, [laughs] but I think we can really learn, and I think it's something that the globe needs – not just the individual communities need.

Paulina: Did you have a chance to meet some Germans and to ask them why they're so interested about your culture, about Aboriginal people?

Warren: I guess only really through the university. So I don't think I had much real discussion with a sort of person who wasn't already at the university and already studying English. So that was quite a narrow sample that I had. But no, I certainly know a little bit about the history of the Karl May books and the effect that they had in Germany and the sense that children, especially boys, were being sort of prepared to be enthusiastic about Aboriginal people early on in their lives.

Hartmut: You have that in Poland, too, right? I mean there are groups like that?

Paulina: But I don't think it's as popular. Maybe for boys, but not girls.

Hartmut: When I taught at the University of Szczecin in American Studies, I saw visual materials students had produced, and the illustrations that the students had come up with were really the same stereotypes as those I'd see in Germany.

Paulina: The stereotype is the same, yes.

Hartmut: And it must have come from somewhere. But I don't know about Indianthusiasm in Poland.

Paulina: I don't think it's so popular as in Germany. I haven't heard about organizing powwows or people who live in the same way as Aboriginal people.

Hartmut: But they only do that on weekends and during the holidays.

Paulina: Okay. [all laughing]

Warren: Not full time.

Hartmut: Not full time. There may be some who tried. There is one big event called "The Week" – "Die Woche" – and I always thought that's the village.[33]

Warren: Oh, I see.

Hartmut: And this year there were more than two hundred tipis.

Warren: Wow.

Hartmut: That's a lot. That's somewhere in East Germany, in different locations.

Warren: I think it would be interesting to make a comparison between that kind of performance and the performances that you see where there's, let's say, a Star Wars conference or where people are dressing up. I think it may be very similar. A kind of celebration.

Hartmut: I think it is. I think you're right.

Warren: And a lot of those conventions in North America – I'm not sure how popular they are in Europe – I see lots of photographs of these people who dress up as aliens or ... And that they are enjoying just the fun of being someone alien, you know? And maybe there's a sense in Germany that there's an enjoyment to being someone who is not your daily life, not at all. And you do something very different and you celebrate that.

Florentine: But I think it's different, though. I mean I don't want to contradict our interviewee.

Warren: [laughs] No.

Florentine: I think it's different because Germans have a particular sense of ... space and time. Time because it refers to their often troublesome history, and space because there is that notion of the German *Heimat* and home-land. Germans have that long tradition that was appropriated by the Nazis but goes back to the eighteenth century, of having a close affinity with their forest, with their landscape, the features of the homeland. Germans imagined themselves being better colonialists than the English and the French, if they were just given a chance. So that plays into their idealization of Indigenous cultures. When Germans discovered their love of nature and naturalness, their nature was already on the verge of being destroyed. That ignited the myth about the homeland and the longing for being in tune with the land. And that is something that really resonates when Germans think of North American Indigenous people. But I'm also, of course, a *Heimat* specialist ... and so ... [laughs]

Hartmut: I think you're right. But this wanting to explore and play a role of somebody one isn't, is a major motivation too. And I'm thinking of one of my colleagues. You know Anette?

Warren: Yes.

Hartmut: She was very, very strong in *Indianistik*. She still does fantastic beadwork and stuff.

Warren: Oh yes, absolutely.

Hartmut: She has done several films with her students recently based on *Star Trek* and aliens.

Warren: Oh, yeah?

Hartmut: She is totally into that nowadays.

Florentine: Well, there is that desire – and that has to do with Germans' burdensome history and identity – that desire to be someone else, and I think, no other immigrants than Germans absorb that.

Warren: Right.

Hartmut: And in Poland we talked about that, and in Germany and in Scandinavia, too, you know Viking clubs? People dressing like Vikings, beards and ships like Vikings.

Florentine: We talked about that in your seminar, too, I think, that there is that enticement for Germans ... to imagine themselves as victims when they are known to be a nation of perpetrators, right? It's so extremely psychologically attractive to be a victim [for] once.

Hartmut: Yeah. You can forget about German guilt and be a victim for once.

Florentine: Yeah, because it's a nation of perpetrators, and being Aboriginal ... and that's what makes it different. Nobody wants to be a Turk, but being Aboriginal, being a pure victim, for once in your national history, or to imagine that on the weekends, it seems just unbelievably attractive.

Warren: Crucially, a victim of someone else. I think there is a sense that in Germany, they've done bad things, and in North America as well. Those ideologies, not just in North America, but that are attached to other European nations, have resulted in atrocities, too. I think this idea of identifying with the victims of a different nation [is significant], because obviously identifying with the victims of the Holocaust is not going be something they would be able to do.

Florentine: No. That's psychologically very disturbing to do.

Warren: That's very interesting. See, whereas here in North America there is, I think, becoming more and more a kind of a suspicion of non-Aboriginal writers who write ... Aboriginal stories. And there was a real beginning in the eighties, a very strong reaction against that, sometimes for very good reasons, for the "appropriate appropriation of voice debates," as they're called.

Paulina: The one question I had in all is, [do Germans] lack interaction with natural environments? [And is this why they are] organizing powwows and trying to behave like *indians*?

Warren: I see, yeah. Again, I don't know from my own experience. Much of the time we spent in Germany was actually up in and around Greifswald, in areas which are relatively forested and which would seem, compared to the average part of Germany, I guess, much more wilderness or natural. Hartmut, you found this, when you went to Saskatchewan: it reminded you of back home, and for us, you know, going to Germany and seeing, in and around Greifswald, seeing the canola fields, seeing the forests, actually didn't seem that different from back home. But yeah, I think it's a good point: in a nation where there is not very much wild space left, there may be more of an attraction to [ideas of wilderness].

Hartmut: It would be interesting to know whether Indianists come predominantly from urban backgrounds. Or whether there are any people who are from villages, you know? I would think that most of them are urban ones.

Florentine: So were the *Heimat* enthusiasts in the nineteenth century, right? On the weekend, they would go out and pretend to be hiking in the forests.

Warren: Yeah, so that's very interesting. Do you remember, you were trying to tell me, the *Kleingartens* that we've seen, is that only an East [German phenomenon]?

Hartmut: That was also in the second part of the nineteenth century, sort of part of social democratic or socialist politics. Let workers have a piece of land where they could relax on the weekend and also produce some of their own food, and breathe clean air, and all of that. That was a big, big movement – a social movement.

Florentine: And the garden was called "Schreber" after the one who "invented" the gardens.

Hartmut: Yeah, *die Schrebergärten.*

Warren: I mean that may be a similar kind of thing, in a way.

Hartmut: I think so.

Warren: Because it seems that you'd say it's very reflective of class.

Hartmut: Yeah, it is a class movement.

Florentine: Absolutely.

Warren: I don't know to what extent the Indianthusiasts are invested in class identity as well, but that would be interesting.

Hartmut: Interesting also in a comparison East–West.

Warren: Yeah.

Hartmut: Research should be done on that. But I can't do it. [all laughing]

Warren: You got a few books that you're going to work away with. [all laughing]

Florentine: Well, do you have more advice for us?

Warren: I don't know. I think my answers were fairly nebulous.

Hartmut: No. No. I don't think so.

Florentine: I think it's great. Thanks for your time. Thanks so much. Wonderful.

JO-ANN EPISKENEW

When the gaze turns in both directions ...

Live interview recorded in Jo-Ann Episkenew's office at the
Indigenous Health Research Centre, University of Regina,
26 November 2012

Hartmut: First of all, thank you for agreeing to be interviewed. And I ask
the first question, which is not mine, but we took that over. Maybe you can
explain your – as it says in the question – tribal affiliation?

Jo-Ann [giggles]: My tribe? I'm a member of many tribes. I'm the tribe of
educated Native women with PhDs. I'm the tribe of mothers, grandmothers,
and great-grandmothers. I'm also the tribe of the Métis Nation of Manitoba, now transplanted to Saskatchewan. I'm the tribe of trashy paranormal
romance readers. And I could go on and on.

Hartmut: Well, the second question is about your contact with Germany.
How did you get into contact with Germany?

Jo-Ann: By the way: Did you ask Germans what their tribal affiliation is?

Hartmut: Yeah, yeah.

Jo-Ann: Oh good, do you think that works?

Hartmut: Yeah, it works. They come up with different definitions, most of
them regional, or they go to something like what you did now, and they
say okay, this is my affiliation, and I am associated with this, and so on. But
usually it's regional and by descent, you know, where they come from.

Jo-Ann: I think it was about 1990-ish that I met Professor Dr. Hartmut Lutz,
but I don't think he was a "Professor Doktor" then, just a doctor, who was a
visiting scholar at the Saskatchewan Indian Federated College, where I was

an undergraduate student. And I became his teaching assistant for his first-year English class, and then I took a class with you, Hartmut, and I think I got to teach half of it because then you had to go home. So we got to know each other, and that's where I learned more about Germany than I ever knew in my life, because I didn't really know anything. I had met some people from Germany but, you know, I didn't know much. And also the whole weird and wacky relationship with the Indigenous people of the Americas!

And so I think our paths crossed a few times over the years. You came back and visited, and I learned about the PhD program and how it worked. And being that I'm old, and not really prepared to up and run away to do a PhD. Plus at the time I was doing it, I can't think of anybody in Canada who actually had as much academic training in Indigenous literature as you did. There were some people who were supervising, but that had not been their area of specialization – they'd learned it on the fly through their careers. And so, just the system of "all research"[34] – that I could do it from a distance – worked, and I asked if you could be my supervisor, and you said yes. So the interviewer was my PhD supervisor, and I've been to Germany on four or five occasions.

Hartmut: The third question goes in a similar direction. There are a few Native people, Indigenous people, who did PhDs in Germany. There are also Germans who do PhDs in Indigenous Studies or aspects of Indigenous Studies. Do you have any comments on that?

Jo-Ann: I think after you were here, several of your students came over and did their master's – Magister – research here. Kerstin Knopf,[35] that's the one I remember the most. So, I think there are more people coming from there to here, from Germany to Canada, than the other way around.

So I only know myself, Jeannette Armstrong, and Janine Willie who've done their studies [in Germany]. There might be others, but I don't know them. I thought that was a really good idea for the German students. I'm having an issue at the moment with my colleagues in the humanities, partic-ularly in literary studies, because we like our humans well mediated through text. We don't really like the real-life ones. They're too messy. And so, for those students not only to learn the text, but to actually get their butts over here to meet the real-life people in their real-life context, I think that is very good. More Canadians who study Aboriginal literature should have to do that, because they don't necessarily.

Hartmut: Do you know any sort of work done by Germans on Indianthusi-asm, or has any of that phenomenon that I call Indianthusiasm – you maybe call it differently – influenced any of your work?

Jo-Ann: In a way, no. I find myself defending a lot of Germans and dealing with stereotypes of Germans by Aboriginal people. Because people over here think that every German, all eighty million of you guys, are all Indianthusiasts. And it has not been my experience. I've met [German] people who aren't even remotely aware of Indigenous people in North America. You know, there may be several thousand [Indianthusiasts], but when you add that up to eighty-two million, I think it's still quite a subculture.

And I [am] actually a little annoyed that some people, when I say I do my PhD in Germany, and they say, "Oh, they'll pass anything. They just love this." And I'm like, "No, no, I had to work my butt off to get that thing!" And the people who are on my committee, like yourself and Kerstin, are incredibly knowledgeable. I mean, even the very first time I went to Germany, I was invited to teach at that autumn–summer school for New Literatures in English, and I asked the ones who invited me, what could I expect, as far as the knowledge level of the students. And they would go, "Ah, no, nothing." So I'm preparing to teach like an introductory undergraduate course in Indigenous Literatures ... Oh my god, those students were all ... like, they knew as much as, if not more than me. It was quite embarrassing, and I was surprised they invited me back. But I wasn't prepared for the level of knowledge. They'd been to North America, they've been in communities, they knew people. So I didn't find people who had these romantic notions.

Hartmut: Maybe does that have to do with your moving in academia? So those people were already educated a little about that?

Jo-Ann: Yeah, 'cause when the second time we went to that conference, and we were billeted with one of the student's families in Berlin, they didn't have a clue. They knew nothing, no. And it was really good. We did a lot of exchange. They didn't speak English that well. But at the same time, you know, in Berlin – my husband being a lot more visibly Aboriginal than me – we went to a bar one time, the students from the class, and we all talked. There was this guy who was half-cut for sure, if not over the top, who had been to Saskatchewan, who'd been to the North, and lived in the ... I don't know if he lived in the Dene community or if he was just camping. But he'd been here and considered himself to be quite the expert, and he was asking my husband about this and that. [My husband] grew up in a traditional family but he had lived in the city since the sixties, and, you know, has spent his life having to work in everything, in an integrated environment. And this guy was asking about all of these really northern things, and my husband is a prairie guy, and then [this expert] says to me, "Well, I guess he's one of the tame ones." Oh! But you know what, you get idiots in Canada who would say the same thing being half-cut, too.

Hartmut: Yeah, they're everywhere. There must be a nest somewhere.

Jo-Ann: Yeah, yeah. [laughs]

Hartmut: You know, I want to ask something out of my own interest. You said that some people thought, when you were getting your PhD in Germany, "They'll pass anybody, because of Indianthusiasm!" That was something that I feared might happen. Has that changed, after your book came out?[36]

Jo-Ann: I hope so. And it wasn't necessarily academics who said that. It was more like other people, who just had this idea that Germans were crazy about *indians*.

Hartmut: Because, when I talk about that, I always find myself explaining why you did it in Germany and not here. And you gave that explanation yourself, you can't move to another place, and so on. Our program is so different from yours, in that it's solely research-based and no classes [to attend], right?

Jo-Ann: That's right.

Hartmut: But I don't have the feeling that our students, our PhDs, know any less compared to Canadians.

Jo-Ann: Well, you know, someone gave me an explanation of the difference between your system – and the Australian, and, you know, a lot of the world – and the American system. And they said in the American system – and Canada is quite a bit like the American system – there, the assumption is that you will be trained through all these classes, and what not, to therefore have the qualification to go on and produce a significant work. In the German system, and elsewhere, you are expected to already be an independent scholar ...

Hartmut: Exactly!

Jo-Ann: ... who is able to produce significant work, and then you have to. So first I had to read this book, which led me to this book, and I spent all my time mining bibliographies. And geez, I read psychology and poetry and different studies. So it's just a different philosophical underpinning, I suppose. And being that I wasn't a kid, you know, and that I had already taught for many years, and being a part of academia, it made more sense to me, really. [And] ... I got to work with you!

Hartmut: Thank you. [Jo-Ann laughs] I think the nice thing about so-called mature students is they know why they're doing it, and they're not – as a rule – doing it because they want the title, but because they also want to make a contribution to scholarship, or there's something that really concerns them, and they want to explore that.

Jo-Ann: Though I have to say, it was a really interesting experience having those letters after my name. It was like I'd been in a room, and I looked at the wall and I didn't know there were doors there. And then, all of a sudden, people on the other side opened the doors and said, "Oh, you can come in now." I mean, there are statements that I made before I even finished secondary school, when I was a poor, single mother without a university education, and now people go, "Oh, you're an expert!" It was really weird.

Hartmut: It's amazing that for some people, recognizing someone as a human being comes with a title or a certain degree. That's very common.

Jo-Ann: Oh, and a little creepy.

Hartmut: How did you perceive Germans and Germany? And a second question linked to that, from your previous expectations: Did your perceptions change, or were they confirmed? In which way? What was your first expectation?

Jo-Ann: Well, I actually thought it was a single country, with a single culture. [laughs] Yeah, so the first time I go there, it's Schleswig-Holstein and Kiel ... I mean, people don't even *look* the same in other parts of Germany as there. And then I went to Hamburg, it's different, and then I went to Berlin the next time, or no, I'd gone to Greifswald, but that was a pretty speedy trip that time. So I didn't really get to see around Greifswald. But then ... I did get to see skinheads on the train! They were just babies, these little blond, blue-eyed, angel-faced babies!

Hartmut: They are no angels!

Jo-Ann: No, but to look at them! I had imagined monsters and here they were, children![37] And they had these badges – in English![38] And I'm going, "So who is? That is an economic development opportunity! There is a marketing person, there!"

Hartmut: Oh, absolutely.

Jo-Ann: But then, the next time we were there, we were in Berlin. And my husband was with me. We were loving Berlin! We were at the market. We were talking to people. People were friendly. I'm with the students that I'm teaching, and I said to the students, "Oh, I just love Berlin. It's so friendly!" And they were from other parts of Germany; and they all look at me like I'm half nuts, and they're going, "Really?" [laughs] "We say that Berliners have ... they wear their hearts on their tongues, and if they like you, they're very friendly, and if they're mad at you, they'll really let you have it." And I'm going, "Yeah, but when I was in Hamburg," I said, "nobody would look at us or make eye contact. And we're all just like living in a little bubble." And then my one student from Hannover said, "Well, we think that is friendly. We are respecting your personal space."

Hartmut: Exactly!

Jo-Ann: And I said: "Oh, it's really interesting." And then I went to Greifswald, and I didn't really get to meet anybody, really, outside the university thus far, and I just thought about Greifswald, because it's so beautiful in my own opinion. And last year I went to Grainau.[39] We stayed in Munich for a few days, my son and I. I'm loving Munich. It's ... I mean, it's a wonderful tourist trap. You know, you walk, there's this, there's that, and people are very friendly, and there's the market. And then, when I went to the conference, I mentioned to Ruth about that, and I said, "I'm guessing this is the place where all the German stereotypes come from?" And she said, "Yes. That's why we 'hate' them." [both laughing]

Hartmut: You know, the other thing is, if you come from the north, you grow up sort of "hating," not hating ... but with antagonism against Bavaria. And each time I go there, and Ruth says the same, "The people are so friendly!" And then we say, "It's a trick! They're trying to really derail our stereotypes!" [both laughing] I find it interesting that you say there is not one monolithic Germany in your expectation.

Jo-Ann: Oh gosh, no.

Hartmut: So, what were your expectations when you went there? I mean what was your image of Germans made of?

Jo-Ann: Well, I was born in 1952. So I spent my entire childhood, once we got a television, watching war TV and war movies. So I don't know what I expected about the people, because I mean I'd met individuals, but ... I guess the biggest thing was, there were just so many different cultures. Also, really interesting to be there and to feel the East–West tensions! Oh my goodness! You're hearing the westerners going: "Oh it's these darn Easterners! Get off their butts, and get working." It very much sounds like some of the things here, against Aboriginal people! And the people in the East going: "We wanted reunification. We didn't want colonization!" I don't think I've ever heard anybody use that word, but with us it is the same. We didn't ask to have our educational system wiped out. And then in Berlin my husband got one of the shirts with the little sign, the WALK sign on the street, because that had become symbolic of the Western domination. The Westerners even wanted to change the little [crosswalk] man.

Hartmut: Das *Ampelmännchen!*

Jo-Ann: Yeah, the walking [man]. So hearing those tensions, that's the thing I didn't [expect] ... You know, the stereotype I had? I expected everybody's house to be perfectly, absolutely clean, tidy, and neat.

Hartmut: They are! [laughs]

Jo-Ann: Yeah? No! We stayed with a student the first days in Kiel, and I have to say her house was not clean, tidy, and neat. And the poor girl was trying to be this wonderful hostess. She was so wonderful to us. And I finally went – 'cause it was myself and my daughter; I'd never been overseas, so I was too chicken to go without a relative, so I took my daughter – and we started doing dishes. And the poor hostess says like, "Don't. We don't do that here. It's not our culture." And I thought, "Yeah! We got computers, you know! You're feeding us!" We were almost two weeks with her and her boyfriend. I think the other surprise was how well travelled the students were. I felt like a hick from Hicksville.

Hartmut: That's changed!

Jo-Ann: Yeah, not that much, though! There were flights to Hamburg every two weeks, so I ended up having to stay for two weeks. So I went to Walmart and bought me the biggest suitcase they had. And then we got to her place, and it was a fourth-floor walk-up! And here is the student, and her boyfriend, and her brothers. And they [had] travelled all over the world ... And they're looking at me like, "Am I dragging a suitcase, like really?" I was so embarrassed! So these hefty young men are carrying my suitcase everywhere. So it's become my mission in life not to look like a hick from Hicksville. Actually, I went to India for two weeks on carry-on. It has become a mission to look like I know the heck what I'm doing. But you know, their fluency in so many languages, they're well travelled! Really, this kind of makes us North Americans not look too good. It's actually kind of embarrassing.

Hartmut: You gave an example of this guy who was half-drunk or drunk, who said something to you or Clayton? What were your other experiences with racism in Germany?

Jo-Ann: Well, just one. When I taught in Berlin, we were talking about people living in contemporary times. And this student made the assertion that "If you are Native and you weren't living traditional, what was the point?" And I kind of said, "You know, we're not like a living museum, here for the amusement of European visitors. We have to earn a living. Cultures that don't change and adapt, die!" So I was a little ticked at the student for that.

I think she'd done a lot of travelling. But I think a lot of Native people really *play* Germans ... You know, being the Native, giving them what they think they want. Being the "oh so wise," or the "this or that."

Hartmut: Can you comment a little more on that? There is also not just a cultural, but also an economic side.

Jo-Ann: Yes. Well, there are people who sell a ceremony. Doing things like that, I think, is terribly tacky. I think there was a little reciprocity going on with a few of your students,[40] because they were all females, and they all just managed to have themselves a lovely *indian* man while they were here: you know, beautiful, exotic German girl, and beautiful, exotic Aboriginal man. So there were just a few temporary romances. Bernie[41] used to shake his head, "Uh-oh, what is going on with these students?!"

Hartmut: But, you know, maybe instructors here [in Canada] would worry about that. In Germany nobody would. Because our students are about one year older than yours. They're not chaperoned at all. We are not responsible for their moral well-being, or at least we don't have the feeling. But what you say about the exotic, that certainly is true.

Jo-Ann: And our students, the Aboriginal students, are not children. These were not babies. They were men who had been around the block. You know, in Aboriginal education, and in research, we talk about the four Rs: respect, responsibility, relevance, and reciprocity. There's a lot of reciprocity going on! [both laughing] Everybody had a story to tell when the year was out, you know?

Hartmut: Well, that's part of learning.

Jo-Ann: Yeah. Nothing like getting inside on the culture!

Hartmut: You did some presentations and some readings in Germany. And when you compare that to presentations or readings you did or do here, what was the difference in the audience? Was there a difference? What was it like?

Jo-Ann: Sometimes I think I'm funny. And I don't know if this is part of my culture. Well, it *is* part of my culture. There's always that black humour, and the teasing and everything, and self-deprecating humour. As you know, I ended up being an academic dean before I even finished with a PhD; it was bizarre. But when you work at a small, underfunded Aboriginal institution, you end up doing things that you're not qualified to do.

And so one of the commitments I had made to myself – because I had this contract and it said: We want you to be acting dean for a year. If it doesn't work out, you just go back to your old job without any loss of benefits and this or that ... I had a feeling, at the time, that being the dean there would be a lot of incentive to put on a mask, or create a persona, being phoney, and I didn't want to. This was kind [of] like one of those pivotal moments in life for me.

And actually, to bring Métis humour into negotiations has been ... You know, being an administrator, it's lots of fun, because a lot of time it's been: "Well, the White people went to the same public relations courses and communicate the same and everything," and then you come completely way out of left field; it throws people right off. So, it's just my way of being. I'm trying to be completely honest and be myself. Which means that I make all these sick jokes all the time, because I'm always, you know, "What the heck?!"

I think that actually deserves a lot more study, because as Aboriginal people our humour has changed a lot. I asked my husband, because in my family, if you make a mistake, they wipe the floor with you. Their teasing can be pretty brutal. And I asked him, his dad, who was born, like, in the 1890s, I said: "Was he like that?" And he said no. So I started asking Elders about their Elders and humour. So contemporary humour is very different. But meanwhile, that's the way I live!

Hartmut: So you think contemporary humour is more sarcastic?

Jo-Ann: Oh, yeah.

Hartmut: And how did your humour get across, I mean in Germany as compared to audiences here?

Jo-Ann: Yeah. [laughs] I think sometimes the students just kind of looked at me like ... puzzled, [I] don't know, what the heck.

Hartmut: And do the audiences here get it?

Jo-Ann: Yes, on different levels. Like that talk, the one I did at the University of Fraser Valley on Indigenizing the academy, there were a lot of Aboriginal people, and they got it. And the others were like, looking around somewhat uncomfortably. My friend who is a Haida, Musqueam, she said I "spit in the soup." That's what she says, when I talk I name the elephant in the room! I identify it. So, for White people, when you're talking about racism now, it's a little uncomfortable. The humour kind of helps to ease it along, instead of just being strident, you know? But I don't think Germans ... [students] I don't think they're expecting their professor to be cracking jokes all the time.

Hartmut: No, they don't. They have to get used to it. I think also that Germans aren't very well known for their humour! There is a regional difference,

I find. I always think that in Schleswig-Holstein there is a lot of irony. And you tease a lot. But you can only tease those that you know very well. Because you don't want to hurt them, really, you know? But humour is one of the most difficult things between cultures, to get the other's humour.

Jo-Ann: Yeah.

Hartmut: And so, I'm not surprised. When you got there, I mean apart from the humour, were there any other things where you found the audiences react differently?

Jo-Ann: Well, I think there was a bit of a disappointment in me, like I mentioned to you last night. They looked at me and went, "What?"

Hartmut: Because you didn't look ...

Jo-Ann: Didn't look the part. That's why they were chasing my husband around. Maybe having lighter skin made me have less authority, as an authoritative voice.

Hartmut: Well, you don't confirm their stereotype. Did you have to do something to sort of deconstruct their stereotypes first, and sort of open their perceptional windows, so that you, as Jo-Ann Episkenew, could be there, and not just their expectation?

Jo-Ann: Well, I don't think I did, and I think perhaps I should have. Like for me, the first time I was quite taken aback, because they were at a much higher level than I expected. So I was just playing catch-up. I hadn't done my PhD at the time, so I almost felt a little intimidated.

The second time, you know, it's kind of a feeling like, "I'm a visitor, I'm a guest in your house," so I tried to do it kind of subtly, but maybe I should have been a little more bold about how much rattling your cage can I do? I should have.

Hartmut: Well, you can do it with humour, too. I sometimes do that. I say, "All Germans look alike. Look at me. We're all tall, blond, and blue-eyed." [Jo-Ann laughs] And that sort of solves it, sometimes.

Jo-Ann: I'll have to get myself an invitation to go back to that again, 'cause I think I'd feel a lot more confident now.

Hartmut: You certainly are! Your work does not engage with German Indianthusiasm, does it?

Jo-Ann: No. Although I can think of a couple of people who have been involved. There are a couple of German scholars that I've been engaged with.

Just the other week, a medical doctor, a pediatric respirologist, from the University of Manitoba ... Now it's interesting, I mean, there is nothing he said to indicate he was [an] Indianthusiast. Yet he came to Canada – only going to be here for a short time – and then he's done an enormous amount of work in Aboriginal communities.

Hartmut: And is he from Germany?

Jo-Ann: Yeah. He is a lovely man. You know there was nothing that came out of his mouth that was about stereotypes. Although, when I first met him, he did kind of tell me about the reality compared to what he imagined. He was in remote northern communities, so it was a bit of a shock. And then there is this other one, who's done work on suicide. And I can't for the life of it remember where I met him, but that's just me being senile probably, but, oh, he loves me. Every time I see him, he's hugging me. I think my generalization is based on two people. There seem to be people being drawn to, or doing something ... And immigrants here have a really interesting relationship. I think new immigrants have to be reminded. Because a lot of times, new immigrants to Canada have this idea that, "Oh, we weren't the colonizer," you know, and that "We're really here to help. We're on your side, and we're buddies," and everything.

Hartmut: We're on your side – on your land?!

Jo-Ann: Exactly! Yeah, they have to be reminded that their prosperity is based on ... "Whose land are you on?" So I've tried to do that. That was where she said that "spittin' in the soup" thing. Because, you know, at CACLALS, the Canadian Association for Commonwealth Literatures and Languages – it's the non-White people literary studies, kind of a home for Aboriginal literature – And they're always thinking, "Yeah, we're all the same! Buddies! We face racism." "Yeah? Not quite," I say, "because you guys are on our land, prospering. I've heard where you come from." They forget about that part. And so, I felt with a lot of the Germans, you know, they really want to help Aboriginal communities and people; they might have to be reminded a little bit about, "You're doing well on our land."

Hartmut: We talked a little about the economic side. Have you met any German hobbyists?

Jo-Ann: I met the ones who worked in the office in Greifswald. I have my lovely beaded necklace with the jingles on it. And everybody is like, "Oh, is that ever nice, where'd you get it?" German Walmart. [laughs]

Hartmut: That was Anette, hmm?

Jo-Ann: Yes.

Hartmut: She is a great beadworker.

Jo-Ann: You know, again being a visitor over there, I don't feel ... I did ask one of the students something like, "I don't get it." Like, "Why don't you go back to your own pre-Christian traditions? Why are you borrowing ours? I don't understand!" And then they explained to me the whole relationship with the Nazis and that it becomes forbidden.

Hartmut: Yes, it becomes, not really forbidden, but in a way it's ...

Jo-Ann: Too connected?

Hartmut: ... contaminated, tabooed. Or some of it is ruined, or spoiled, you know. Because, if you go to some layers of German culture, a lot of it [had] been used and misused during the Nazi period. You don't want to identify with that. So you always have to sift things through. So it's very complicated. You can end up with very strange bedfellows that you don't really want to have anything to do with. I think that the Nazi period – this took me ages! – but if any nation has an ethnopoesis that tells them who they are, for Germany it's the Holocaust and that time! Everything comes back to that, and it's also how we are seen. Although, as you've explained, you saw all these war movies, and then you realized, "Oh, there's more to it." But the first approach is always through that, and that makes, I think, being German complicated – although young people now don't feel that anymore.

Jo-Ann: That's good.

Hartmut: Yes. I think that's good. They have it a little easier. But then sometimes when they go abroad, of course, they have to encounter it.

Jo-Ann: It seems to me, well, the first time I went, where it seemed to me that students were carrying the guilt. Now they're a little older. And I'm going: "You weren't even born!" It's kind of almost the polar opposite of Canada, because Canadians, they've got the lovely myth, and they're just blindly going through life not realizing, not wanting to acknowledge: prosperity is built on somebody else's loss.

It's almost like polar opposites, and a position in the middle might be a little more comfortable, or more useful because you can't crap about yourself and your country all the time. I don't want my students to feel that. I want them to acknowledge the truth in history, and then become allies, not just going around beating themselves up. People can't sustain that, and I often wonder if some of that skinhead attraction is: "I'm tired of feeling guilty, damn!"

Hartmut: Sure. And if you think of Hitler coming to power, that was part of that, too. After the First World War, which, in my perception, was something that was started by a number of European powers, not just by the Germans, but the peace conditions were very oppressive afterwards, and somebody came and said, "We are not shit. We are superior to the others." So a lot of people bought into that.

Jo-Ann: Absolutely. And even today, you know, when I see the protests in Greece, and all of a sudden the Nazis grow like trees.

Hartmut: That's a good example of how the old stereotypes are sort of dormant. And then in times of crisis, they all come up again. If they can be used, they come up.

Jo-Ann: Ironically, antisemitism can come up at the same time. It's quite fascinating. And I mean to me, my experience in Germany, people have been really good to me.

Hartmut: How do you feel about Indigenous dancers and singers in Germany?

Jo-Ann: The ones who are living there, or the ones who just go over there and visit?

Hartmut: Indigenous people who go, for example, to Karl May festivals and perform there. They usually come in groups in the summer, but there are also some who have stayed, or who are GIs, who have German families. So there's far more interaction and intermarriage than met my eye before, I must say, but through this project I'm learning more about that.

Jo-Ann: Yeah. My grandson's girlfriend's grandfather lives in Stuttgart. He's lived there for years. He's an artist and a traditional dancer. You know, I think of that particular family. Well, they were just devastated between residential school and then the child welfare system. So maybe for him, being there, where these Indianthusiasts actually honour and appreciate him for an identity, maybe that's a better world for him than here, facing – well, we call them the "micro-aggressions," you know?

I wonder what people who are visibly Aboriginal – and I know this because of my own family – they keep going along, happy life, go to work, day to day, and the next day, you all of a sudden get whacked with a racist something. And there's always the question, that crazy-making second-guessing, of "Is your world a safe place? Is the waitress at the coffee shop just having a bad day, or is she a racist?" So maybe just being in Stuttgart just makes life a lot easier. And he can be this person he wants to be, reclaiming identity between residential schools and the foster care system. So people might have different reasons.

And I also think for people like dancers and that, a lot of those people are poor. They're poor kids, living on the rez, and this gives them an opportunity to see the world, and be appreciated. I've heard more people go, "Oh, I was over there, and White people were even nice to me!" Like this is a big deal! So ... I mean I'm not too crazy about the guy who does his five-grand sweat lodges and stuff like that.

Hartmut: That's a whole "industry" of its own.

Jo-Ann: It's nice to go ... Even me, I felt like: "Oh, this is what White people are like who didn't actually come and take our land! How nice!," you know. [both laughing] "This is them in their own terrain, how they live and act, and ..."

Hartmut: That's where their stories belong.

Jo-Ann: Hmm. "That's where their poop is!" [giggles]

Hartmut: Exactly! And their ancestors'!

Jo-Ann: I'm quoting Tomson Highway, here, for the record. I'm not just saying that.

Hartmut: Okay. [both laughing] Chicken! No, you're not plagiarizing, okay. The other side of the coin: What do you think of Germans dressing up as *indians*, doing powwow and all that?

Jo-Ann: I don't know. It's weird. [laughs] I don't get it. It's ... Yeah, I find it just weird! Taking on a culture ... This is not a hobby, you know. Maybe beadwork could be a hobby, but ... I hate particularly the "culture of expertise," like, "I've done *all* this research, and I can speak the language," and then this, and then that ...

Hartmut: Well, then you're not getting it.

Jo-Ann: No, you're not, because unless you've actually suffered the oppression, the history, the continuing racism, you can do all the anthropological research, linguistic research you want, and you don't get it.

Hartmut: Of course, what you just said is right, and how can they possibly get it, because they haven't gone through that experience, but what I meant is, you sometimes get German "experts" who tell Indigenous people, "This is the wrong pattern," and "Your people don't do that, or didn't do that." And that is really worrisome.

Jo-Ann: Oh, big time! And it's also situating people frozen in time ...

Hartmut: ... and in the past.

Jo-Ann: Yes. So, you know, if it changed in the last two hundred years, then you're doing it wrong? What gives you the right to say? You know, I see people all the time changing. You can't go to a sweat lodge these days without having a requisite meal after, along with the berries and bannock. Oh, how authentic is that? But now, everybody has got to have salmon and corn next together. And neither salmon nor corn are from here. But, you know, somebody really liked it. And a lot of things, that people like. When you're making feast food, you typically are honouring somebody who died, and making something that they liked, you know, like macaroni soup. That is our tradition!

Your cultures change, and to go and critique some cultures' adaptation!? And just the whole thing of doing it looks creepy. You know, I've never seen it in real life, but I've seen that, *If only I were an Indian*,[42] that thing from Bulgaria.

Hartmut: That's from the Czech Republic, I think.

Jo-Ann: Yeah, and I pitied those people. You mean, you have absolutely nothing of your own?! This is but the whole imitation thing.

Hartmut: It's such an interesting film. What disturbed me there, I mean all the Indianthusiasts or hobbyists, okay? I think I feel about them the same way that you do – but the cameraman! I think he was a North American. Remember that scene where they come out of the sweat, and they're naked, and instead of taking the camera away, he follows them. And I thought, that's sort of "North American voyeurism." I think we are very laid back about nudity, relatively, but you respect people, so you don't look. But this cameraman! It's an interesting film.

Jo-Ann: And the fact that they were living like that three hundred and sixty-five days of the year! Because, they seem to.

Hartmut: Did they?

Jo-Ann: Yeah, they were living like that full time.

Hartmut: I thought it was just the holidays ...

Jo-Ann: If I'm right. I'm pretty sure I remember it correctly.

Hartmut: There is an event in Germany every year called "The Week." They have a whole week where those come together, and this year, I learned, they had three hundred tipis. Three hundred. That's a lot.

Jo-Ann: I've never been anywhere with three hundred tipis.

Hartmut: Nor have I been. I was invited once. Anette said, "Don't you want to come?" And I said, [laughs] "Anette, I wouldn't want to wear a loincloth!" Would have been interesting. I went to a powwow once. They organized one in Greifswald.

Jo-Ann: Well, I can't say that my feelings are representative, you know. I can't remember, but my husband didn't find it as creepy as I did. He kind of thought, "Oh, that's interesting." So, this is very much my own feeling. But yeah, I just find it creepy.

Hartmut: Yeah, there are some observers. There is a film made by John Blackbird. He is from Meadow Lake. He is Cree. He is in Calgary now. And it's called *Indianer*, which is a twenty-minute documentary. (He has also one about *Powwow*, but that's powwows in North America.) In *Indianer* he filmed German powwows. He did East and West [Germany], and he interviewed people – also some Indigenous people who came over as dancers, or who helped the German groups along. They had very, very varied opinions. It was very interesting, ranging say from "It's amazing how well this drum group can sing" to "They got it all wrong."

Jo-Ann: Yes, I mean, even if they do it *technically* right, but oh, there is so much missing in their understanding. You can't have – and I say that from the point of view of somebody who very much lives in an in-between space, looking the way I do, and having the family I have – but, yeah, they can, you can go out in this world and live without people hurting you for what you look like. And that makes your experience in the world very different.

Hartmut: I think I told you about Renae Watchman?

Jo-Ann: The Navajo scholar?

Hartmut: Exactly, who's got a PhD in German, speaks it fluently. She lived in Germany quite often. She did a very wonderful, very well-researched article on powwows in Germany and interviewed a lot of people. But she also said there were things like using the drum as a table and things. Yeah, I see your eyes widening.

Jo-Ann: Yeah.

Hartmut: But, I'd say they might make an exact replica, but that's it. Some of the essentials are not going to be there.

Jo-Ann: Yeah. I'd be very interested to hear why she did the study. Like my son also, he took German, he was very interested. So when the gaze turns in both directions, then it's kind of ...

Hartmut: Do you have any comments on European, German interests in spirituality, Indigenous spirituality?

Jo-Ann: I think some of the foundational principles of things can be very common, you know. Some things! Again, I mean spirituality is very much tied to culture, and when you have to go get somebody else's, I find it kind of sad that you don't have your own. I mean my spiritual beliefs are very individualistic. There is stuff in Aboriginal spirituality that I might practise, and stuff that I don't. That's another thing, I'm not too crazy about being mediated by other people. I actually follow Dan Coleman.[43] Did you read his book *In Bed with the Word: Reading, Spirituality, and Cultural Politics*? I have it right here. I love it. I love the way he writes. Do you know Daniel?

Hartmut: No.

Jo-Ann: Oh, I thought you did. He was around as a master's student about the time when you were here.[44] And then he's gone on to McMaster. Yes. And he's a White guy who grew up in Morocco with missionary parents.

Hartmut: So he's come a long way, obviously.

Jo-Ann: But he defined ... 'cause I never knew what spirituality meant. I could tell you in a heartbeat what a wounded spirit meant, but what did spirituality really mean? Again, he talks about your relationship with self, with others, and with the universe. I can live with that, as far as somebody who has strange feelings about the Christian goddess, one's imaginary friend, and stuff. So when people were searching, you know, doing this, and this, and this, it's just kind of sad. Their culture isn't good enough for them. It seems kind of needy.

Not that I have not done that, you know. I was younger, too. I was a Baha'i. So, I mean, I've done that, and so I know it was kind of sad and needy when I did it. So I guess, the other people feel the same about it. Hopefully they'll find a place where they're comfortable with their own identity.

Hartmut: Okay. If you think about this general topic again, German Indianthusiasm, or Canadian or North American Indigenous and German, or European, relations on the whole, is there something you wanted to say and you didn't have a chance to, because I didn't ask? Or something that you would like to get off your chest, or criticize, or add?

Jo-Ann: Well, I think, the first time I heard – because I never knew about this German Indianthusiasm – when I heard about it, I was talking to other people in the communities. Everybody was like, "Oh, they're White people, and they like us. That's really great!" Because that hadn't been their experience with White people here. So, I think, people have kind of mixed feelings about it. I think they think it's funny, especially ... the powwows and all that. They think it's funny. The experts really tick them off. But the concept that somebody likes them, that makes people feel good. Yet, at the same time, as people have become more aware of it, it almost can reflect internalized racism, like "Oh, you guys are really sick, because you really like us." You know, not really sick, but ...

Hartmut: Weird.

Jo-Ann: Must be something weird about you, 'cause "normal" White people don't like us.

Hartmut: Actually, you know, as a White person working here, but interacting with White people – and the same when we were in California – I had questions like that: "Do you really like *indians*?" and "Why are you working there?" And I know a colleague who worked here [in Regina], who is in a wheelchair, [he] was asked by this Indigenous student: "Do you only work with us because you're in a wheelchair?"

Jo-Ann: Whoah.

Hartmut: So, talking about internalized racism on the one hand, and "real" racism on the other, if you work here as a non-Indigenous person, you get a lot of comments which expose things.

Jo-Ann: Yeah. It's just the same when people get paid to dance powwows and that. People almost see it like a scam, instead of "Geez, we're really valuable. And these people appreciate us."

Hartmut: You know one of my theories is ... why Germans love Winnetou? Winnetou loves Germans, and there a very few people who love Germans. And all of a sudden you have this image of somebody who loves Old Shatterhand because he is German. That's a very nice message. You don't get that very often. Okay. Anything else?

Jo-Ann: No. I'll probably think of something at three in the morning.

Hartmut: And then you'll say, "Shoot!" [both laugh]

Jo-Ann: Sending an email at three in the morning.

Hartmut: Okay. Thank you.

AUDREY HUNTLEY

This is where I feel at home but part of me is back in Germany, too.

Phone interview by Florentine Stzelczyk and Hartmut Lutz,
27 November 2012, Calgary to Toronto

Hartmut: Can you explain your tribal affiliation?

Audrey: I have mostly settler and some Indigenous ancestry (Scottish, German, and Ojibway). My mother's side is easy as she immigrated here from Germany and her people have lived in the same village forever, but my father didn't know his father who he has his Indigenous ancestry from. He was told by his mother that his father's mother was Ojibway but record searches for his community of origin have not proven successful. It's been really frustrating until recently; my second cousins found me through social media and then I met my grandfather's half-sister, so I am finally making some connections. They all have knowledge of our Indigenous ancestry, which has been validating, but no specifics unfortunately. Since I moved back from Germany almost twenty years ago, I've lived and worked as an advocate in the urban Indigenous communities of Vancouver and now Toronto. This is where I feel at home, but part of me is back in Germany, too.

Hartmut: We get so many different wonderful answers. I am really glad about this question, because some people totally self-identify, while others go by lineage, and so on. It's really interesting. You know that our overall frame is German Indianthusiasm and reactions to that experience. Can you please explain your first German contact, how you got into contact with Germany and also went to Germany?

Audrey: Okay. Well, I have an early part of my life where there was a connection to Germany, and then a later part of my life, and, sort of a big chunk in between without a whole lot.

My father was in the army, and he met my mother, who lived in a village close to a Canadian base by Hagen and Hemer.[45] My dad was posted back to Germany when I was about three, and I lived there 'til I was about five. We didn't live on the base, we lived in my mother's village, and I lived with a lot of extended family. We came back to Canada when I was five, and I didn't return to Europe until I was a teenager.

And then, later on as an adult, I went on a two-month backpacking trip that turned into eighteen years. I discovered free education and went to university and completed a master's. Yeah, it turned into this much longer stay, involving universities but also political organizing and becoming an activist.

Hartmut: How long were you in Germany then?

Audrey: As a child, just a couple of years, and then of those eighteen years in Europe, thirteen of them were in Germany. I came to Marburg in 1986 and returned to Turtle Island in 1998.

Hartmut: You know – well, of course you know – that there are some Indigenous people getting PhDs in Germany. There are two or three. There are also German academics who are doing PhDs on Indigenous issues, Indigenous literatures, and so on. Do you have any comments on that?

Audrey: Well, you mentioned two things. One, Indigenous people doing PhDs – I think I know who you're talking about – I think it's great! I'm happy to see there are real people over there! Because for me in the mid-eighties to early nineties it was a real struggle, just introducing people to the "real *indians*" who are not frozen in time such as the ones that Germans imagine, actual Indigenous people from here, and not just their ideas about what Indigenous people should be. And there were a lot of fake shamans in Germany as well.

Hartmut: Yeah! Okay, maybe we come straight to that, because one of our questions was to hear your comments on the European and German interest in spirituality. And that brings us to the shamans. What were your experiences with that?

Audrey: I hardly know where to begin; the fascination with a noble savage idea of Indigenous people is everywhere in popular culture. After having been in Germany for a while, I became very motivated to deconstruct these romanticized ideas of "imaginary *indians*" that are so prevalent in Germany along with cultural appropriation. I found it really infuriating.

Although I also remember as a child buying into the fantasy. I remember wanting to impress my friends who were fascinated with a TV show called *Winnetou* with my dad's grandmother being Ojibway.

Later on, once I had become involved in political organizing, I was thinking more critically about my own identity, and I was very influenced by the work of Chrystos.[46] I translated a body of her work.[47] So part of what I was doing, what I felt was important with my activism and my *Magisterarbeit* (master's thesis), which was published as a book,[48] was that I wanted to deconstruct these ideas that people had. But I also wanted to challenge them, like their appropriation of Indigenous culture. And Chrystos is really strong about that. In her poetry there are a lot of poems where she strongly speaks out against that, like "Ich bin nicht eure Prinzessin."[49] We were on a book tour together, so we had a lot of really intense confrontations with people who would come out to hear her read, and who would want to be almost like a disciple of hers. They were greedy and very needy.

Hartmut: Making her their guru, huh?

Audrey: Yeah. She asked them quite pointedly not to start sweat lodges. And some people would listen, and would try to understand, but a lot responded very violently and very aggressively, and wanted to just take and partake. And I've had big arguments with people even in Canada. I remember being on the Journey for Justice, which we organized in Vancouver when I was working in the Downtown Eastside. It was a research trip using rafts on the Fraser River from Prince George to Vancouver. We stopped in several communities along the way to talk about violence against women and children. One of the women working for the rafting company was a German woman. I had huge arguments with her, because she knew someone, a German, who runs a sweat lodge for money over there. And I strongly objected to that and tried to explain what I thought was problematic about it.

I encountered another instance of this type of behaviour around the time of the uprising in Oka (1990) when I started a solidarity committee and we did awareness-raising actions at the airport in Frankfurt. There was a key moment when people's lives were very much in danger (people were locked down at the treatment centre). I was in close contact with people who were in Kahnawake, in the band office, who were fielding solidarity calls, and they were calling for people around the world to break through the media silence, because everything was focused on Iraq, actually, on Saddam Hussein marching into Kuwait at that time. And they believed that they were going to be massacred if they didn't get some international attention on what was happening.

We staged a small demonstration, which we knew would get police attention very quickly – and be ended very quickly – at Frankfurt Airport, before a Montreal-bound flight. Although we did not anticipate it, most people on that flight were actually soldiers! So it was a pretty heated situation.

We got what we wanted. In less than twenty minutes we had enough media attention to break the Oka story in Germany.

During that time, I did a lot of speaking about what was happening at the stand-off: once I had the most awful experience of arriving at a gym somewhere close to Darmstadt, I think, and noticing that people were calling it an "*Indianer* Festival." People were wearing loincloths, and they had a tipi set up.

Hartmut: Hobbyists, huh?

Audrey: I didn't know what that was at the time ... I just wanted to leave. But some of the organizers were sincerely interested in the situation at Oka, so I decided to stay. It was a pretty packed audience by the time it came around to my talk, and they were showing a few other worthwhile documentaries as well. I ended up being glad that I stayed, and did that work. Oka was such a big moment for so many people, such a turning point for me and some of my family members in thinking about our Indigenous ancestry.

Hartmut: So you were in Germany during the Oka time. I was in Saskatchewan.

Audrey: There were people all over the world working to show support for Kanesatake. There were a lot of people who had a personal connection to Toronto and Montreal or who had been to Kahnawake perhaps, who were in other cities in Europe. There was a lot of dialogue at that time, people going back and forth and supporting each other.

One explanation that's always been offered to me for this German hunger for anything *indian* is the Holocaust. It's easier to appropriate a romantic and noble trope rather than own their own history. Chrystos used to challenge people in Germany to go beyond that, to try and discover what is Indigenous about their own culture. I found that could get problematic, though, and it really bothered me when Ward Churchill toured Germany and would call on the left to get in touch with their Teutonic values. He would talk about how the Romans colonized Germans, so the Germans know what colonization is, so all they need is to get back in touch with their Teutonic roots. Um, no. Please don't.

Hartmut: It's *a little* far-fetched, if you think it was two thousand years ago, and there were no "Germans" at that time, just different tribal peoples.

Audrey: It's very simplistic. Since I've actually been living here again on Turtle Island, and I have been more connected to Indigenous people and communities, I've become more open in my thinking about who should be able to partake in spirituality, because I have met elders, who I consider to be my teachers, who admit anyone to ceremonies who has the desire and is respectful. And I don't think I am in a position to make judgment calls around that stuff ... I just feel humbled by their wisdom, and I don't question. I actually just appreciate that inclusive approach.

Hartmut: Yeah, but you mentioned the example that somewhere somebody was actually selling ceremonies, right? I think that's not right.

Audrey: And I would differentiate between hobbyists and those who have a sincere need and are looking to connect spiritually. I would totally not put those two things in the same category. I have a much stronger rejection of hobbyists than I would with someone seeking a spiritual connection.

Hartmut: Did you have any contact with them, besides the experience in Darmstadt?

Audrey: No, actually, I never did. But I have heard people here tell jokes like the one about German beadwork. "If you are in a powwow somewhere and if you notice someone has really good beadwork, then you say, 'It must be German.'"

Hartmut: Yeah, I heard that a lot, and I know someone who does very good beadwork actually.

Audrey: I never went to any of those hobbyist gatherings except for that experience in Darmstadt. There was nothing like that in Marburg. I mean, there would be the local bookstore that would have really weird window dressing sometimes. You know, that kind of appropriation of Indigenous symbols seems to be everywhere in Germany all the time, but that is different from hobbyism, too.

Hartmut: Has your experience with Germany and Germans influenced your work?

Audrey: Yes, very much. I was there for thirteen years. I think I had very important learning experiences in that time. I really respect the teachings that I got at university there, or in talking to activists in particular, people who were very committed – around the world. I admire the history that Germany has in that regard, and it certainly challenged me to have very ethical standards around any of the work that I do with regard to research or activism. No, I really much appreciate and am happy that I was influenced in the way that I was.

Hartmut: Okay. That partly answers another question that I have here. Has scholarly work by Germans on Indianthusiasm influenced you or your work?

Audrey: I haven't heard of any, actually. I haven't had the opportunity. I have not been so in touch with Germany in more recent years but do hope to visit soon.

Hartmut: I'm touching wood. I wish you all the best with that, Audrey. How did Germans react to you in Germany? I mean, you talked about your childhood and how, as a child, you found it quite attractive to be special. Later on, during your student years or so, if you identified as Indigenous or part Native, how did people react?

Audrey: Usually, incredulously. They didn't believe me 'cause I don't look Indigenous enough in their view. So I often found myself having to defend or explain. You know, that's a classic situation that I have here, too. It doesn't happen only in Germany. But it's even more so in Germany. People have a really thick stereotype in their mind. People in Toronto at least have some concept of blond and blue-eyed Native people, never mind being familiar with lighter-skinned people, because down east people have been mixing for a lot longer.

You know, I really didn't think about my ancestry until around Oka. Through Oka, I learned, actually discovering my own connection to my ancestors. I read a lot of literature, and I talked to people having similar experiences to me around Oka. So, I would come out to people about it in a very politicized community. So, I guess the experiences were fairly positive, just because people had some sense about those kinds of issues. Also, I was very involved in the Palestinian solidarity work, and there was a lot of feeling of overlap, actually, between the experience of Palestinian people and Indigenous people here.

Hartmut: Talking about that, didn't you find that that issue is very complicated, or more complicated in Germany?

Audrey: Of course! And what's so strong at that time has become a lot more a subject of controversy since I was doing that work in the early nineties. There were a couple of key articles that looked at the antisemitism of the left.

Hartmut: Well, I say this as a German: you're almost enviable because you can opt out of that.

Audrey: I am part German, too.

Hartmut: I know, I know. I'm just saying it is very, very complex. Complicated because, well, like everything in Germany, you open a cabinet and there's a skeleton there, it's all around. So very often what we say is historically compromised, even if we are fully aware of the history. There is another area, when you mentioned antisemitism: what were your experiences with racism in Germany?

Audrey: Well, Marburg was a bit of a haven, being a progressive community. But we were very aware, doing a lot of anti-racism work. I was part of the *Ausländerausschuss* (committee of foreigners). So a lot of the work we did was either challenging systemic racism that had to do with "Ausländergesetze und so weiter" (foreigner/immigrant laws, and so forth), but also experiences that people would have with fellow students or just German citizens.

I have light-skin privilege, so I think the experiences that I had, they also had to do with who I was travelling with: "Ausländerin" (female foreigner) as opposed to, you know, a bunch of Germans. I would have different experiences, depending on who I was travelling with.

But, you know, definitely those were times when we had a militant Antifa (anti-fascist movement/activists in Germany), and we did things like go and protect the refugee homes and we had systems in place to deal with that. They were, you know, kind of intense times.

I lived in a mixed (foreigners/Germans) housing co-op. It was called *Bettenhaus* (literally: "beds house"), and it was supposed to have a quota of foreign students and the goal was to foster the spirit of international solidarity between students but there were serious political divisions between the White Germans and the foreign students. There was a lot of racism and sexism. Awful, awful conflicts. So, yeah, I had experience with both institutionalized forms of racism and individual ones. I always felt as though the debate was kind of lagging behind what people were doing and talking about in Canada and the US, or thinking about like the writings of people like Audre Lorde.

Hartmut: Did you feel that things were more progressive in Canada with regards to literature by writers of colour?

Audrey: Yes, but that started to shift in Germany as migrants and the German people of colour began speaking out. And it had overlap with the work that I was doing, having Jeannette Armstrong's work published,[50] and having Chrystos's work published.[51] All those things were eminent in the work that they did and that they talked about, too. So there were publishers starting to give attention to that in Germany, you know – Orlanda Verlag publishing Audre Lorde's work.

Hartmut: Yeah, and in Osnabrück we were publishing a series called *OBEMA* [Osnabrück Bilingual Editions of Minority Authors], which went in that direction, too. We also had a special issue on Audre Lorde,[52] and Jeannette[53] was in there as well. But those were little islands, I guess.

When I look at *Germanistik* [German Studies], what people do in Germany seems to me often to be very conservative. But when I look at *Germanisten* [scholars of German studies] in the US, Canada, or Australia, the few that I know, they seem to address more progressive, more up-to-date issues.

Then, when I look at Canadian Studies, Canadian literature, and particularly the study of Indigenous literatures, I find that some people were teaching that in Germany when it was not taught at English departments here. So it seems that the view from outside sometimes makes things easier, perhaps?

Audrey: Absolutely. And also you're not on stolen land there.

Hartmut: Exactly.

Audrey: Big difference.

Hartmut: And how would you politically utilize that? Or you have, I guess, in your work.

Audrey: Well, I don't know if I've utilized that ...

Hartmut: I don't mean in a negative sense.

Audrey: But there's also other discomfort zones that you have out there! So the key is to bring it back to how people connect to it. And in Germany often it does have to do with a romanticization, a projection of unsatisfied wishes and dreams, which is appropriate and inappropriate, I think. So, I'd often find myself challenging that romanticizing view for those reasons. In the same way that activists would do that, say, with the Zapatistas.

Hartmut: Many, many years ago I sometimes did presentations at *Volkshochschulen* [evening classes at so-called "people's colleges"] about contemporary issues in Native America. And people would flock to that because it said *Indianer*, but when I started talking about Sinti and Roma, they didn't want to listen. So, I think that perhaps is typical. But then sometimes one can use that in a positive way, I think, just to catch attention, and then to turn around and make transfer possible.

What do you think about Indigenous dancers and performers who come to Germany on a regular basis, quite often to dance in powwows or to go to the Karl May Festival and present Native dances and Native culture?

Audrey: I have a very uneasy relationship with folks who do that although my position has softened over the years. I'm certainly not as much of a purist as I once was in regard to immediately rejecting or labelling someone. I don't have that harsh a view. But it makes me very uncomfortable to see that consumed by Germans. I have developed more understanding and sympathy for Native people's motivation to go and do that, now that I've been back here awhile and have actually talked to people here as well, as opposed to when I was living in Germany.

I remember being really, really disgusted back in the day (the nineties) when Dennis Banks was dancing around Germany and would not give a statement on the Mohawk uprising. That was happening at the very same time that he was participating in the Run for Peace in Germany with some Japanese people. I think they were calling attention to their shared connection through uranium extraction and survivorship of the bombs in World War II ... And they were doing cultural performances. So we showed up at one with a big banner, you know, talking about genocide, ongoing genocide happening right now with the Mohawks at Oka. And we asked him publicly as a former member of AIM to at least say something about what was going on there and to draw attention to that cause. And we kind of had to shame him into doing that. I thought that was sad, but if you are going to go and perform culture for the consumption of Germans, at least use the opportunity, and talk about what's really going on with ongoing colonization, as opposed to just going and making a bunch of drums to sell!

I understand why people do that. People are hungry – there's a lot of poverty over here. That's the stuff Germans don't generally want to hear about. I'm not going to judge an Indigenous person for ending up choosing that lifestyle, maybe being in Spain now, doing drum workshops. There are AIM leaders doing that now. Maybe they have earned the right to do that, but I can't help but have an uneasy feeling about that.

Hartmut: I remember Howard Adams saying, "Those are bread and butter issues, and they come first." Because you have to eat first, but I absolutely share your views on that. I used to have nothing but ridicule for them. And now I talk to some who do that and others who interact with them. I have a much more, I don't know, "lenient" sounds condescending, but a much more flexible ... I think I understand that better. Maybe we just get a little less righteous.

Audrey: The lines get blurry in a lot of ways, and it's not always simple.

Hartmut: You know, I think we've covered most of the questions that I have here. Is there something that you would like to, from your side, say about this project? We look at Indianthusiasm and the artistic and scholarly reactions to that, plus at people – Indigenous people – who have lived in Germany and who have stayed there and have their own experiences. I think the overall question is also how stereotypes of Germans come into play, or stereotypes about Germans, and how maybe the reality does not confirm the stereotypes people have who go there. That's not very clear what I just said, I realize. [laughter]

Audrey: Are those the types of people that you're interviewing?

Hartmut: Well, some of them. You know, I should explain this. What I learned in those weeks that I've been here, and mainly talking to Renae Watchman and John Blackbird and some others, and to more and more people who have been to Germany, they tell me – Jeannette, for example, or Jo-Ann Episkenew and Warren Cariou – that they had relatively positive experiences in Germany.

As a German born in '45, I always expect people to comment on the racism and how unfriendly people are in Germany, and all that. They see that, but they also have a lot of positive experiences. What they comment upon is the impact of the Green Party, or environmentalism or so, and maybe my own stereotypes about Germany are being expanded – I wouldn't say shattered – but they change. So, this is also a learning experience for me.

I don't know how it was for you, when you came to Germany the second time. Did you have specific expectations in your mind, and were they confronted?

Audrey: I know. I ended up liking Germany, despite myself, because I actually never wanted to like Germany, given its recent history of fascism.

And I had always been drawn to other parts of Europe. I rejected Germany as a teenager and wanted to go to places like France, Italy, or Greece. I was always more drawn to Mediterranean culture, and it was kind of in spite of myself that I ended up there ... It all started when I took a bunch of kids on as an animatrice for a summer job, and I ended up close to Marburg, and then was really drawn to the political activism there.

I was in university in Grenoble, France, at the time, where the Front National was pretty much the strongest player, and it was frightening to me to see how passive the left was. And I was becoming politicized myself, but was so much more comfortable with the culture of activism in Germany that I ended up wanting to move there. I had a bit of the best-of-both-worlds experience. You know, Marburg was very much an "idyllische linke Hochburg" (idyllic leftist citadel). So, it didn't really feel like you were living in the real world. It wasn't as intense as like Hamburg, or Berlin, but it had an undercurrent of social movement.

So, I never really knew the German stereotype, because I didn't really have to do with that world so much. And I don't think Germans, when they are romanticizing – and these hobbyists – they don't at all get the thing that

I find most striking. They simply don't get the connection to land. And that's the very basis of Indigenous spirituality. And that gets completely obliterated, when it's been exported and taken to a whole other place. And so, it just falls flat.

Still some of my best friends are in Germany and they are people that are actually political activists in a way I can identify with more and better than I do with the left here. It's a bit of a dilemma for me that I probably will never resolve. Hopefully, I will be travelling more and can reconnect … I feel so split apart.

Hartmut: I think I can sympathize with that.

Audrey: Interestingly I do have some German friends who have moved to Toronto and live in my neighbourhood. Someone I knew from the Antifa Bonn, a German person of colour and his German wife. We have this strange little colony of Germans who were activists in the late eighties and nineties. I really appreciate having them in my life, because there's an intellectual stimulation that happens that I don't have with people here. That has to do with a shared history of a very specific type of political culture. I hope that doesn't sound arrogant, 'cause I don't mean to suggest it's better, just different.

Florentine: No, not at all.

Hartmut: No, no. It sounds very understandable to me. I remember moving away from Tübingen and ending up in Cologne and being totally uprooted politically and frantically looking for connections. Then, also even moving from West Germany, from Osnabrück to Greifswald in East Germany. It's a totally different political culture. And Florentine was just saying the same here.

Audrey: So, I think to wrap it up, there's one thing on my mind that I wanted to add.

Hartmut: Yes, please.

Audrey: I don't know if people that you have talked to – who go over and, say, dance in powwows or go for ceremonial reasons – have talked about prophecies at all?

Hartmut: Prophecies? No, not yet. We haven't come across that.

Audrey: Because that was one thing that sort of changed the way that I think about these things, at least in terms of what I consider to be appropriation or not. When I look back, and when I was living in BC, I had the opportunity to visit a place called Round Lake, which is in the Okanagan. And people told me there that the prophecies say that the medicine teachings are to be shared, and that we are coming into this time where the prophecies say that Indigenous people will become the leaders. That we will start bringing those medicine teachings back to people, so we can stop the catastrophe that's happening with the environment.

Hartmut: I think that's a project that Jeannette is very active in. And with her dissertation,[54] I think that's something she has done, also for the first time at a European academic level. You know, she's taken it right to the lion's mouth, and I think there's a lot to be said for that. And she talks about re-Indigenization, not in the sense of blood, but in the sense of place, and what you mentioned, the land. And I think there's a future there, and there are more and more people in Europe who realize that. You know, one of her co-supervisors was Konrad Ott, who has the only chair for environmental ethics in Germany. And he's a Habermas scholar. At first he was a little condescending, or very insistent on Enlightenment priority. But he learned a lot from Jeannette, and she also learned a lot from him. So things are coming together, I think. I hope.

Audrey: So that's very positive to hear. I'm happy to hear that.

Hartmut: Yeah. And when you think of a sort of medicine way, when you think of Black Elk's dream, or the prophecy, the Red Road that has to be followed again from west to east,[55] I think that falls into that image. Personally, I come from a materialist background, and I have a hard time with prophecies, but I have had – with regard to Indigenous peoples – so many "coincidences" in my life, that I have a hard time explaining them rationally. And Jeannette once sat me down and she said, "Hartmut, relax, it's all connected, just relax and focus." [Audrey laughs] And she's right. She's right. So, yeah, thank you. Is there something you want to add?

Audrey: No, I think that was it.

Hartmut: Okay. Thank you very much, Audrey.

Audrey: Okay. We'll be in touch.

THOMAS KING

The thorn is in my side when I'm talking to Europeans, who begin lecturing me on indianness.

Interview over dinner in a Calgary restaurant on 20 November 2012 with Helen Hoy and Thomas King, by Renae Watchman, Florentine Strzelczyk, and Hartmut Lutz

Hartmut: There is an increasing number of Indigenous people who live in Germany or who have lived there.

Thomas: Really?

Hartmut: Yeah. And their experiences very often are very different from some of the things that are taken up in literature. I wasn't aware of that, and it was through Renae that we came to that and thought we could combine that. And we're now interviewing people like you who are dealing with German tourists coming, and so on.

Thomas: Very badly ...

Hartmut: But then we also look at people from here, who go to Germany and, for example, dance or meet with Indianthusiasts. So that is the gist. [To Florentine] Maybe you want to add something?

Florentine: I was initially interested in writing that dealt with or picked up this German fascination for anything Indigenous. But with Renae's input we're also talking about Indigenous people who make their lives in Germany. We are interested in your work also, which had to do with some of the German references to characters and things German in your work.

Thomas: My experience has been very limited. I've not been to Germany to talk to other Germans. I haven't been to some of the *indian* clubs that are in Germany to see exactly what happens. Now I've been to a couple of *indian*

clubs in the States, and they're pretty awful. Most of my experience really has been from meeting Germans at powwows. And we've got a drum in Guelph [Ontario] now. We used to have eight singers on it. Now there are about four or six of us who remain. And from time to time at the events we go to, we would run into German enthusiasts. We took the drum somewhere ... I forgot where we took it. We had a guy who was German, but he was living outside of Germany, one of the European countries like the old Czechoslovakia or Yugoslavia or something like that. I forget where he is from. And evidently he sang and he wanted to sing with us and we had a drum there. We were doing a public event and all of a sudden this guy comes up and wants to sing with us. This happened a lot! But normally they weren't Germans, but this guy happened to be. And he was fairly put off that we said no. And of course, we said no because, you know, our rule was that if you didn't practise with us, you didn't get to sing with us. And the last thing we wanted is ... you know, as we are doing this [*Thomas uses his hand to demonstrate a steady drumbeat on the table*], this guy is doing this [*switches to offbeat drumming on table*]. And my experience has been that the Germans tend to – this is not just the Germans – There is a sense that they have a stake in or that they own a part of Native culture, that because they've taken it on, that that's *theirs*. And if you suggest that "No, it's not ..." But it's dressing up. You know? It's play-acting. But they were more enthusiastic about it than that.

Florentine: Yeah, they're quite serious about it.

Thomas: And depending on how serious they are and how – dare I say it – obnoxious [they are] about that enthusiasm, that's what my reaction is based on. I can get fairly testy about it. Most of the time it feels as though they're testing you. So, some will come by the drum for instance and say, "So, did you guys smudge with western sage?" or something like this, or they'll ask about dancers, you know? "Did this person do that?" or "Is that authentic, from the tribe?"

At the Toronto Powwow we used to get a fair amount of that, and it's okay, you know? As I got older, I've gotten less concerned with it, but every so often you get somebody who really is pushing it.

And they even go so far as to suggest that this singing group isn't singing the way they should. And when the guys [around the drum] hear that, it's sort of like the heads snap around: "What's that?" And a lot of the drum groups tend to have a good sense of humour. Black Lodge used to sing songs for kids. And they're not traditional powwow songs.

Renae: Mighty Mouse.

Thomas: Mighty Mouse, yeah.

Renae and Thomas: [both singing] "Oh my god, it's Mighty Mouse." [both laughing]

Thomas: What's that other one? [Starts singing another song, drumming on the table] "Mickey Mouse, Minnie Mouse, Pluto, too. They're all movie stars at Disney Land ..." Those are fun songs, but for the real enthusiast those are a little [inauthentic]. And most of the time, I'd sing at powwows and at Indian Days on the Blood Reserve. Some of my writing is based on that. And you can see 'em [the Indianthusiasts] coming a mile away.

Florentine: Oh yeah?

Thomas: Leather vests, beads, everything else. One guy wanted to get the fry bread recipe off of one woman who was cooking fry bread, and she told him: "You haven't got enough money!" And he said, "Oh yeah, I do. I do! I can buy that fry bread recipe!" And he was determined to get it. She was determined not to give it to him. He was really obnoxious, really obnoxious about that. He wanted that fry bread recipe, sort of like he had gone hunting for a trophy elk. And he wanted to shoot it and take it home with him.

So, I'm the wrong person because I deal with the same stereotypes that I create about Germans. But I put them in *Lederhosen* with tubas on the reserve. Or I put my Natives in *Lederhosen* with tubas just to make the Germans feel at home.

Hartmut: Do you see any connection between this obsession that those Indianthusiasts have and the reception of your work in Germany?

Thomas: Well, I have no idea how my work is accepted in Germany. I've never been there, but I know the book that's published there by a reputable press. I've not seen any reviews of the books – if there were any reviews of the books. They've never hauled me over there for a book tour, so I don't know.

Hartmut: Eva Gruber, and others?

Helen Hoy: You know Eva Gruber took her first course in Native literature from me.

Florentine: Oh really?

Helen: That's sort of where it all started!

Florentine [joking]: So it's your fault!

Helen: My fault! But that was really interesting, she came over to study something in the sciences, and she took my course because it fit in the schedule.

Thomas: Well, with Eva, she came over and interviewed me for the book. But the book is made up of all sorts of people, not necessarily Germans. They're all over the place. So I just don't know.

Helen: But she also wrote a book in which she wrote a chapter on you. Her first book – one of her earliest books.[56]

Thomas: Is there? Okay. I don't know. [joking] I don't read. I'm traditional. She reads for me! [pointing to Helen]

Helen: He doesn't read anything about himself.

Thomas: I can't stand to read stuff about myself. I can't manage it. But really, my take on all of that is very limited. I have a bias that I play out in my literature. And I mean, probably if I went back and wrote those books again, I might be more clever than I was originally. But I was having so much fun. And I think, probably, the enthusiasm that overtakes Germans, and the French for that matter ...

Hartmut: Oh yeah, the Czechs and the Scandinavians, too. It's all over.

Renae: Russians.

Hartmut: It's not just in Germany.

Thomas: I think part of it is just sort of escapism – fantasy. I mean, that's what Karl May was all about. May never came to the US.[57] But there was this fantasy for you to be free, with nothing to encumber you: You could ride around with the wind in your hair.

Florentine: Naked.

Thomas: Naked, yes.

Hartmut: That's part of it.

Thomas: There was a film made by the National Film Board called *If Only I Were an Indian*. And those Cree, coming over the hill and seeing the Czechs down there all naked. The women were going: "Ooh, so embarrassing."

Hartmut: I think that was also a North American documentary. Because you could see the women were not comfortable with being filmed, but I'm sure it was a male cameraman who thought, "I get a free shot ..."

Thomas: Right. That's right.

Hartmut: And I don't think a European cameraman would have done that. We are more laid back about nakedness, but if you see somebody naked, you'd look the other way.

Renae: Well, it was John Paskievich's film …[58]

Thomas: You know, what's funny is there is this European idea, the *indians* are completely uninhibited. Whereas a matter of fact, the opposite is probably true. I mean, the tribes I'm familiar with are pretty uptight about stuff like that. [to Renae] How are the Navajo?

Renae: I'd say we're very modest, very conservative. Very superstitious. That's just part of our culture.

Thomas: Yeah. So it's funny how people see us – and how we actually are.

Hartmut: I think there was a movement in the 1920s for going out into nature. It's a projection, I think, of freedom. And I think they are projecting this to Indigenous people or *Indianer* because they think there is that freedom that they are seeking. It's their own.

Thomas: It's a spinoff of that sort of utopian idea.

Florentine: Yeah, exactly. [all agreeing] Jean-Jacques Rousseau.

Hartmut: It's like all stereotypes: They tell you everything about those who carry them, and nothing about the people they think they depict.

Thomas: Sure. The joke is, though, that none of the Germans, nor the Czechs, nor the French, want to emulate contemporary *indians*. None of them get dressed up like me or like you, Renae. It's all "dead *indians*" they want. They want to dress up and look like "dead *indians*."[59]

Florentine: And that's why they take the right to say that you're not the real *indian* because you don't [resemble the stereotype].

Thomas: I don't know how many times I've been told that overseas, you know? How disappointing I am to them.

Florentine: Oh, really?

Thomas: Really.

Renae: I'm still disappointing. [laughs]

Thomas: A little beadwork and some feathers and you're all right! But they want to decide who is who: "I wish we had someone who looks like what we imagined *indians* to be."

Florentine: So why were you so disappointing? They told you?

Thomas: Well, I had a moustache at the time.

Florentine: Oh, yeah?

Thomas: So I looked like either Fu Manchu or a Mexican bandit. And one woman – actually, a photographer – told me that I wasn't an *indian*, that *indians* didn't have facial hair. Those clichés and stereotypes are hard to break down. Germans wind up with the same motion pictures that we wind up with. The big movie in Germany was *Dances with Wolves*.

Florentine: Oh, yes.

Thomas: I have a German poster of that.

Florentine: I do, too.

Renae: The first time I saw that, I saw it in Belgium, so I saw it in French with the subtitles, and I couldn't believe it – I was watching this. Wow! I don't have it easier. I was telling Hartmut and Florentine that I was often mistaken for maybe a Turkish woman or some other Eastern European woman. And that racism that's directed toward Turkish people in Germany would manifest in introductions. I would be introduced as Renae and then whomever was introducing me to another person would say: "Und *sie* ist *Indianerin*!" [And *she* is an *indian* woman!]. Then the person would suddenly be interested in me [because I wasn't Turkish].

Florentine: Oh yeah, there is a racist hierarchy.

Thomas: Hold a big sign: "Ich bin ein *Indianer*." [laughs]

Florentine: Or hold a sign: "I am not Turkish."

Renae: I would never say that. I am a Shiprocker.

Florentine: Of course not.

Thomas: Of course, you could have said: "Ich bin ein Berliner." It's not gonna stop because what the world has decided is that there is this block of dead *indianness* that really is the stereotypes and clichés that are all wound up. The cover of my new book[60] – that artwork was originally a poster for an Italian cruise line that was advertising trips for North America in the thirties and forties. So that's how Europe saw North America.

Hartmut: It still does, if you look at the yearly catalogues or agencies that advocate trips to North America. There is always an *indian* on the cover.

Helen: Still?

Hartmut: There still is. It actually becomes a tradition. You show a piece of landscape and an Indigenous person. So if you advertise Lapland or Sami-land, you have the landscape and then a Sami in a blue dress or so. Or you have the same for Thailand. So, it is always the combination of landscape and an Indigenous person. And that hasn't changed. If you see a country like Canada, the embassies pushing Canada abroad, inviting people to invest money, how do they present Canada? It's the West Coast, it's totem poles, it's Indigenous people. The Canadian government does that very, very consciously.

Florentine: Oh, absolutely.

Helen: This happens in Ottawa every July. There always has to be some Native dancing at whatever Ottawa events are happening.

Thomas: Or the Calgary Stampede. We used to leave the province whenever the Stampede was on. Just to stay away.

Renae: I do that, too!

Hartmut: It is commodification that takes over, and I think that is something that both sides – not the Indigenous people, but the entrepreneurs of the West, in Europe and here – advertise.

Thomas: No, they're great North American symbols and nobody's going to give them up at any time. So I suppose I shouldn't be worried about the Germans because they're not emulating me.

Florentine: No. Absolutely.

Thomas: Not me, nor my family, or you. It's a story about you ...

Hartmut: It's a story about themselves.

Helen: They're playing off what the government gives them.

Renae: Could I ask a question?

Hartmut: Sure.

Renae: I think this topic is tied to, you know, Natives that live there. Some of whom may be men who dance for money. What are your thoughts about that?

Thomas: Well, it depends. You make a living as best you can, I mean. There are Cherokee guys in Cherokee, North Carolina ...

Renae: That's true.

Thomas: Who've been doing ... It's called "Chiefing" where they put on a full-feather headdress that the Cherokee never owned – Germans maybe, but not [Cherokees]. They get their picture taken with a tourist for a certain amount of money. There was one guy down there who probably put his kids and his relatives through college doing Chiefing, who was famous for it. Do I have any objection to that? [all say yes and all laughing]

Yes, I suppose a little bit, but you know, I'm not going to tell him how to make a living.

Hartmut: You call that Chiefing?

Thomas: Chiefing, yeah. It's called Chiefing. That's what they call it.

Renae: I understand that. It's a bit different, because with people that live in Germany that are Natives, they are actually from Plains tribes, so they're justifying that they are depicting actual cultural dances from their tribes, like Blackfoot or Cree or whatever, you know? So, it isn't as far-fetched as Chiefing.

Thomas: I don't know. I don't really mind. If I went to Germany and ran into a bunch of Lakotas, and they had a drum and they said, "Listen, do you want to sing with us?" I know a couple of Lakota songs; sure, I'd sit in and I'd learn some. I'd do that. But I'd do that for me and for the group. I wouldn't do that for the tourist. But if we were on display, and they say, "Oh we're gonna go over to Berlin, and we're gonna sing a couple of songs at this event, would you come with us?" You know: "You haven't got a good voice, but it's okay, we'd need someone to fill in, on the lows." I'd probably say "Sure." And do it. But, I mean, when you go to powwows ... This is the dichotomy of the powwow: we're doing it to show other people what we can do. We're also doing it for ourselves. It really is a reminder for ourselves. So it serves both purposes at the same time. The Navajo have public ceremonies, the Hopi have public ceremonies – no, they have private ceremonies. Well, the public ceremony you can do for the public or for ourselves, for the community.

Hartmut: I had a German term: *Indianertümelei*. There is no way of translating that, or I didn't know. You know that "-tümelei," it starts with "Deutschtum." If somebody thinks that everything German is first and is just so wonderful. And we really talk about it. It's sort of ...

Thomas: So, sort of "Deutschland, Deutschland über alles?"

Hartmut: That is too aggressive.

Thomas: Oh, okay.

Hartmut: No, Deutschtümelei is ...

Florentine: Is more cozy.

Hartmut: It's a form of cultural nationalism.

Florentine: Yeah, it's liking your oak furniture and your cuckoo clock.

Hartmut: It's believing in the stereotype of Germany and in your homeland.

Florentine: And that also doesn't exist, right?

Thomas: My God! Oh, I hadn't thought about that.

Hartmut: So, that's what I was thinking about *Indianertümelei*, because that's what it does: it fetishizes this stereotype, I think. And I didn't have a way of translating. So I came up with Indianthusiasm.[61] I thought it would be a fun term. Maybe it's not the right term, but it's there now.

Thomas: Now you got me thinking of terms I can make up for you.

Hartmut: Sure. She [pointing at Renae] came up with Powwowthusiasm.[62]

Renae: Yeah.

Thomas: Powwowthusiasm?

All: Yeah.

Thomas: That's not bad.

Helen: We sure get that!

Thomas: At the powwows, I mean. You put a powwow together and you could actually have Europeans running – racing each other – to get a good seat.

Florentine: Oh really?

Thomas: They're pretty powerful. I mean, you know, I enjoy them.

Helen: At a book fair years ago, there was an unscheduled drumming moment with the Red Something Singers. As the drumming started, we were in the hallway and we could just see people just running towards the drum.

Thomas: I forget the name of the drum. We almost got trampled because the head singer hit the drum once, and then you hear that beat go –BAM ... All of a sudden the room begins to move and Helen and I were, like, *Woah!* ... The stampede starts coming right at us.

Helen: They were running past Tom, because he is not what they were looking for.

Renae: You're not the *indian* they had in mind?

Thomas: That's right. Well, and the nice thing about that was that the guys [that] were singing on that particular drum were all young kids. They were teenagers. They were a fun bunch of kids, very nice kids. All they do is hit the drum, and they'd have a crowd. Just like a magnet. But you don't see much of that in Europe. I mean even with all of the enthusiasm, with the *indian* clubs and what not, I doubt that you see a lot of powwows, or a lot of dancers, or a lot of singers. During the powwow season, we can, you know, we can go any place and sing.

Hartmut: Yeah, there are powwows. There are powwows in Germany. I went to one once.

Thomas: How was it?

Hartmut: I thought it was very strange and I left after a short time.

Thomas: Strange because?

Hartmut: Because I had the feeling those people were pretending to be somebody they weren't.

Thomas: They are.

Hartmut: Yeah!

Thomas: But that's not a sin.

Florentine: No.

Hartmut: One of the organizers was a colleague of mine, and I used to have nothing but ridicule for them. But then I got to know her, and how serious she is about things. And she is a good person. And then I realized: for her it's just a hobby in a way, and she's now into *Star Trek* and does films with her students. So she's found another – she doesn't say this – escape or whatever. But she is a fantastic beadworker. She really does very good beadwork.

Thomas: I tell you where the thorn is in my side, and that is when I'm talking to Europeans – they could be German, they could be French – who begin lecturing me on *indianness*.

Hartmut: Oh yeah.

Florentine: Yes. They like that.

Thomas: Now, it's not that I know any more about it than they do. They have made a lifetime studying it, but I don't like or appreciate it.

Hartmut: I can understand that.

Thomas: It makes me feel as though they're trying to say: "Well, you know, you may be Native by blood, but you don't know shit about *indians!*"

Hartmut: That's a common reaction. When people come and lecture me about Germany, I think it's weird. And on the other hand, what happens if you're in another country, you become the expert.

Thomas: And sometimes I get asked questions or I get into a conversation with someone who wants to know all the intimate details of our culture, but I just felt like, you know, I am not interested in talking to you about that particularly. I had a weird experience happen. We used to get invited out to the Sundance at the Blood Reserve, had friends there. And we go out there every year. And there were people out there who were not Blood. These were not Natives. They wanted me to be their informant. They wanted entrée to certain people at the Sundance ground. I'd say, "No, I'm not gonna do that. That is not my job and yeah, you wanna do that? Go right ahead. I don't know you. I don't know who you are."

Hartmut: This is just for the record – I think I know the answer – but for years on the cover blurbs of your books, there was this German connection. You know the question?

Thomas: Yeah.

Hartmut: It was always Cherokee, German, and Greek.

Thomas: Yeah. [It is now] just Cherokee and Greek.

Hartmut: Now, since *Truth and Bright Water*,[63] it's just Cherokee and Greek.

Thomas: This was my fault. My grandmother, her family name from Europe was Eschelmann.

Hartmut: Eschelmann?

Thomas: Eschelmann. And I even got the Eschelmann Bible. And it was a Dunker Bible.[64] It was a religious group. And for some reason I thought she was German. German-German. And my grandmother's mother's people. And when my first book came out, I wanted to honour all the sides of my family, my Cherokee side, my Greek side, and my grandmother's side. That was the German side.

And my mother said, "What's this German stuff?" And I said, "Well, for granny." My mother says, "She's not German. The family was Swiss." And I said, "Well, were they at least German-speaking Swiss?" And she says, "I don't know." So I thought, "Oh my god. No German at all. It was Swiss at the very best." So I thought, you know what? The two major streams of my life would have been Cherokee and Greek.

Renae: So your mother, you said your grandmother, was Greek?

Thomas: Yeah. My grandmother, when she married my grandfather, he was from Greece. She learned how to speak Greek fluently. The people in the neighbourhood didn't know she wasn't Greek, as a matter of fact ... I mean, the household ... They'd speak Greek until my grandfather died. And then it sort of melted away into the melting pot pretty much. And he died when I was about two years old. So it wasn't a long time that I knew him.

Since we were at a restaurant, our meal came to the table, so we abruptly ended the interview and enjoyed our meal, chatting about unrelated matters.

DAVID T. McNAB

You can deal with stereotypes! At least you're dealing with some knowledge.

Phone interview by Hartmut Lutz

Hartmut: Can you introduce yourself? Your background, and then say something about how you got into contact with Germany.

David: I can do that. My name is David McNab, and the full name is David and then the middle name is Thornton: David Thornton McNab. I was named after Thornton Wilder, the writer, because my mother, that was her favourite American writer. She always felt that I would become a writer.

I'm a Métis historian, and I teach at York University in Toronto. My home department is the Department of Equity Studies, where I teach Indigenous Thought, and my secondary department – it's a 60/40 split – is the Department of Humanities, [where] I teach Canadian Studies.

Hartmut: And before you met Ute,[65] did you have any contacts with Germany? And what type of expectations did you have about Germany?

David: Yeah, I did have quite a bit of familiarity, born in Kitchener-Waterloo. Besides, I was born free. I was born outside [of the] hospital, in the back seat of a taxi cab.

Hartmut: Oh? [laughs]

David: Born free because the driver of the taxi cab was in such a state of trauma that when my father came out to pay him, he had left. I'm free. I love that story. That's my creation story.

So, as you know, Kitchener-Waterloo is in Waterloo County, and Waterloo County was part of the original Six Nations Reserve. So I was born on the Six Nations Reserve, but the original one. The original one was in 1784,

139

right? The Haldimand Grant.[66] And the Six Nations chose that piece of land six miles on each side of the Grand River ... because of the name of the river and of the fact it was good for farming and hunting. And the name of the river originally was the Bear River. If you go back to the early maps of the French regime you see that the river was originally known as the *Ours* River. That's for Bear. It was Bear River originally. Very few people know that. [I learned that] through my land claims research.

Hartmut: Now: contacts, expectations about Germany?

David: Yeah. And of course, after the reserve was created because of [Joseph] Brant, then it was leased and all kinds of other things happened to the pieces of land and the communities in Waterloo County. And the area was supposedly cleared for settlement, and it was seen not to be Six Nations reserve land. So one of the early peoples from Europe into Waterloo County were Germans. And one of those families, who are still buried in the nearby cemeteries, was known as the Huehns. And the Huehns of course as you're German you know, were "Hühn."

So they were one of the first settlers. And it appears [that when] my family came to Waterloo County, they set up shop, so to speak, in the area and they intermarried with the Onondaga, who are a Six Nations people.[67] I've been down to the graveyard, and all the names are in German, from the early settlers, the Huehns. And so that's on my maternal grandfather's side, who was Edward Huehn, and he was born in 1898, and he passed away in 1967. And he met my maternal grandmother, whose name was Mabel Kennedy [of Métis /Cree/Algonquin descent], born in 1898 as well. And she only passed away in 1993, [at] 95. So they got married, and they had my mother, and I was born on October 28, 1947. And one of the very first things that caught my ear growing up in Kitchener-Waterloo in the 1950s was German, because both my maternal grandparents spoke German at that time.

We were around the corner, so you know how kids are, we'd just go, and we got introduced to it without even knowing about it. And that's the reason for my second language.

So, but of course the Huehns, because of the racism in the First World War – they were born in Berlin, but of course it then became Kitchener, the British Imperial name, in the First World War – so as a result of that [racism], most Germans in Waterloo County, including the Huehns, didn't want to call attention to themselves. They only spoke German until ... I think it was after the First World War.

Hartmut: That was a general pattern – that they tried to sort of tone down their Germanness because of the war.

David: They didn't speak German except in the house. I remember clearly, that that was the case. They would only speak German in the house in the 1950s. That was the impact of racism in Waterloo County.

Hartmut: How do you spell "Huehn"?

David: H-u-e-h-n.
They're just "Hühner" (chickens), right?

Hartmut: Yeah, yeah, *klar*.

David: And they were from Elsass [Alsace]. And they came over to Waterloo County, probably because of the Napoleonic Wars.

Hartmut: Yeah.

David: Now, on my mother's side, she has a very interesting family history, going back to the late eighteenth century, in which her great-great-grandmother was married there from Cumberland House.[68]
Her husband was Alexander Kennedy (ca. 1770–1832), who was a chief factor of the Hudson's Bay Company. And that carried forward: one of Alexander Kennedy's sons, William (1814–1890) came and worked in the fur trade as well. He was at Fort William on the Ottawa River. Sarah Stevens (ca. 1810–1858), who I think was a daughter of Chief Peter Stevens, of the Algonquin Nation, was a member of the Bird Clan. William Kennedy's son, he was a Bear, and the bears and the birds are very compatible, 'cause they look after one another, you know? Because the birds are above, and they overlook the bears, 'cause the bears are on the ground.

Hartmut: And are busy down there.

David: Good, it was a good thing. So, William was there working for the Hudson's Bay Company in the 1830s and then he got moved to [the Ungava Peninsula in what is now] northern Quebec, as a trader, but of course in those days, you couldn't take your wife and your children with you. So, because William's father, Alexander Kennedy, was very, very wealthy, he left his family seven thousand pounds in his will when he died in 1832.

Hartmut: Incredible.

David: Yeah, so William chose to use fifty pounds and bought a [100-acre] farm on the [east side of] the Bear [Grand] River [in what became part of Waterloo County]. I ended up being born in Waterloo County, on the Grand River, and actually we still live there. Ute teaches German Studies, by the way. We live about a couple of kilometres from the Grand River ... still today, in that place.

Hartmut: Wonderful.

David: [William] Kennedy bought the lot [for Sarah, his wife, and two sons]. Kennedy and then one of his two sons [also named William (1835–1925)] had a [trading] merchant business. They [bought and sold] grain, various kinds of grains, with the Mennonite farmers. And they also, along the way, they also liked to hide, because of the racism in Waterloo County. A number of generations married into first-generation German families. So they married the German women that came over from Germany to Canada. So the whole family is on one side, all through seven generations, Indigenous, Algonquin, Cree, Métis, who actually married with the Germans *to hide*! Which is absolutely remarkable – it's the best thing to do. Nobody would suspect you're *indian*, married to a German who was born in Germany. And of course, that's why I married Ute. [Hartmut laughs] Now forty-three years.

Hartmut: Sure.

David: Another story. So anyway, one of the first things that I learned – when I was about four years old – was from my German-Onondaga grandfather, Edward Huehn. He and I were in a backseat of a car and he said: "David, it is very important for you to remember, and the way to remember is to see something outside, close your eyes, open up again, and say the name or the word and the place four times. And when you do that, you will never forget that." It's my very early training, from four years old, in Onondaga, remembering. That's why I remember everything from at least the age of four and up and became a historian.

Now, so that's the German influence there, as well as the Onondaga influence, because the Germans are very like that, too, in terms of the knowledge of history, right?

Hartmut: Well, I hope so. [laughs]

David: Well. Okay. It's a compliment, Hartmut.

Hartmut: Yeah, I know, I know. I hope we deserve the compliment. [laughs]

David: Public school in the 1950s: the first course in Canadian history came up ... ahh, that was in about, what ... 1958, the first course in Canadian history. Well, who should I have my first course in Canadian history with, but a Moses. His name was Jim Moses.

Hartmut: Oh.

David: Six Nations!

Hartmut: Is Daniel David Moses related to him?

David: I don't know.

Hartmut: Well, he's Delaware, David is.[69]

David: No, that's not him. He was from the Six Nations. He was a young history and phys-ed teacher in the mid-1950s, and he actually taught in the public school there [in Kitchener]. What he would do, was to ... what I say is, unlearn our history using the Six Nations pedagogy. The first thing to do, to remember and to learn, is you have to unlearn. He just talked about what it means as an Indigenous person to learn Canadian history. And what Indigenous people [originally] brought to Canada.

Hartmut: So you were exposed to German culture and language at a very early age.

David: Yeah. I was on a – without realizing it – on a Two Row Wampum[70] journey.

Hartmut: Yeah. And now when you look at Indigenous Studies or so, you know there are increasing numbers of – or a few numbers of – Indigenous people from Canada who study in Germany or got PhDs in Germany. And vice versa, you also get German scholars coming – or students coming – to Canada pursuing Native Studies here. How do you feel about that?

David: Oh, Hartmut, I think that's absolutely "tragic," because that destroys the whole history of the Two Row Wampum, in that the Germans, because of their enthusiasm for *indians*, they *marry* them.[71] And that was a good thing, right? Because in the Two Row Wampum each person is in their own canoe, their own ship.

But if they marry, that's immensely the bond and the basis for Canadian history ... and the relationships between the Germans and the *indians*.

Hartmut: So you don't think there should be Natives coming to Germany studying there or vice versa?

David: Oh both, yeah. I think there should be a two-way. Because of that history.

Hartmut: Okay, then I misunderstood you. You said it's "tragic," and I thought, "Why?"

David: I think that more hasn't happened. There should be more of it!

Hartmut: I agree with you, absolutely.

David: Whenever we go to Germany, with Ute's research and everything, I'm very happy, and everybody is.

Hartmut: How do people react to you in Germany?

David: But that isn't true in Canada. The racism is still [prominent here] today.

Hartmut: So you find people react differently to you in Germany than in Canada?

David: Absolutely. If I come, they always want to know who you are, who I am, right? They don't give a shit of how white I am. But the Germans, because of their enthusiasm, they want to know who you are. You look different. I know my own personal history ... and they are very intrigued.

Hartmut: Don't you find that their being intrigued, or so, is also full of stereotypes?

David: Yeah, but you can deal with stereotypes! At least you're dealing with some knowledge.

Hartmut: Yeah.

David: Here, there's no knowledge, right?

Hartmut: Yeah, okay. I hope that [what you say about Germany] is true.

David: I've been going back and forth to Europe since 1970 with Ute. That's been my experience forty-three years later. It's almost every year.

Hartmut: You have travelled a lot, so do you find differences in European countries regarding Indianthusiasm?

David: Oh yes. I think the Germans are more ... What is the term? More knowledgeable. Even though the stereotypes are there. They're much more intrigued, and they're inquisitive, and they're curious. So that's an opening, right?

Hartmut: Have you taught German audiences?

David: No. I haven't.

Hartmut: Does your work engage with German Indianthusiasm? Or has that influenced your work, your research?

David: Yeah, Ute and I wrote, of course, that article about the German film.[72]

Hartmut: Okay, yeah, that's right.

David: And you know, we also met people there on our research. Eventually we may, when we retire ... we'd like to write a book on the subject of German films.

Hartmut: Yeah, that would be interesting.

David: The last time, or one of the times we talked in Germany, I came back from a chat with a ... What's his name, the hero of the East German film?

Hartmut: Oh, Gojko Mitic.

David: Remember that?

Hartmut: Yeah.

David: You were critiquing me on that.

Hartmut: And you know there is an Indigenous filmmaker working on Gojko Mitic: Neil Diamond, you know? The Cree? He did this film *Reel Injun* about the Hollywood *indian*.[73] And he's now working apparently on Gojko Mitic.

David: Wonderful! And Gojko Mitic, even though he wasn't German, he was Yugoslavian, he is very respectful as well.

Hartmut: Yeah, that's what I heard from other people, too. Apparently, he is a very nice guy. People in the former GDR, they just love him.

David: Once you met him, you know why. He's amazing. Amazing guy.

Hartmut: Have you met any German hobbyists?

David: Not really. We haven't got into that part of the research.

Hartmut: How do you feel about those guys?

David: Well, they're good and they do their homework and their research. They don't bother me.

Hartmut: And when you think about the sort of New Age approach to Indigenous spirituality and the interest that there is in ceremonies, and also some Indigenous people catering to that interest, who come to Germany, how do you feel about that?

David: Well, I think two things. One, they're very authentic and sincere in what they believe. So we have to respect that. And they're so far off the mark, that it's basically laughable. So, as an Indigenous person, you know that whether it's false or not. That's it.

Hartmut: But you really think you have to respect their desire, huh?

David: Yeah! Sure. Why not?

Hartmut: Do you have any thoughts about why there is such a hunger for spirituality?

David: Because of the state of Europe since the early nineteenth century. Two world wars.

Hartmut: I think – or some people have said – that sort of hobbyism and Indianthusiasm is also a way for Germans to escape their own history and guilt feelings and enter a realm that is free of guilt feelings.

David: It's a way of signing their own health for them.[74] I can't disrespect that urge. Otherwise I'd be disrespecting myself. Because we're all humans, right?

Hartmut: Sure. That is the nice thing. [laughs]

David: It is part of the Two Row Wampum, which I live by.

Hartmut: When you think of Indigenous dancers from Canada and the US and singers who come over to Germany and work there during the summer in some of those camps, or at Radebeul at the Karl May Festival – how do you feel about that?

David: Well, I'm very intrigued because almost every time I go over, first I see one in Germany or, say, Prague, or wherever, I encounter these people going over. Going over at least since the early nineteenth century as troupes, and so I'm very intrigued by that. My research hasn't taken me in that direction, but every time that I encounter one of those groups, I take digital photographs. And I include them in my lectures.

Hartmut: What do you say about them in your lectures?

David: Well, basically, there's one way to open up and approach representations of Indigenous people and stereotypes. Again, because the students in Canada, they really don't know. They never met any *indian* except on TV or on show, right? You have to open up things based on the issues.

Hartmut: So you use those pictures that you take to talk about the representations or the dissemination of stereotypes?

David: Yeah.

Hartmut: So if you see that in the context of stereotyping, do you criticize those groups going over?

David: Of course not. No, no, no. No. Then I show them why it is that the people are doing things like this. I ask the students: What are the issues that this event is taking place in Prague or in northern Germany or southern Germany?

Hartmut: Yeah.

David: Because they don't *know*.

Hartmut: No.

David: How else would they know?

Hartmut: That's true.

David: Photographs, for example, that I have accumulated, which I put in my lectures. I can go on for at least half an hour to an hour in terms of letting the students know about the various understandings, what it means to walk the tightrope, which is the name of our book.[75]

Hartmut: Ah, yeah.

David: Representations of Indigenous people, right? That's why Ute and I did those books – because we wanted to open up the field to understanding of Aboriginal people. And that's why, when we did those books, we deliberately chose ... We were inclusive, but we deliberately chose Indigenous voices being part of those. Because they're actually wonderful teaching tools.

Hartmut: Yeah, I try to include as many Indigenous sources as I can. And if I have a choice, I take Indigenous speakers or writers or artists.

David: You and I think rather alike, I know.

Hartmut: I think so, yeah.

David: 'Cause you're German. I'm just teasing you!

Hartmut: [laughs] Yeah, I know, I know. No, you know what? One thing I'm learning – we've talked to a number of Indigenous people from Canada who've also lived in Germany and worked there, or have family there. And those that have been travelling there, the picture they have of Germany – or what they tell me – is so positive that I, as a German born in 1945 with all this guilt and so on, really have a hard time accepting, because that's not my take on Germany. But it's also very pleasant, you know.

David: That's very important, in what you just said. In terms of my relationship and my marriage to Ute, for forty-three years, she came over to Canada when she was ten years old. She came alone, right? And the very first thing [she did] when she got to the top of the old Malton airport [Toronto], she looked out on the gangway to get down, she looked around in Canada, and she said, "I wanna go back. There are no cowboys and *indians* here." [Hartmut laughs] And of course she ended up meeting one. [David laughs]

Hartmut: You know, when I was five and my brother eight, we played Cowboys and *indians*. And of course, I was the *indian* and he was a cowboy. And all the other guys in our street were cowboys, too. And once they tied me to a tree at the railway embankment, because I was the only *indian*. And then they forgot [about me]. And then I was missed at the dinner table, and my brother came to rescue me. Maybe that should have told me. [Hartmut laughs]

David [laughs a lot]: I love it! What a great story.

Hartmut: To come back to those people who come as performers, or also if you think of some books by Indigenous people that are translated, or artwork that is being sold – there is also an economic side to the whole thing. Have you any comments on that?

David: Ute and I really don't know the actors or performers over there. But one person we are working on is the person and the family of Louise Erdrich.

Hartmut: Oh yeah?

David: That was the first thing when we met Louise in the year 2001 – she said in a bookstore ... She told me to stop talking. And then she turned around, and she said to Ute: "You have to write my German family history 'cause nobody else is interested in it."

She sold many, many of her novels. And we have accumulated many of her novels, because she is a national bestselling writer, right?[76]

Hartmut: Yeah.

David: They've been translated into many languages, but most of all into German.

Hartmut: Yeah, I'm asking this because this is something that I've heard from a number of Indigenous writers and also visual artists. You know, they bank on the German market.

David: I agree with you. I agree, but that's my take on it. That's not really part of my own research. An observation based on many trips back and forth.

Hartmut: I've gone through my list of questions and I'm wondering, do you have comments or something you would like to add, or something you want to get off your chest, or that should be in a book *Indianthusiasm: Indigenous Responses?*

David: No, no. Like I said, I approach it very respectfully, going back into my family history and into the early nineteenth century, as of the Two Row

Wampum. And we have to respect both sides of the Two Row Wampum. That's where the knowledge is, right – in the actual Two Row Wampum? And that's the approach that I take. And that's the reason Ute and I met in Eastwood Collegiate in Kitchener, in our joint German class. Her name was Lischke. Which is, as you know, Czech. It is not a German name – a Czech name from Prague, which is "fox," right?

Hartmut: Yeah!

David: So we got together in German class [in high school]. She would always get 99, and I would bum along at 62, right? I would actually cheat [off] her, because I'd look over her shoulder to at least get the last half of the German sentence.

Hartmut: You know, this is what you call a "German connection." [Hartmut laughs]

David: Exactly. And then finally, after five years, we went to the same university – Waterloo [Lutheran University] – and in the second term, I invited her out for a date.

And after that, in the end of our third year, we ended up getting married, on August 28, 1970. So now we've been ... we are in our 43rd year. So, there is living proof Germans and *indians* can do it.

QUENTIN PIPESTEM

It's been my job to not only entertain them through my dancing and singing, but also to educate them in the actual original traditional stories.

Live interview with Renae Watchman, recorded over lunch at the Grey Eagle Casino buffet, Calgary

Quentin: My name is Quentin Pipestem. I am from the Tsuut'ina Nation on my mother's side, and my father comes from the Siksika Nation, the Blackfoot people.

Renae: When did you move to Germany, and would you consider it home?

Quentin: I moved to Germany in 2007. And the reason I went to Germany was for work. I work as a Native American dancer, singer, storyteller, flute player. That's my profession. Five years ago, I found there was a place north of Berlin in a town called Templin. The name of the place is "El Dorado Western Town," a Western town theme park. They were looking for a Native American entertainer, performer, dancer – more or less what I do, and so I started there. At the beginning it was supposed to be for a month, but after one month they really liked what I do as a performer, and they invited me to stay for the rest of the season. And then after that, it went to the next season, and now it's been five seasons, and I'm still working there.

Renae: And how long do you plan to stay?

Quentin: Well, that's the question. I do plan to be living in Europe for still a few more years, and I imagine I'll be working at this place, El Dorado, while I'm still in Europe.

Renae: I understand you used to work somewhere else in Europe before that, right?

Quentin: Actually, I used to live in Italy before that for seven years. I was doing my shows there in Italy. I would organize performances at Native American *indian* festivals in different towns and doing all sorts of festivals in Italy. Yeah, I was working there before moving to Germany.

Renae: Okay. And are you fluent in German?

Quentin: No, *ich spreche nur ein bisschen Deutsch!* [I speak only a little bit of German!]

Renae: How do you get around in Germany?

Quentin: I get around pretty well. This place is north of Berlin. So, I spend a lot of time in Berlin, and in Berlin there are many people who speak English. So, it's not so difficult to get around in Berlin.

Renae: Do you know any other Native people that live in Berlin?

Quentin: Yes, there's another Peigan Indian, Murray Small Legs. Technically it's not Berlin, its actually called Potsdam, the town right beside Berlin. He lives in Potsdam, and I've known him since I've been there. Before I moved there we used to work together with these Native American festivals. We also used to do other shows throughout Europe. We have a little network of Native American people who live in Europe from Spain, France, Germany, Austria, all dancers and singers. Sometimes, when I used to live in Italy, we would organize these three-day Native American festivals, where I would invite all these different Native people from the surrounding countries, and we would come together in one place, and together we would put on shows, conferences, craft workshops, and stuff like this. So yeah, we have a little network of Native people in Europe.

Renae: How many do you think live there now?

Quentin: Oh, well, the ones that I know ... There's at least eight to nine people that I have worked with over the years. There's another Lakota who lives in Italy, and he's a poet and actually he knows many of the Lakota stories; his name is Gilbert Deville. And there are two Natives who live in Spain, Kendall Old Elk, is one of them, he is a Crow Indian, and I work a lot with him. And there is a group that live in Paris, who work at the Buffalo Bill's Wild West Show [at Disneyland Paris], and there are three people that I always work with normally, and one is another Crow Indian, his name is Kevin Dust. And then there is a Nakoda, Kevin Moostoos, and then there is the Navajo. He's a good friend of mine too, and I can't think of his name, it just blocked my mind.

Anyways, in Austria, there's a Northwest Coast Indian, and his name is Ed Bryant. And there's another Ojibwe lady from Quebec. I just started working with her last year, and her name is Anita Assiniboine. She's a jingle dress dancer. She lives in France on the outside of Paris.

Renae: Obviously, you've been living in Europe for so long, and you've made some contacts, and they do the same thing you do. How do you perceive Germans, in Germany? Or Europe?

Quentin: Well like you say, I have been living there for quite a while and I do have my ideas of the different countries, but mainly Italy and Germany.

Well, first of all I should mention that my connection to Italy is that I have a son in Italy, and his mother's Italian. That's why I actually originally moved to Italy at the beginning when he was born, and that is why I actually still stay in Europe, because I want to have my connection with my boy. I still have a strong connection with my son. When I'm not working, I'm spending time in Italy with him, or when he has his holidays in the summer or during the Easter breaks, he comes to me in Germany. So that's actually the main reason why I'm still in Europe, and probably will still continue being in Europe. He's eleven years old, so I think at least another four or five more years I'll probably be there to be a part of his life.

So that's my connection in Europe, and living in Italy I learned a lot about the Italian culture, the people, and I do even speak the language – well not fluently, but pretty good. Italian people are very interesting people; actually I enjoy Italy as one of my most favourite countries in Europe, next to Germany, because now I work there and I got to know the German people. But the German and Italian people: it's like black and white – totally different mentality, way of life, philosophies! Germans are really dedicated, very straightforward, they really focus on what they want, and they do what they want and they're very, how would you explain that ...

Renae: Rigid, no? [laughs]

Quentin: "Rigid" yes, is a good term, is a good way to say it, but then you know it's ... I really respect that, because they really have a lot of respect for doing things in the right way. Maybe too much respect for this, because they always follow the rules, never stray off the path, they are always very oriented, minded in this way, keeping to the rules, the rules are the rules. And then – going back to black and white – Italians are the opposite. They can get around the rules, or bend the rules, or forget about the rules: that's the way they manage their way of life. Sometimes Italians, politics, culture, just the way of life, can be sometimes, like living on one big reservation [laughs]. Because you know, in the way of politics, it's like, "You do me a favour, I do you a favour," this sort of thing. And there's still this way of life, with even the people and taxes! They're always trying to find a way around the taxes, but in Germany it's opposite. They pay their taxes, they work hard, they really strive to make a good life for themselves.

Renae: I asked you what you thought of Germany. I feel like this is a question that's loaded, but when they come to your shows, do they have expectations? Do you fulfill them, or do they – do you think they're more educated? I mean, I've been going back for twenty years, and I have my own stories to share, but how do they perceive you?

Quentin: Actually, they really have a great, wonderful fascination with the Native American people. Both in western Germany and in the former East Germany. Well in the west, you already know about Karl May and his books, and so many people, not only in Germany but Eastern Europe, grew up with these books. So that's one part of the fascination [with] the Native American people.

But the other part is, where I work now was formerly the GDR, and back in the old days, they never were allowed to read or watch anything from the west side. So it meant no books, no western books, no movies, or anything western. So in the former GDR time, what happened was that they actually made their own movies. They made about nineteen movies, and in the cowboy and *indian* movies that they made, because they're also anti-west in the former East Germany, the Native Americans were the heroes, compared to the opposite in the old black-and-white cowboy and *indian* movies in America, where the *indians* were always considered the bad guys. And so that's why the mentality – you know in the old times in America, the *indians* were always considered like the bad people.

Renae: Wagon burners?

Quentin: Yeah, the wagon burners, you know, the savages. But then, the former East was actually the opposite. I mean, it still told some of the stories that happened, where the *indians* were defeated, but they portrayed it in a way where the Native Americans were the heroes. And so a lot of the old people nowadays, they still have this fascination with the Native American as a hero. So it's a really positive outlook [on] the Native people, as opposed to some places here in America, where it can still be considered negative to be Native American. In Europe it's the opposite. It's actually a positive thing, and more in the east. But also throughout Germany, and actually throughout Europe, when you meet somebody, they're very fascinated, and very interested in where I come from, and who I am, and then on top of that for what I do as a profession, as not only a performer, but like a storyteller, flute player, and also one of my specialties is the hoop dance. I've been world champion three times in the past. I've never had any problems within Europe, and people are very fascinated. So that is why I really enjoy what I do there.

Renae: You were telling me about the positive image they have of Natives, and you're saying it's still there. So, are you telling me that when you perform, – they're very respectful people?

Quentin: Well they still have some sort of Hollywood version of Native people as in the tipis, and also with the totem pole in the middle of the camp. Of course, the totem poles come from the west coast, and that's not a part of our culture from the Plains, but for them they still have this notion that it's a general Native American theme, but other than that … No, they really have a great interest and fascination.

And it's also been my job to not only entertain them through my dancing and singing and that, but also to educate them in the actual original traditional stories. Whenever I do any sort of dance, or sing, drum, or flute, I always first of all explain the traditional story of the origin of each dance, and everything that I do. And the people really appreciate this because then they are not only entertained, they're also educated. And then they come and talk to me after, and they're happy to know that they're learning something – not only being entertained, but learning something that they never had a chance before to learn.

Renae: Are you the only one who works in Templin?

Quentin: Yeah, well for the season. I work from April to the middle of October, and for most of the season I work as a solo performer. But then, the second weekend in May, we have what we call our "Indian Days," which is one of the highlight events of the season. During the season there are different highlight events, like American Car Weekend or Biker Weekend, or just different things; we have a certain event once or twice a month, and in May we have what's called the Indian Days. It's four days of just the Native American theme. I invite the people I talked to you about before, who live in Europe. I also invited Moontee [Sinquah] and his two sons this year. I brought them in from Phoenix, and they came as part of this festival, and so we had about nine Native American dancers perform there. The Native American, or Indian Days, is the biggest highlight event of El Dorado season. It gets the most people, it's their biggest event, and that's what I'm in charge of. I organize it. That's just to show again how interested they are in this Native American culture. It's their biggest event of the season.

Renae: So there's that [fascination]. My colleague says Germans still have many issues with racism, like toward Turks who have lived in Germany for generations and are still considered outsiders, and other groups are still considered outsiders. But, at the same time, there is this fascination, and the love for Native people they have. Have you encountered any of these contradictions in Germans' behaviour?

Quentin: No, I have never had any problems with this at all, and mostly because of the fascination with Native American cultures. It's a positive thing. But also I heard stories that even at the time of Hitler, he actually had a fascination with Native American people. So that kind of went down [to neo-Nazis], I guess, throughout the years. I heard that the racism, mainly from the neo-Nazi people, is still a big problem in Germany. I have seen and read in the newspapers this problem that exists in Germany, this racism towards non-German people. But I heard that the neo-Nazis look at Native Americans not really as equals, but that they're better than the other [minority] people.

This is something that, like I say, I've never had any sort of negative problem at all [with] when I've been there the last five years. Not only that, like I said, not only the twelve years I've worked there, but the last twenty-some-odd years I've been working as a performer. I['d] travelled to Germany many times beforehand, so I've been to Germany many times in the past twenty years, here and there. I've never had a bad experience with this sort of thing, this negativity.

Especially where I work, it is really considered to be an area where there's a lot of these neo-Nazi groups. And even some of the people that I work with at this company – El Dorado – I'm told that some of them are in these groups, but then I make friends with everybody there, everybody that I know is really good friends with me, and I've never had any negative experiences at all as a Native American, I have to say. But there is racism toward other cultures, that are not German, not neo-Nazi, so I know that this does happen.

Renae: That's interesting; that's the same thing I thought. I was telling Florentine and Hartmut (when they interviewed me), when I lived in Germany and when my German friends would introduce me to their friends they'd say "Hi, this is Renae," and the people that they were introducing me to would often not care who I was until my friends would say, "and she's *indian* from the States." Then those people would suddenly be interested in me as a person. It was like they had some sort of [racism towards me, before finding out I wasn't Turkish] … It was weird to me, I don't know if you get that? I never asked the people who were suddenly fascinated, so I don't know what they thought I was before: to treat me kind of weird until they found out I was *Indianerin*.

Quentin: A lot of people always think first of all that you ... that *we* come from South America, and so they think right away: South Americans! South Americans: you see them all over Europe, they're on the streets, they're performing, they're always playing their music and trying to be Native Americans wearing North American *indian* clothes, so Germans always perceive, "Oh, okay, from South America." But then when you say that you're North American Indian, then that's where the fascination kicks in, and then that's when they become interested. This I also experienced many times.

Renae: What do you think of that?

Quentin: Well first of all, when they say, "Oh I thought you were from South America," I always say: "Well no, first of all, I'm too tall!" [both laugh] I actually, for the fun of it, as a busker, I performed on the street. I didn't have any traditional clothes on, I just had sweat pants and shirt, and I did a hoop dance. This was just right down one of the main streets from the Colosseum, the Colosseum was right in the back of me. And these guys, this South American group, these friends I know, they had their street stand there. For fifteen years they've had the same place. So they're friends of mine, and just for the fun of it I went out there just to do it. And I did a hoop dance show there, not in my traditional regalia, just the hoops and black outfit, and people really loved it. So it was fun in this way, to do something like that.

But the South Americans, they borrow and they take the Native North American culture, and they incorporate it into their music, more as a marketing tool. They know there's the fascination with the North American *indians*. That's why you see them on the street. They have their war bonnets, and they're dressed like North American *indians*, not like South America from their tribes or their culture, but they dress like Native Americans and they do their music. In a way it's kind of like stealing or borrowing ... For them it's business. It's how they earn their money for their families, I imagine. And for this I can understand why they would do it, and so I don't really mind, in a way. They're still Native people but from South America and they're still *indians*, Native Americans, but from South America. I really don't mind it; like I say, I made friends with a few of them over the years in different areas, but I still feel funny to watch them do it, and more annoyed because I'm always compared to them. When people don't know who I am and we first meet, like I say, they think I'm from South America. No, no, no, I'm sorry, I'm not!

Renae: That's the same thing when I say where I'm from. My home is Shiprock, New Mexico. They always hear just the Mexico part, not the *New*

Mexico part, and that bothers me too, because I have my own unique culture and identity as a Diné woman.

I brought this up already: this term Indianthusiasm, which is when people are in love with all things *indian*, basically. Did you work with hobbyists? Do you know any hobbyists?

Quentin: I do know some hobbyists, and I have worked with them in the past. I've worked with a group that comes from Czechoslovakia [*sic*], and I worked at another Western town in Germany, Pullman City, where they have their own Indian Days, and they hired me to be there, and they also hired this hobbyist group.

I got to know these hobbyists really well, and actually they became friends of mine. Well, at first, when I saw these hobbyists, I was a bit taken back, and I was wondering, "Why?" But then, getting to know this group, I found out that they were very respectful in what they were doing, in the sense that they were doing the dances, like the traditional, jingle, grass, fancy. And what they tried to do was they made it as authentic as possible as we do it here, and the outfits and the dancing styles and even learning the stories of the dances. But one thing that I learned is that they don't say or try to pretend to be Native American. They say: "Of course [we] are hobbyists, and this is [our] hobby, and what [we] do." But they are very respectful to the culture. So that's what made me understand, or made me appreciate what they do. It's because they are really respectful, and they're not trying to be Native American. They just enjoy doing this, being part of this culture, and dancing, and doing these shows, because they have their own groups, and they do their own shows. So I appreciate it. But I only know the dancing part. I've heard there are many camps where people actually live like Native Americans, but this I haven't had any experience with.

Renae: Have you been invited to any of those camps?

Quentin: No, not really. I haven't been to any of those. Part of it is that one of my friends, Murray Small Legs, has experienced it. From what he told, some of these [hobbyists] are actually more than just fascinated, they're more of fanatics. They learn everything they can about the old ways, [how] we used to do things: skinning, tanning hides. They really become so fanatic that they actually think that they're better than Native American people.

And this is where I don't like it, and it's what I don't appreciate. Because these people in these camps live like *indians*, like for maybe two months, two weeks at a time. With respect that they do know a lot of the old ways, a lot of old traditions that they learn mainly from books, but then they practise them over the years. Thirty or forty years they've been doing this maybe, and they do know a lot of these old ways, but ... they look at the modern *indians* today as us losing our old ways. And so for them, they think of themselves better than *indians*.

This is what my friend Murray told me. So he actually had troubles with them in the past. But me, I've never been invited to these camps, but I *have* been invited to a powwow, different powwows. I actually did a performance at one powwow in Poland. I was just a guest to do my hoop dancing, my performance there, and they appreciated it, and they liked it, and I was actually quite surprised in how they organized their powwow. It was actually exactly like you would do it back home. They had three or four groups of singers, the singing was a bit different [laughs] but not bad, I mean they're still doing their best. There were many, many dancers and they even had arts and crafts, selling, and vending.

[Food arriving]

Renae: Okay, the Polish powwow: did they do round dances and friendship dances and things like that?

Quentin: Yeah, something like that. Well, actually I did a round dance with them as part of my show, but then they had the Grand Entry, and they had somebody do an opening, and then they had all the different categories, just like at a regular powwow back home. But it was in Poland! I was the only real Native American there, so it was really strange, it was like a twilight zone! [laughs]

Renae: It's funny, the first time I went to a powwow in Germany was in 2002, or 2003, and, at first, I felt really strange. Like you said, it was like the twilight zone, and you walk into this place and you almost want to leave. After I gave it some time, I appreciated everything I was learning from, you know, the powwow.

Quentin: But you know, that's the thing. Two years back I actually was invited to a powwow some place in the United States. I can't remember where, along the east coast somewhere. It was quite a while ago, but it was a hobbyist powwow. In America they have these hobbyist powwows where only White people do these powwows. But, see, the difference was that their regalia were not authentic as the way we do it. It was more of their own fascination [with] what they thought there should be in Native American regalia; and so some people had furs on that looked more like barbarians. But they were more standoffish, when I was there in the States. And they had their own perception. They made [their powwow] what they thought Native American culture was. But like I was saying before, in Europe when they – the hobbyists – when they do it, they try to make it as authentic as they can, as we do it over here. So there's this respect of trying to maintain the authenticity of what they're trying. The more correct, the better they feel. [European hobbyists],[77] they do things better, compared to over in America, where these [American] hobbyists have their own fantasy, and their own thoughts ...

Renae: I'm glad that you brought that up. I forgot about that because I used to live in Atlanta, a long time ago, from 1994 to 1997, and I hated those east coast powwows. They were really sad to me. And I remember that now: all of the fur [laughs] – fox tails on women's outfits, and things like that. It was really bizarre, but I totally blocked that out of my head [laughs]!

Quentin: Trying to forget it [laughs]!

[interruption]

Renae: What was his name again?

Quentin: Kuno D. is half Ho-Chunk and half German. His mother is Ho-Chunk and his father was German, but he was raised in Germany, yet he still has the connection with the Ho-Chunk people. He is registered on the Ho-Chunk band, and he has two sons and one daughter that are also registered to the Ho-Chunk band, and they travel to America. They visit with the family during the summer, and so he knows all his relatives on the Ho-Chunks. He has all the connections with the reservation, but always lived in Germany, so he is more German than anything. He has really more of the German perspective of this thing [Indianthusiasm] but still has the connections with his people, his family back home. His mother lives back home now, back on the Ho-Chunk reservation, and he was there this last summer with his sons for a month or so.

Rob, my other friend, he is a Lakota and he has actually been living in Germany for the last twenty-odd years, but he came from America to live in Germany because he wasn't doing so good in America, and it was better for him to move out of the country. But he's doing really well. He had a really rough and crazy past, but in the last few years he's really doing good for himself, and he's a carver. He carves sculptures out of rock, different kinds of rocks and marble, and he sells them over there, and he's got the other kind of perspective, where he comes from America, but now living in ... more like what I'm doing now. And so they really have a good idea what it's like to live in Germany.

The last years that I've worked in Europe, between Italy and Germany, and working with this group of guys, its always been difficult to find a Native

American woman dancer. But just this year there's this girl I told you about
before, Anita Assiniboine. For the first time, I've been able to have a female
perspective of the Native dancing. I never had this. It's always been the male
perspective – male dancing. If there are other Native American females who
live in Germany, it would be interesting to know if they're dancers, and if
they are, then there's work in the sense of performing. Where I work now,
I'm stuck in – well, not really stuck, I shouldn't say stuck, I actually really
enjoy where I work now because it's one place.

In the past, when we used to do these shows, we never had this female
perspective and it was always just men performers. These other guys, they
travel to different shows, different festivals that are throughout the summer,
from June they take time off from their work. So, if you're a Native dancer
living in Europe it's possible to find work throughout the summer, different
shows here and there.

Renae: Does it pay well?

Quentin: Yeah, it pays good. Well, there's two parts to it: there's the pay that
you get for doing the performances, but then a lot of these guys do their
own craft work.

Renae: And so they sell on the side.

Quentin: So we have always like a market, whenever we do these shows
where you can sell stuff. This is another thing that people really enjoy, having
their own handcraft made by Native Americans; it's good business. If you're
a craft person you can make money in this way, too. And with the shows it
gets decent enough to go from show to show. I do very well where I work, so
I really appreciate the work that I do. Actually, I'm one of the main persons
at this place where I work.

Renae: So you can make all the rules or whatever? So what's your day-to-day
life like – do you mind? You get up and have coffee [laughs] ...

Quentin: Well, this year was a really busy year for me. Because I actually had
two jobs where I work. I was working as a technician for the shows. Where
I work, it's a Western town theme park, so of course there's the theme of
"Cowboys and *indians*," and so I do two shows a day, myself, and I have my
own area, my own performing area, with tipis in the background and a place
for 200 people to sit, a stage, and seating area. So I have my own shows, and
then the other shows are done by stunt guys, professional stunt people, and
they do three shows.

Last year, there was a comedy show, and then two stunt shows: one big
show in the show arena, and one main street stunt show, with stunt fighting

and professional stunt people that really do high falls, air explosions ... this sort of work. My job with them, I was a sound technician, a sound sampler. So I have the keyboard when they do their fighting scenes, the "punch-punch," slap, the "ooh-ahh," or explosions. I started this two years ago, and last year they hired me to do it full-time. I was doing six shows a day! The park opens at ten, so I'm up around nine or whatever, and then my first show is at eleven o'clock, just a twenty-five-minute music show: I do drumming, singing, some contemporary pieces also. And then from there I would have half an hour break. At twelve o'clock is the comedy show, where the stunt guys do slapstick and I'm the sound sampler, so that's a half an hour show. I have my lunch break, and then at 1:30 I do this hoop dance show, and it's inside, and they have a big stage, with lighting and sound. That's about a half an hour show. Then at 2:30 is the big outside stunt show that goes forty minutes. My next show is at four o'clock, which is outside in the big show arena again, and that's another half an hour show. From there I have a break again until 5:30, where they do the main street stunt show, where I'm also doing the sound sampling, that's a twenty-minute show and then at six o'clock, more or less, the park closes.

Renae: It's a full day!

Quentin: It's not so bad. There was one point in the season, where it's really hard – actually three points. There's the opening, which is two weeks straight every day, and that's in April, that's the beginning of the season. Then there's the high season, which is seven weeks, where the park is open every day, and so seven weeks of performing every day ... once I get through that, the rest of it is downhill. The end of the season is open two weeks again for holidays. And in between, actually I don't complain at all, because last year they changed it around, where it was only open on Saturday and Sunday, and so I had five days free and two days working. But my salary never changed over the years, so I got more free days. Yeah, I'm really happy with what I do. I even saved the company some money this year. That I will tell you another time ...

Renae: Okay! Thank you!

WAUBGESHIG RICE

I was definitely an ambassador. And sort of a mythbuster in a lot of ways, too.

Phone interview from private home in Calgary on 27 November 2012, by Florentine Strzelczyk and Hartmut Lutz

Hartmut: The first question we have is a good one, which Renae Watchman came up with: How would you define or describe your tribal affiliation?

Waubgeshig: Anishinaabe. Also, commonly known as Ojibway. I'm of the Ojibway branch of the Anishinaabe nation. Originally, I'm from a place called Wasauksing First Nation in central Ontario. It's near Parry Sound, Ontario, which is on Georgian Bay, about two hours north of Toronto. The traditional lands of the Anishinaabe are sort of around the Great Lakes.

Hartmut: How did your contact with Germany come about?

Waubgeshig: You have time? Okay, good! [laughing] I was in Grade twelve at Parry Sound High School, and I wasn't exactly sure what I wanted to do in terms of a career, or a profession. And I still had one more year of high school to go after that, but I really was clueless as to what I wanted to do in terms of where to go to school, and in terms of a career.

So I was walking down the hall of my high school and I saw a poster that read: "Have you ever considered spending a year abroad? If so, come to the seminar at lunchtime."

So, I went to the seminar, and it turned out to be a Rotary student exchange seminar. There was a member from the Rotary Club from Parry Sound who was there giving an overview of their program and saying, you know, "These are the things you can do if you're an exchange student." So I thought, well, I have basically no direction right now, I don't know what I

162

want to do, so maybe I'll apply to do this because I always had pretty good marks in school. I was a pretty outgoing student, and so I figured, hey, spending a year elsewhere would be a really cool experience.

It was a long application process: I had to do a bunch of interviews and fill out all kinds of forms and that kind of thing. The Rotary Club at Parry Sound accepted to sponsor me and, basically, what they get you to do with Rotary is just put a list of countries down that you want to go to, and they'll select the appropriate one for you, and then that's where you'll go. So I wanted to go anywhere in Europe – really, it didn't really matter to me at that point – so, I randomly put down the Netherlands, Germany, Belgium, and France, and figured that if I go to any one of these, that'd be cool – I'm really excited either way. So they picked me to go to Germany. They found a Rotary Club in northern Germany, in the town called Brake an der Unterweser, which is about a half an hour north of Bremen. They found a hosting club for me there, and I went through a bunch of orientation sessions, and then I went there in July of 1996 and spent a whole year there. So it wasn't like Germany was in my sights, I wasn't directly focused on Germany. Germany was an option for me, and it ended up being the place I was selected to go to, but in the end, it was obviously the best outcome because I had pretty much the most amazing year of my life over there, for sure.

Florentine: What made it so amazing?

Waubgeshig: Well, I guess, generally, having such an eye-opening experience at such a young age. I was only 17 when I left. The overall exchange experience was amazing. That was the most exciting. But I think that the welcome I got in Germany and just the enthusiasm that I found for my background and my culture was something that I hadn't really experienced in Canada up until that point, and it was really bizarre sort of ... [Florentine and Hartmut laugh] ... because I flew overseas to this totally foreign country, where the people were more interested in my culture than in my own country of Canada, right? The way I perceived it, anyway. So it was, in that sense ... I don't know if I can just attribute it to me being Aboriginal, but that really helped.

Hartmut: I'm sure it did, but it must have also made it complicated. Don't people have a lot of stereotypes, which you have to get out of the way before they can meet *you* as a person?

Waubgeshig: Absolutely! But those provided for some pretty funny stories in the end too. I was in the *Gymnasium* in Brake and – I think my first day of school was just a week after I got there – it was a Monday, I went to school and, basically, I was flocked just outside of the school by a whole bunch of people who were in my class, because they had heard that an *Indianer* was coming.

They were thrilled, right? Well, not thrilled, but they were intrigued, I guess you could say. So I was surrounded right when I got there by all kinds of people and then I thought, well, this is cool. I wasn't really nervous anymore after that because I'd received such a warm welcome.

A couple of weeks after that, the guy who would eventually become my best friend there – we were outside having a coffee and a cigarette – he pulled me aside and he said, "You know what, Waub? The day you showed up we were actually really disappointed." And I said, "Why? What do you mean?" You know? I kind of took offence to that. And he was like: "Well, you were wearing normal clothes, you were wearing jeans and a T-shirt." [laughs] "I was hoping for a kind of Winnetou image, you know?"

Hartmut: But they didn't show that, huh? They didn't show their disappointment right away?

Waubgeshig: No, no, not right away, but at the same time he was sort of half joking and half serious. But I mean, he and everybody outright told me after that: "This is all we know of *indians* really ... It's what we've read in Karl May books and that kind of thing." This predated the widespread use of Google or any sort of social media, right? So, it's not like they had easy access to modern Aboriginal imagery or anything like that. So in that sense, I was definitely an ambassador. And sort of a mythbuster in a lot of ways, too.

Hartmut: You know, there are a lot of contacts, also academically, between people in Germany and people here, and you have Aboriginal people getting degrees in Germany. You also get people in Germany doing degrees in Indigenous literatures and Indigenous cultures. Do you have any comments on that?

Waubgeshig: Well, to tell you the truth, I wasn't aware of the profound number of Aboriginal people in Germany within academia, until I met Renae [Watchman] at Mount Royal [University]. When she told me about how many were actually over there, I was pretty floored, but at the same time really enthused because it was a nice surprise to hear about that.

And, yeah, I have known about academics from Germany coming to study First Nations culture. There was a guy named Franz Koennecke who was studying in my home community of Wasauksing back in the 1980s, and he actually did his dissertation on ... sort of a history of my community.

Hartmut: Was he an anthropologist?

Waubgeshig: Yeah, yeah. He passed away, unfortunately. He died about twelve or thirteen years ago. So he was actually really my first exposure to German academia. I was aware of people coming over; I wasn't aware of us going over there, I guess.

Hartmut: You said earlier that your choice of Germany was really random and they selected that out of a list? On your list were also the Netherlands, Belgium, and France? Can you explain why you selected this cluster?

Waubgeshig: Because they were all Western European countries, and they're all within close proximity with one another. I basically wanted to experience Europe, and those seemed like the ideal four options.

Hartmut: How did it work out, language-wise?

Waubgeshig: Oh, it worked out very well. I didn't really know that much prior to going, you know, I hadn't taken it in high school or anything like that, and in the couple of months before I went I studied books and tapes, but in vain, because I didn't really pick anything up before I went. There, I had a tutor and I guess after about four months I was pretty comfortable speaking it and then, after six months, I was speaking it all the time, so ... *ich, ich war damals fleißig, äh ... ich finde es ein bisschen schwer jetzt, uh, zu reden, aber ich verstehe noch, äh ... ganz viel.* [I, I was diligent, uh ... I'm finding it a bit difficult now, uh, to talk, but I still understand, uh, a lot.]

Hartmut: *Ja, das glaube ich.* [Yes, I believe that.]

Florentine: *Das klang gut! Das klang richtig gut!* [That sounded great. It sounded really great!]

Hartmut: *Bist du mal wieder zurück gewesen in Deutschland?* [Have you been back to Germany?]

Waubgeshig: *Äh, zweimal ... in ,99 und, äh ... 2002.* [Uh, twice – in '99 and 2002.]

Hartmut: So you still have friends there.

Waubgeshig: Still have friends there, we're still in contact, but I haven't been in ten years now, which is unfortunate. I hope to get back sometime next year just because it's been way too long.

Hartmut: Okay. We have a question: you must have had some ideas about Germany, stereotypical or not, but what were the ideas that you had of Germany or what you knew about Germany before you went over?

Waubgeshig: I think, having been in high school, the thing that sticks with you the most is the twentieth-century history, I guess.

Hartmut: Yeah, the Holocaust.

Waubgeshig: Yeah, things like that. So a lot of those sort of negative moments in history, but those weren't first and foremost, those were just, you know, what you learn in school and that kind of thing. And culturally I knew about a lot. Mostly from Bavaria in the south. Where I ended up in the north is obviously nothing like [laughs] Bavaria at all. In Niedersachsen [the federal state of Lower Saxony] and the Wesermarsch, it's all flat, right? [laughs]

I guess it was fortunate because one of the host families I had, they did a lot to send me letters and pictures and stuff before I left, so that I could figure out what I was getting into. The Rotary Club was really good about that too because it was a cultural exchange, essentially. They wanted to make sure they did everything they could to make sure both sides benefited from this arrangement.

Hartmut: That sounds really good. You said there was twentieth-century history, and culturally there was Bavaria. Anything else?

Waubgeshig: Popular culture. I mean, popular music. You have The Scorpions, the rock band, that's what I knew about. Uh, athletes, there was Detlef Schrempf, who played in the NBA, he was a basketball player. Small little nuggets of … examples of Germany in popular culture, but not really a whole lot.

Hartmut: And how did your image, and those two other realms, how did that develop or deconstruct, when you got to Germany?

Waubgeshig: They weren't necessarily deconstructed. I would say a more prevalent image was constructed once I was there. Because when I got there and I got to know my peers and my friends were teenagers who were in the *Gymnasium*, I really got to learn about what modern German culture was and what the modern attitudes were, especially toward Germany's history. And, you know, you come from a country like Canada, where people wave the flag all the time and they're so proud to be Canadian and they have maple-leaf tattoos and Canada Day is a huge day. I think it was especially eye-opening for me to come to Germany and see that national pride wasn't really there, and the impression I got from my peers, from the young people my age, was that there was a shameful history there and that they wanted to acknowledge that, and they didn't necessarily feel the pride in their country. [They had] pride in their culture, in a lot of the strong sort of traditions that have maintained over the years – but in terms of the history, that really overshadowed a lot of things. This was in the mid-1990s, too, right? Almost twenty years ago that I was there, and not long after German unification, either, so I think the German identity or the unified German identity was still coming into shape.

Hartmut: It still is being developed, yeah.

Waubgeshig: What I learned the most from my peers was that there wasn't a sense of national pride like there was in Canada, for sure. That was the most striking thing for me as a seventeen-year-old kid. But at the same time, there was an amazing amount of interest in my own culture as an Aboriginal person. And that was hugely eye-opening for me and really heart-warming, too, because as I mentioned earlier on, I'd never seen people in Canada be as interested in my culture as Germans were, really.

Hartmut: Have your experiences in Germany influenced your work?

Waubgeshig: Oh, absolutely, yeah. Well, my experiences in Germany are what led me to become a journalist. Prior to leaving, there were two newspapers that were published in Ontario, one out of North Bay, Ontario, called the *North Bay Nugget*, and another one called *Anishinabek News* that was published by the Union of Ontario Indians. I was approached by them before I left – well, from the *Anishinabek News* particularly, they spearheaded it because they hadn't heard of a young Ojibway kid from our communities in Ontario doing an exchange like that before. So they asked me to send monthly articles about my experience, and they published them in the newspaper. So, prior to that, you know, I always enjoyed writing and I always enjoyed storytelling, but I didn't really see how it could translate into a career.

But when I was in Germany and I started writing about my experiences as an *indian* in northern Germany, I had a lot to write about, specifically that experience with my friend who said he was disappointed. I wrote about that because I had a lot of these funny and really eye-opening experiences, and it really ignited a new desire within me to write for a living. And that's how I got into journalism, essentially. So, by writing about my experiences there I was able to figure out what I wanted to do in terms of a profession.

Hartmut: And that's what you wanted to find out, right?

Waubgeshig: Yeah, exactly, and also what I mentioned before about how there was this strong desire on behalf of Germans to know about Aboriginal culture. I guess there was a lack of that back in Canada. You know, when I discovered this option of journalism, I thought, well, when I go home, my job is going to be to educate Canadians about the Aboriginal experience in this country, and the best way to do that is through journalism, essentially. Well, not the best way, but one of the easier ways to do that is through journalism. So the whole experience set me off on that journey, definitely.

Hartmut: What were your experiences with racism in Germany?

Waubgeshig: Honestly, I didn't really experience anything negative. To tell you the truth, people were very respectful, you know, after a while ... I think the visual effect of me showing up and being a regular everyday person really sort of dissolved a lot of preconceived perceptions or images that anybody had, so I don't know if that eliminated any sort of negative or racist thoughts or if people were maybe too ... afraid or too timid to say negative things to me. But I didn't experience anything negative at all while I was there.

Hartmut: And with regard to other ethnic groups?

Waubgeshig: Oh, I definitely saw harsh attitudes towards Turkish people, for sure. And, I mean, I guess that is what it is, right?

Hartmut: Have you contacts with others who have had similar experiences – like you or Renae or maybe other Indigenous people who've been to Germany or have that experience?

Waubgeshig: Actually my stepfather was in the Canadian Forces. He spent a few years in Germany, but he was well into adulthood by then – he was in his thirties, and he was in the military, so it wasn't that similar of an experience. But with people who have done exchange programs? Yeah, I've met a lot of them. But not really any Aboriginal people who have spent the same amount of time that I did in Germany, anybody who's spent a year there at a young age like I did ... except for Renae, I mean, and she was there many years before I was.

Hartmut: Yeah. And she is very knowledgeable about people in Germany, Indigenous people in Germany and their networks. That's a world I didn't know anything about, really. Although I've worked in Indigenous literature for years and years, I wasn't aware of that. I knew there were GIs, but people living there permanently and having their own associations or so, that is a minority in Germany that most people don't know anything about, I think.

Waubgeshig: And when she told me about that, it pretty much blew my mind.

Hartmut: [laughs] Same here. You as a journalist or also creative writer, did you do any presentations in Germany? And how would they compare to presentations here – or the reactions of audiences?

Waubgeshig: Yeah, I did them quite a bit, actually. Once I was able to speak German well enough to give presentations, I was asked to do them in different classrooms in my school and at the Rotary Club as well. My one presentation at the Rotary Club of Brake, basically the whole premise of it was to myth-bust, really, to sort of break up these stereotypical images that they had. And one thing I said was – I think I got up and the first thing I said was – *"Wir leben nicht in einem Tipi"* (We don't live in a tipi!"). [laughs] There was a guy from the local newspaper there, doing an article about it and that was the headline in the paper the next day: *"Wir leben nicht in einem Tipi!"* [laughs]

Hartmut: So you found that, in order to really get your message across, you first had to get rid of or make conscious the stereotype through which you would be perceived otherwise, right?

Waubgeshig: Yeah, absolutely. For sure.

Hartmut: I think that's what most Aboriginal people are confronted with when they address German audiences; that they have to, sort of, deconstruct the perceptional frame that otherwise they're forced into or are seen through.

Waubgeshig: Yeah. I was serious about it, but I always sort of took a lighthearted approach to it, because, you know, humour and comedy is such an important part of traditional storytelling, and I kind of wanted to convey that.

Hartmut: Yeah, it gets it home but makes it more digestible. And it doesn't antagonize people, I guess?

Waubgeshig: I agree with you!

Hartmut: Did you have similar experiences here in Canada? I mean, would the German audience be different from audiences here? Or maybe you can't say.

Waubgeshig: It's hard to say ... I think – and this is only speaking very, very generally – doing the same kind of talk in Germany, you come up against a crowd that, back then, really would have no current knowledge of the situation. Whereas in Canada, I think, you can generally say that people do have a general idea of what's going on, but maybe they choose to ignore it. Or they choose to ignore the truth because they're forced to confront a lot of the harsh realities of what Canada really is. And that's it's a pretty shameful country when it comes to the treatment of First Nations people, right?

People are uncomfortable with accepting that fact that Canada has a really shameful history and that, in a lot of senses, it's a pretty bad country, because of how it treats some of its people. So some people refuse to accept that. And I think it's harder to really convey the contemporary situation to them because they just don't want to hear it. But that's speaking very, very generally.

Hartmut: I think, probably, there's a lot in that. If you take that look back at Germany, maybe that also explains in part why Germans are fascinated with Indigenous people far away.

Waubgeshig: Do you mean because of Germany's own history?

Hartmut: Yeah. And I think it's easier for us to fantasize and idealize a people that is far away from us and that we have no negative dealings with as a nation. Okay, there may be individual encounters that are negative, but for us, it's a guilt-free realm.

Waubgeshig: Yeah, I never really thought of that at the time, but I can definitely see that. It makes sense to me and just in the fact ... as I was mentioning to you before about my peers who refused to accept or refused to acknowledge anything good that their country was at the time – because that shameful history overshadowed that – I guess, in a lot of senses, looking to North America, to Native people, was a form of escapism. And I don't recall anybody really saying that to me directly but I could sort of hypothesize that for sure.

Hartmut: I think we've got most of our questions answered, but, you know, there may be a couple more: You know there are Indigenous people who go to Germany and other countries in Europe to dance and to perform and to take part in powwows. How do you feel about that?

Waubgeshig: About Aboriginal people from Canada going there to perform?

Hartmut: Yeah.

Waubgeshig: Oh, I think that's great. I mean, the more the merrier, right? [laughs] When I went there, I brought some things with me, like I brought some of my traditional shirts and my pipe and things like that, but I was just one person and I think to have full troupes of people going over to really demonstrate ceremony and tradition, it goes a long way, it's hugely effective.

Hartmut: I'm pretty certain you must have noticed that a lot of – or some sections of – the German population are very interested in Indigenous spirituality. How do you feel about that?

Waubgeshig: I think that's good, I mean I grew up with a lot of that, those traditional ceremonies and teachings. They're positive. They're about love, they're about respect and humility and some very important teachings, so

I think if anybody could follow those general principles, then it's good for people as a whole.

In terms of the folks over there who sort of took it upon themselves to re-enact things, I [never] saw that when I was there. I don't know if people would mention it to me. You know, they'd ask me if I'd heard of it and I had – I had heard of that before I left – but, I didn't really know enough about it to really seek it out or anything. I'm not sure if people would tell me but they wouldn't ask me if I wanted to see it or anything like that, and I don't know if it's because it was so far from northern Germany, or if it was because they didn't want to expose me to that. I'm only speculating here, as to why I never saw that while I was there.

Hartmut: How do you feel about that?

Waubgeshig: Uh ... [laughs] I think it's strange. I remember thinking it was strange when I heard about that while I was there. I mean, in hindsight I would have liked to have seen it while there, but I'm not sure how I would have reacted at the time. In one sense, I might have been flattered that, you know, you had these people so far away paying homage to traditional North American culture, but, at the same time, it's so far removed from it, too.

So, I mean, I would like to see that before I die, I guess, just to see what it's like. But at the time I'm not sure how I would have reacted to that. And I think maybe that's why nobody offered to show me.

Hartmut: Okay. I think we've done our questions ... Florentine?

Florentine: Is there anything else you would like to let us know about?

Waubgeshig: No! I just want to really thank you guys for this opportunity. I think it's really cool that I happened to meet Renae at Mount Royal last month and then, this has led me to you guys and the great work that you're doing, which I think is amazing. So I think you guys should really keep it up. I'll definitely want to read the end project of what comes of all this.

I think I'll always have a special place in my heart for Germany. As I told you, it was one of the best experiences of my life. It really helped open my eyes to my own culture, but also to my people's place within Canada. And it got me on my career path that I'm on today. I'm forever grateful for my experience there and the more I talk about it the more guilty I feel about not having been there in ten years, so ... [laughs]

Florentine: Can you imagine writing a novel about it at one point?

Waubgeshig: Oh, definitely. I'd like to. If I ever get to be a full-time author, then I will definitely write a novel about my experience there, for sure.

Hartmut: Okay! You know, in a way, you had an experience that I think all of us have if we go to another country as a young person. We learn a lot about ourselves, and our own culture. And I think that is a wonderful experience, and I wish more people would take the opportunity and go abroad.

Waubgeshig: Yeah, and I credit the German people, and the people of Niedersachsen and northern Germany, for really welcoming me and being so supportive and being so interested in my culture, you know? That went such a long way. And who knows where I'd be if I hadn't gone there?

Hartmut: Okay. Well, thank you very much for letting us talk to you.

Florentine: Thanks for your time and we'll be in touch with the manuscript and the interview.

Waubgeshig: Okay, *danke schön!*

DREW HAYDEN TAYLOR

You can't underestimate the influence of Karl May's Winnetou.

Live interview with Drew Hayden Taylor by Florentine Strzelczyk, Renae Watchman, and Hartmut Lutz in Drew's hotel room on the University of Calgary campus

Hartmut: We have a number of questions, and the first question that Renae taught us to use is: What is your tribal affiliation?

Drew: Tribal affiliation? Ojibway, Anishinaabe, Mississauga band of the great Ojibway nation. I am from Curve Lake First Nations #35. It's very easy to find – just go to the centre of the universe and you're there!

Hartmut: Can you say something about how you got into contact with Germany, and how that started?

Drew: I'm not even sure. I remember the first place that I went to was Marburg. I think that I was asked to come and present something at a conference on Canadian Studies. I remember being there – it was, like, three days of presentations on the hydroelectric dams in Quebec, the effect on the Cree people, and all this sort of different stuff. I found myself really a stranger in a strange land, because there were all these papers being presented on various Native topics, half of them in English, half of them in German. And I was sitting there in the middle of this.

Part of it was held in a rebuilt castle. Somebody told me the castle was originally built around 1100 AD, and I remember thinking, "Wow! All this is happening in a place that's older than original contact." So, I think that's basically it. I was originally asked to attend a conference in Marburg, and I think that's where I met you. Then we went from there to Osnabrück. You were my glorious introduction to the wonders of Deutschland.

Hartmut: Then, in Osnabrück you bought *Lederhosen*!

Florentine: Would you believe that?!

Renae: Did you really? [laughing]

Drew: Beautiful, beautiful, gorgeous ones.

Florentine: Do you still wear them?

Drew: Yes, I do! And on days I'm not retaining water, I can fit them.

Hartmut: There is an increasing number of people who study Indigenous literature in Germany. There are also Indigenous people who go to Germany to study there, or they go there to perform, some of them, others to read, like you. Can you comment on that, I mean this exchange?

Drew: Well, one of my first major contacts in Germany was Albert-Reiner Glaap,[78] who was in Düsseldorf, I believe, working in Düsseldorf. It's been so long since I've sat down and had a conversation with him because he's been retired, but he's one of the foremost experts on Native North American theatre. And he kept bringing me over to talk. He had a class on translation where they translated something of mine into German, *Toronto at Dreamer's Rock*,[79] which was then later done as a radio play on WDR. And he ended up doing – with Cornelsen Publishing – an annotated version of *Toronto at Dreamer's Rock*.

So, my introduction to Germany started with me being a Native playwright, through people like Reiner Glaap. Then as my literary career grew, as I began to get more and more into writing creative non-fiction, novels and stuff like that, it became more of a widespread interest in much of my work, and my visits to Germany began to have a broader appeal than just the theatre. I was often asked to lecture on Native humour, on Native literature, and it even got to the point where I've been asked to talk about Native sexuality based on the book, *Me Sexy*.[80]

So, I've done fourteen trips to Germany so far, and each time it gets much more intense and much more creative. One of the things they're trying to do in Lüneburg is to develop a course based completely on my work and trying to arrange with the English Theatre in Hamburg, trying to get them interested in doing a production of *The Berlin Blues*.[81]

Renae: Have any of your pieces, your plays, been performed in Germany?

Drew: Just a radio play, based on *Toronto at Dreamer's Rock*, and the first act of *In a World Created by a Drunken God*,[82] at Lüneburg. And I was the second act, where I got up and I lectured on all that sort of stuff. One of my plays has toured. It toured the Czech Republic, and quite a few places in southern Germany. But it was a Canadian production.

Florentine: Can you comment on the German characters in your work a little bit?

Drew: Well, there's only German characters in one of my works, *The Berlin Blues*, and *The Berlin Blues* is the fourth part of what I refer to as the Blues Quartet, a series of comedies I've written exploring and deconstructing the world of Native humour. And they have all, of the four, they've all explored different aspects of Native culture, everything, from powwow play to children being raised without a father, to elders falling in love. And with the fourth one, I wanted to use my experiences in Germany, having been there fourteen times, and write about this bizarre preoccupation, this interest, in some corners of the country, this obsession with Native culture, that I've gone across Germany and discovered. And I wanted to present a very ... I didn't want to do anything nasty, or mean-spirited, or rude about it. One of the first rules of humour that I subscribe to: Humour should amuse, not abuse.

And so I thought, "Wouldn't it be funny if a group of Germans came over and they knew more about Native culture than Native people?" Because one time when I was up in the north, it was either Greifswald or Rostock, my girlfriend at the time was given a beaded leather pouch. One side was Prairie beading, the other side was Eastern Woodlands. And my reserve has a huge arts and crafts industry. And I was looking at it, and I swear it was indistinguishable from the real stuff. And I remember looking at it, being absolutely amazed.

Driving through Lüneburg, I saw three tipis. In Vienna, I told you about the Christmas shop with the dream catchers and the medicine wheels. In Vienna, there was also a North American Native cuisine restaurant I came across, that sold all North American wild meat. So all this stuff, and of course the whole *Winnetou* legend, all that sort of stuff, I thought, "This is all ripe for caricature."

So, I just thought, I want to sit down, write something where these Germans show up and they know more about Native culture than the Native people do. And, as a bit of cross-osmosis, the Native people end up learning more German than they had expected. And the characters were just completely made up. I just decided to take one and run with the stereotypical German: very efficient, the fuss bucket, the person who says, "We're seventeen minutes early." [laughter] And the other guy, who's much more in touch with the roots of the Native community, who's just sort of along for the ride because of this interest.

One of the characters is named Birgit,[83] and I do know an academic in Germany named Birgit[84] – it is not based on her – and the guy who is the artistic director of Native Voices, a Native theatre company in Los Angeles, his name is Randy Reinholz. So I have a character named Reinhart Reinholz. And I just did it as an homage to him, trying to develop and promote Native theatre in the States.

So just, basically, it was an opportunity for me to start up my own carnival and go and play. And that's the way I viewed it. It was just a wonderful chance to tackle all these different topics, one after the other, and make fun of everybody. I make fun of the Germans, I make fun of the Native people. I mean, you can't have a character like Trailer, right, a Native character. I just have so much fun making his life miserable.

Florentine: So when you go reading from a play in Germany, how do Germans react when they are confronted with their own stereotypes?

Drew: They thought some of it was stereotypical, where Reinhart says, "I bring you greetings from the Teutonic people" or "Teutonic nation." I find students overall to be very serious. Especially ... not just in Germany, I find this all over. When you go to some of these places, they're very intense. And they found that a little stereotypical.

But overall, their responses have been absolutely fabulous. Everyone seems to realize that it's good-natured joshing. As I said, it's not malicious by any manner, I think that's easily recognizable, because I turn around, and I poke just as much fun at the Native people, too.

Renae: So it's been well received?

Drew: Wonderfully, wonderfully. It's been taught for four or five years in Lüneburg and in several other places. And, like I said, they are seeing if they can get a production up and running in Lüneburg, Hamburg.

Hartmut: How do Germans react to you in Germany?

Drew: I always found it funny, because I'd go over, and as I said over dinner, I look more German than Native. It doesn't seem to be an issue; they keep throwing money at me! [obviously joking]

I'm going to put it this way: I've gotten less flak and less comment over there about the way I look and being Native than I have in Canada. People seem to just accept me for the way I am. Of course, things have changed a lot in the last twenty-five years. For one thing, I've developed a name for myself as a Native artist, so that I don't have to confirm that I'm Native or prove that I'm Native. It's generally accepted.

And I often start off my talks by talking about the fact that I grew up on a reserve, but I'm half Native, a blue-eyed Ojibway, the "Occasional,"[85] that sort of stuff. So I immediately set the groundwork for explaining who I am, where I come from, and how I look. The response has been absolutely wonderful, everywhere I've been. I can't, off the top of my head, remember any negative experiences, to the best of my knowledge. You know, I get the usual silly questions about what's it like living on a reserve, what are the houses like. I get some of that occasionally, but not as much as I get in Canada. I think I was once asked how frequently do I go hunting. [laughing] And I say: "For a good dry cleaner?" [laughing]

Renae: When you said that you don't have to justify, that you've never had any negative experiences, do you find that you're protected by your phenotype? Because when we were talking about this in another conversation ... the question is: Do people find you more interesting when they know you're Ojibway? Or are they always interested because you're the famous author, Drew Hayden Taylor?

Drew: It depends on the audience. I was just telling Hartmut that three nights ago I was playing poker in a small town next to my reserve, and this guy who had been invited by somebody else showed up, and he was sort of half-drunk, with his wife. We were playing poker and he just – someone told him I was from Curve Lake – and he just, he didn't care, but when he discovered I was a writer he spent two hours trying to convince me to write his biography. He said he had a really interesting life, "You gotta hear it, let's go outside and have a talk. I swear you'll make a million bucks off my story." I said, "I'm just here to play poker."

And then occasionally I bump into people who ... You heard me talk about the guy who ran a Christmas stall in Vienna, right, who, just when he discovered I was Native, wanted to know if I knew this Elder in the Okanagan Valley. I said, "Not that I know of." So it varies, and sometimes I get weird, weird questions.

I was in Bonn. I was going to lecture on Native theatre in Canada at Theater Bonn, and this young girl came to pick me up. She looked to be about twenty-three or twenty-four, and she was the assistant drama director at the theatre. And we were walking toward the theatre and she was talking about how excited and delighted everybody was at the theatre to learn about Native theatre in Canada. But they were all talking, they were very curious, they said, "Your name, Drew Hayden Taylor, what does that mean in English?" [laughing]

And one of the top questions I get asked whenever I travel – I've been asked this in India, in Australia, to the point where it's just such a silly, stupid question – I get asked, "Do you have an *indian* name? What is your *indian* name?" And it's gotten to the point now where every time I get asked that, I just roll my eyes and say, "My Indian name is Spread Eagle, and my girlfriend is Eager Beaver." [laughing]

Because, you know, having a traditional *indian* name, you don't ask somebody what it is. They can share it with you. It's a thing you personally do share. You're not supposed to ask. You do not put it on a business card. So every time I get asked that, I respond with that. So this young girl is saying, "Your name, what's it mean in English?" For about three seconds I'm trying to think of something snarky. But then she had looked so earnest, so serious, I was aghast, so I just swallowed my snarkiness and said, "Drew Hayden Taylor *is* my English name."

Hartmut: Did you ever explain to them that you don't ask for the name?

Drew: Probably not.

Hartmut: Because it's very different from our etiquette. You just ask.

Drew: Do you remember the story *Ishi*?[86] Do you know what "Ishi" means? It means "man."

Hartmut: "Man," yeah.

Drew: Right. Because names are very special and important in many Native cultures, and the guy, the anthropology professor, knew enough not to ask him what his name was, he just called him "Ishi." And "Ishi" never shared his name with him. And of course, you know, who the professor at San Francisco Museum,[87] who his daughter was?

Hartmut: Ursula K. Le Guin, yeah.

Drew: Yeah, Ursula K. Le Guin, so cool. So, I just figured there's some things ... you could spend days going through all the subtle nuances of a Native culture: the dos and don'ts. Maybe I'll do a book someday, *The Dos and Don'ts of Being Native.*

Hartmut: Has scholarly work by German people or German scholars influenced your writing? Or if there was some influence, how was that?

Drew: Umm, it hasn't really influenced. Scholarly work seldom influences what I write, because I don't understand it. I've read some stuff on things that have been done on my work, and some of it I understand, some of it I don't understand. Maryann Henck,[88] from Lüneburg, did this thing about my trickster character (from *Motorcycles & Sweetgrass*) being interviewed in a psychiatrist's chair, and the whole concept of the psychological background of being a trickster. And I just go, "Somebody with too much time on their hands." [laughing] Now, I am very skeptical of academia. This predates my German experiences.

Are all three of you familiar with *Toronto at Dreamer's Rock*? No? It's a one-act play for teenagers. A young boy named Rusty goes up to a place where kids used to go for vision quests for thousands of years. He goes up there with a backpack full of beer, because he comes from a dysfunctional family. But this is a real place. I've been there; and he can feel the energy and the power. And he goes up, and on his way up, and at Dreamer's Rock, being what Dreamer's Rock is, he runs into Keesic, a sixteen-year-old Native boy from four hundred years ago, and Michael, a Native boy from one hundred years in the future. So you have these three sixteen-year-old boys at the top of this rock, all with different definitions of what being Native means. So they're up there for fifty minutes: they fight, they argue, they talk about girls, they laugh, and at the end of that time they all come away with their own understanding of who they are as Aboriginal youths.

And there's a guy, he's actually half German and half Sri Lankan, Alek Steinwall, who is doing his essay, his master's thesis, on Native theatre back in the mid-nineties. And he was writing chapter three, specifically, *Toronto at Dreamer's Rock*. And he interviewed me, and he phoned me up one day and he says, "Guess what? I've just successfully defended my master's thesis." He said, "I've just defended it, I'm getting it, come on down to the bar, I'll buy you a drink." And I went down there, and he gave me a bound copy of his thesis.

And what you need to know is, when the boys are going up to the top of the rock, they hear the sound effect of a crow cawing. In Ojibway mythology, a crow is a messenger from the Creator. Basically, it's a messenger saying, "Pay attention, something interesting is going to happen." But Alex confused the crow with a raven, and his entire chapter on my work was full of raven metaphor analysis. And as I said before, it was just a sound effect. And I'm reading this, and *it's all wrong*. Meanwhile, he's over there getting tanked. And I'm thinking, "Should I tell him?"

Florentine: Sure!

Drew: And I opted no, I'd better not, he's having too much fun, I don't want to bring him down. Daniel David Moses even coined a term for this. In the early part of the nineties and the late eighties ... most people referred to Tomson Highway's plays as the benchmark for Native theatre, and the way in which all Native theatre should be adapted or understood and analyzed, and [there was] the whole concept of "trickster." And it wasn't legitimate Native theatre unless there was trickster imagery in it. And Daniel David Moses has this great quote. He says, "Most academics suffered from the 'Spot-the-Trickster Syndrome.'"

Renae: That's true.

Hartmut: I've got something: I don't deal with tricksters. There are so many, they all try to capture it. But Trickster is elusive. And I think that's why they love it, because as a postmodern concept, they can put anything in it. I don't deal with it at all.

Drew: But, you know, Native people are not postmodern. We're not post-colonial. We're still colonized.

Hartmut: When I asked about reactions, or whether German academic reactions had an influence, what I meant is somebody like Albert-Reiner Glaap or people inviting you over. They are from academia, right?

Drew: No, and I'm very grateful for all that, otherwise I would not have had the opportunity to see the four corners of Germany. I find it really interesting, being in that environment as a writer, surrounded by all these people who make their living by analyzing other people's work. In fact, I use the term ... it's like I am the chef and they're all food critics.

Hartmut: You could also say, they're the vultures and you're the meat on the table.

Drew: Ah, *that* far – I wouldn't go that far. I just find it interesting how people interpret elements. I had, one of my ... are you familiar with *Funny, You Don't Look Like One?*[89] Do you remember the picture on the cover, my picture of me like this? One class at York University spent, like, one or two classes analyzing the cover trying to deconstruct it and find out what I was saying in that picture, which was just a photograph of me.

Another time I was being interviewed by a woman who was doing a big master's essay or thesis on Native theatre. This one was on *Only Drunks and Children Tell the Truth,*[90] the middle of the Adoption Trilogy. And she sat down and she says, "You know, I think it's really, really interesting. I loved the play and that's why I want to do it. I think it's wonderfully written. And, I think it's a stroke of genius that you named your adopted character Janice." And I went, "Really? Why?" And she goes, "Well, obviously it's a reference back to the two-faced god Janus!" The Roman god, right? The one that can look both ways, past and present. "What a wonderful metaphor for an adopted child!" And I'm sitting there going, "Oh, you caught that." [laughter] "Oh, clever! You're the first one." [laughter]

So as I said, I find all this academia stuff ... I just roll my eyes and say, "Do what you want!" But then I know: I just want to tell a good story.

Hartmut: Do you then feel that once you've written a story – this is not on our catalogue of questions – when you've written a story, that you sort of are responsible for seeing to it that it's understood the way you want to understand it, or is the text out there and anybody can come to it and read it?

Drew: I think anybody can come to it and read it. I don't have time to teach everybody at all, because I'm on to something new. Albert-Reiner Glaap has this wonderful story of the guy who wrote *Educating Rita*,[91] Willy Russell. Evidently he knows Willy Russell. And Willy Russell was visiting some friends ... Oh, Willy Russell also wrote *Shirley Valentine*,[92] but we're talking about *Educating Rita*.

And he [Glaap] says he [Russell] was visiting a friend at some university – this is one of those stories that, if it isn't true, it should be true – a friend at university, visiting, and he found that he was teaching a class on *Educating Rita*. And he decides to audit it. So he goes in and he sits down, and they're talking about that scene at the very end, when Rita is about to leave for Australia. She has sort of grown beyond what the professor can teach her, has outgrown him, and she is going off to be all she could be. And he's left there, being the alcoholic professor. And so, as a going-away gift, she decides to cut his hair, because that's what she does, she's a hairdresser, right? That's how the whole thing starts. And she's cutting, and, of course, the professor goes, "This all goes back to Samson and Delilah. Delilah emasculating Samson by cutting his hair, dah de dah de dah." Evidently Willy Russell stood up and said, "No! She cuts his hair because that's what she does for a living!" And they got into this big fight about what happened and what it actually meant, the academic and the *actual* writer. And Willy Russell absolutely refused to believe that that was the context of that scene. He just said, "She cuts hair for a living, what else was she going to do? His laundry?" And I felt sort of like, "Yeah, you tell him."

Hartmut: So you do think that there is one reading of a text, and that's the writer's view?

Drew: Ahhh, I wouldn't put it in such concrete terms. I think sometimes people take it and run off in the wrong direction with it.

Florentine: I was wondering, you know, we talked about it over dinner a little bit, that there are these hierarchies, racist hierarchies, and that obviously Germans are quite obsessed and fascinated to a certain extent with Indigenous culture ... What do you make out of that? When you go over there, what are the kinds of comments and what are your observations, and how do you make sense out of that?

Drew: One of my observations in reference to the German preoccupation with Native culture is, that above all others, they're obsessive about Plains

Indians. Tipis! You never see a longhouse, you never see a wigwam, it has to be Plains, and, of course, Lakota, if at all possible. You know, I think Lakota had a better publicist or something.

I guess it's just the whole Custer thing.[93] But I just find it ... It's interesting, they are specific. While there is an overall interest in all Native cultures, and everywhere I've been, they have Ojibway, or whatever, and while they found interest in that, even Mohawks or whatever, but it seems to be the Plains Indians that get all the attention.

Hartmut: Have you thought about why that is so?

Drew: Why? As I said, it's because they had more publicity. They had the Battle of Little Big Horn, Sitting Bull and Crazy Horse,[94] and all this great stuff. You never hear about any of the great Ojibway battles, you know, because we were too embroiled in the fur trade. We were partners to a certain extent in dealing back and forth rather than – we weren't enemies of the British, or the Americans, or whatever. So we didn't have that warrior mentality that everybody seems to be interested in. You know that old newspaper saying: "If it bleeds, it leads."

Hartmut: Yeah. I think that's important. I looked at that sort of statistically in US literature, but in Germany, too. It's the Sioux and the Apache that gave the US Army the hardest time.[95] Ideologically, I mean, other people gave them a hard time too, but ...

Drew: If I remember correctly, the Seminole in Florida carried on this guerrilla warfare for a hundred years or something.

Hartmut: Yes, that's true, but they don't figure. They don't come on horseback, and they don't wear war bonnets, perhaps. The Apache didn't either.

Drew: No, no, they just had bandanas.

Renae: Just Winnetou!

Hartmut: Yeah! What were your thoughts, before you came to Germany? You must have had expectations, or an image of Germany, and how was that confirmed, or how did that change? What was your image?

Drew: I don't know, I don't know exactly what my image was, because I think I went over there when I was, like, twenty-nine. I had been off the reserve for about ten years and living in Toronto. I was not very worldly. I knew almost nothing of Europe.

The only thing I knew, really, about Germany, was World War Two movies. That's basically it. I had no idea. Like, my ideas, movies were my understanding, contemporary France was the Pink Panther series, right? [laughter] So, I literally went to Germany with a blank mind. With blank expectations, not knowing what to expect. I think I was smart enough to know that World War Two had been over for a long time, and that you guys had every electronic convenience we had. So I sort of just went there, not knowing what to expect. I remember taking that amazing train ride down the Rhine and seeing all those beautiful castles and the vineyards, and just looking out the window and going, "This is so amazing!" The sense of age, the sense of history that was there!

Tomson Highway has this great saying. He was doing this speech some-where in Europe, and he says, every time he steps off the plane in Europe, he smells the air, and he says, "Europe smells different than North Amer-ica." He says that's primarily because every square inch of Europe has had a war fought over it, not just once but several times. So it has a completely different smell.

Hartmut: Well, a lot of people say that Europe has a lot of history, but there's history here, too, Indigenous history.

Drew: Yes. Our history is mostly verbal or story. Not really buildings, not really suits of armour. Ours is pictographs, ours is stories, you know? There's a book I keep running across that I've never read, *If This is Your Land, Where Are Your Stories?*

Hartmut: Yeah, that's Chamberlin.[96] That was said by a Gitksan elder at a land claims court case, I think. Yeah, that's it.

Well, we touched upon it, but what were your experiences with racism in Germany?

Drew: Yeah, but I never actually came across any directed at me or at Native people. I'd see stuff. I remember once walking down the street and seeing this big poster, a whole wall littered with these square posters, pictures with a stereotypical *indian* face, and *Indianer* [typed] underneath it, and seeing commercials on TV using *indian* motifs.

But for me, the basic, the most obvious form of racism was geared toward – and this is not just Germany, but all over Europe, I remember when I was in Italy, too! – was geared towards Gypsies, or the Roma. Just almost everybody kept saying, beware of the Roma, beware of the Roma, the Gypsies, don't talk to them, don't go near them, don't trust them. And just the obviousness of it took my breath away.

Florentine: Hmm, yeah.

Hartmut: Yeah, yeah, that's true. Is the reception, as far as you can tell, of your work different in Germany from, say, here in Canada? Or if you don't want to talk about Germany, you can talk about other European countries.

Drew: It's hard to say. The only place in Europe that I've ever lectured – that had nothing to do with my theatre – was in England, of all places. At the British Museum, I did a lecture there twice. I get asked – this has nothing to do with Germany – but I just get asked to lecture on the weirdest things. There was a conference at the British Museum on Aboriginal trade and commerce, and they wanted me to give a keynote address on it. And I know nothing about it, but I made it up.

One time, in Prince George, BC, I got asked to come and lecture at a conference on youth and crystal meth. Again, not knowing anything about it, I went and made something up.

I don't know if the German youth really get the humour in *Motorcycles & Sweetgrass*.

Hartmut: You think Canadian youth would, I mean non-Indigenous Canadian youth?

Drew: I think so. I think there's enough cross-references to other things. But I remember being over there and being asked to explain, I don't know, something ...

Hartmut: If humour is explained, that's the end of it.

Drew: Yeah, exactly. What's that line? "The operation was a success but the patient died." [laughter]

Hartmut: Can you say something about the economic aspect of your works being read or published in Germany?

Drew: Well, one thing I keep hearing from all you German types is about how long it takes for all my books to get over there, *when* they are ordered. No, but I've made a ... I think I've made a good chunk; it's hard to say. You know, my royalty statement is not broken down country by country. But I do know that, as I've said, Lüneburg reads a lot of my stuff, I know that they do it in Frankfurt and other places, too. And I've always been puzzled why. Because people like to say that Tomson [Highway] is so much more famous than me. Sherman [Alexie], I think, is more accessible than me, because I study comedies, and comedies are not always accessible.

But I think one of the reasons I am successful is because a lot of my work does not celebrate the dysfunctional aspect of the Native community. I just celebrate the positive aspects of the Native community. I mean, Sherman's stuff can be really funny, but for every time he makes you laugh, he kicks you in the ribs, right? And I can understand that, it's all incredibly necessary and viable, but sometimes you just want a bowl of ice cream, right?

And one of my last plays, *In a World Created by a Drunken God*,[97] was very, very serious. A play that I have being done in Vancouver in March, *God and the Indian*,[98] is about residential schools and it is very, very dark and very serious. So, it's not as if I'm against that.

I remember starting out in Native theatre in the early nineties, that almost every play, every Native play that was being produced was dark, bleak, sad, depressing, and angry. And that didn't reflect the people. You know, all the characters were either oppressed, depressed, or suppressed. And my mother wasn't oppressed, depressed, or suppressed. And I just thought, I want to show what I think has allowed us to survive five hundred years of colonization: our sense of humour!

So I'd go and do that, but I would get flak. They did *Buz' Gem Blues*[99] in Rhode Island, at the Trinity Repertory Theater, and the local reviewer applauded the artistic director for expanding the boundaries of New England theatre by doing a Native Canadian play. He said, "Unfortunately he's found the Native Neil Simon, it's a pity he didn't find the Native Arthur Miller." And ...

Hartmut: How do you read that?

Drew: They wanted something darker. And I get that a lot. In fact, the artistic director of Native Earth – not this summer, but the summer before – when they did *Berlin Blues* at 4th Line Theatre, the artistic director of Native Earth, Canada's premier Native theatre company, came and saw it. Did not laugh, did not respond. And later she told me that she didn't like it. She felt the White audience hadn't earned the right to laugh at those jokes.

Renae: So, do you get that sense of White guilt that's more prominent here in Canada, so that they don't get your stuff? Whereas in Germany, they don't have that. Their guilt is projected elsewhere, you know, World War Two, so that collective sense of White guilt is not there for them. Is that why they embrace the humour maybe, they get it more?

Drew: I think they've learned. God, almost twenty years ago, my first comedy was called *The Berlin Blues* ... No, that was my last comedy ... *The Bootlegger Blues*,[100] right, which is about a sixty-eight-year-old Christian Ojibway woman who, through a series of circumstances, finds herself in possession of 143 cases of beer that she has to bootleg to buy an organ for the church. And it's loosely based on a true story. It was written for, produced, and toured by a Native theatre company.

A couple of years later, I get a phone call from a White theatre company, saying that they've read the play and they want to produce it. And this was the Port Dover Ontario Lighthouse Theatre, which is on the shores of Lake Erie, right across from Cleveland. And so, with the normal process, this was my first play by a White theatre company. We cast it, rehearsed it, went down there, had two and a half weeks' rehearsal, went on opening night.

It's a theatre, summer theatre, specializes in comedies and musicals, and the vast majority of their audience, shall we say, their hair had a bluish tinge. So the play starts. The place seats 311 people. Lights go up, lights go down, the curtain goes up, *Bootlegger Blues* starts. Complete silence. Nothing. Off in the distance you can hear coyotes howling, tumbleweeds went across the stage. [laughter] Nobody was laughing. I'm looking around and I knew the actors were doing a great job, the director had done an amazing job. Let's face it: the writing was amazing. [laughter] But nobody was laughing. All except for eight people in a back, back left row. Port Dover is twenty minutes away from the largest reserve in Canada population-wise, the Six Nations Reserve, over twenty thousand Iroquois. And two of the cast members were Iroquois from Six Nations. So every performance there were from six to ten brothers, sisters, aunts, uncles, cousins. They started laughing from the very beginning, but they were the only ones who did.

And I looked around, and I was watching them, and I saw this most amazing thing happen. So, about five, six, eight minutes went by, nobody was laughing except them. And then around them, a circle around the Native people, the row of White people around them, slowly began to laugh. And then another five or ten minutes went, and another circle of White people began to laugh. It was sort of a rock in a pond, the circle got bigger. By the middle of the first act, everybody was laughing. And it just occurred to me, this was during the height of that era known as political correctness in Canada, and these are Native people: "You don't laugh at Native people. You know what these poor people have been through." Not only that, it's a play about Native people and beer! So they were waiting for *permission* to laugh. When they saw the Native people laughing [snaps fingers], they knew they could laugh, and by the end of the run, the play had exceeded its box office expectations, and I've had four other plays there since.

And a lot has changed since then. They laugh at Native humour now. So, there's been a huge growth in the last twenty years in terms of understanding Native humour, the success of "Dead Dog Café," of Tom King's writings,[101] and such.

Hartmut: You go over to Germany as an author who's reading his plays, or you do lectures on topics that you've been asked to do. There are also quite a number of Indigenous people who go to Germany as performers or dancers, for powwows and so on.

Drew: Yes, I've met many people over there.

Hartmut: Do you have any comments on that?

Drew: Oh, yeah. I envy them. I've bumped into people who went over to dance. I had an uncle who went over to dance in Germany, traditional dance, back in the seventies, and in my trips I've met people who have gone over and made jewellery and found themselves a German woman, settling down. Also in Italy. Have you been to Turin, Italy?

Hartmut: No.

Drew: It's really fascinating. I was given a tour of Turin, and the House of Savoy. They were the people who ruled the city-state at some point. And the House of Savoy was interrelated with the French crown. And during the 1600s, during the French–Indian wars against the Iroquois and the mid-1600s, the House of Savoy sent over a thousand soldiers from Turin to Quebec. And, evidently, a quarter of them stayed. But the others came back, and when the House of Savoy was building a new palace in downtown Turin, they hired an architect to design the things above the windows, like *indians*, with headdresses. So, you look at the top, and they've got this brick outlay of faces, with what are supposed to be feathers coming out, all around the palace. And the thing is, this is the mid-1600s, the architect had never been, had never seen an *indian*. So these are just vague representations of Native people, to honour the battle against Native people. It was very surreal to see.

Renae: Have you been to Prague, in the Czech Republic?

Drew: Yes, twice.

Renae: So do you know that castle?

Drew: Yes, up where Chekhov, no, not Chekhov, where the – oh God, the Czech writer, *Metamorphosis*, *The Trial* ...

Renae: Kafka!

Drew: Yes!

Renae: Kafka, yes. The same thing: on the castle, around the doors, there are Native heads, too, chiefs' heads.

Drew: I didn't see that.

Renae: Yes, they are hidden. They're not in a row; they're hard to find. And I happened to be with someone who knew them, so she pointed them out, just as we were leaving there. There are about four of them [carved into the frames of the castle at various places]. I don't know the meaning behind them. They're so bizarre.

Drew: Interesting.

Renae: Yes, chiefs' heads.

Hartmut: Have you met any German hobbyists?

Drew: Do you mean here? [laughter] Yes, I've met them at powwows. Well, first of all, what's your definition of a German hobbyist?

Hartmut: I'm thinking of those people who, in their free time, dress up like *indians*, who do beadwork, or ...

Drew: No, I have not. Because I'm usually there in wintertime for your ... the academic year. So I'm usually there between October and April.

Renae: So you'll be there this June, so maybe you should go.

Drew: That's one of the things they said. One of the reasons why they want me there in June is to take me to one of the *Winnetou* plays. It should be fun, it should be great. I'm looking forward to that. But no, I've never, I mean I've bumped into people who have. I think there's a magazine of Native North American political issues somewhere in Germany, I know there's also one in Italy.

Renae: *Coyote*?[102]

Drew: *Coyote*! That's it, yes. I was interviewed for that, and I think it's a magazine that has more of a political bent to it. So, I've met people like that.

Hartmut: There's also a lot of interest in Indigenous spirituality. Have you comments on that?

Drew: Oh, I bump into people who want to know if I am a spiritual elder, or ... [laughter]

Hartmut: Have you thought about why there is this curiosity?

Drew: Yeah, I've often wondered about it. I've written about why I think Germans have this interest in Native culture. And I think one is, primarily, the number one reason for me primarily is, Germans originally came from a tribal culture. You keep hearing about ... Was it Caesar who lost, like, four legions against the Germanic tribes? So, there's this whole thing about tribal affiliations among Germans that I think is inherent, still there, and has this sort of, I don't know, either under-conscious or under-cultural appeal or fascination for Native cultures, who are still in that tribal state. So I think that has something to do with it, and of course then, you can't underestimate the influence of Karl May's *Winnetou*, which I think has had a substantial impact on several, God, four, six generations of German people?

Hartmut: Yeah, still. Even if they don't read that, it's part of everyday culture.

Renae: Have you read Karl May?

Drew: I've read the first half of the first *Winnetou*. I had to throw it down when Winnetou's sister threw herself at Old Shatterhand.

Hartmut: Oh, yeah, and he [Winnetou] explains to her that she's not worthy.

Drew: She's a "savage."

Hartmut: Yes.

Drew: But the thing I found really interesting about the whole book, it dripped with homosexual subtext.

Florentine: Oh, yeah.

Hartmut: It's gay literature!

Florentine and **Renae:** It is?!

Hartmut: That's why it wasn't dealt with as gay, because then it wouldn't have been sold. But there are some analyses by academics about that.[103] It's so blatant. Absolutely. And it's amazing. I think that's part of the appeal, because it's not openly homosexual.

Drew: Right.

Hartmut: But I think every reader, male or female, has a certain homosexual potential, it appeals to that, but in a way that is never expressed, so censorship or homophobia never kicks in.

Drew: Yeah. Now, I thought it was very obvious, right? I read one of his other ones, called *Into the Desert*. But again ... and I had to put that down, he was making ... some guy's son was drowning in quicksand, and Old Shatterhand said he'd save him if the guy promised ...

Florentine: Kara Ben Nemsi. It's a different guy, but it's the same character.

Drew: Well, I'll get to that in a second ... But he basically says, "I'll save your son if you promise to become a Christian. Swear right here." And I just thought, okay. But at the beginning of *Into the Desert* he says, there's just a line in there, he says, "You know, when I was in the United States, I was known as Old Shatterhand."

Hartmut: That's actually what turned me off when I read *Winnetou*. In the end, he dies in the arms of Old Shatterhand, and he says, "I've turned Christian." And that, I just thought, "What a sell-out!" I don't know how old I was, maybe ten or twelve, but I just couldn't forgive him for that. I thought, "How can he be such a sell-out?"

Drew: Yeah. Did you ever see that movie, that made-for-TV movie called *Where the Spirit Lives*? 1989, the first movie about residential schools? It was shot in Waterford, just near Pincher Creek, on the Blood Reserve. In fact, the school is St. Paul's School, there. Anyways, at the very end of it, when the girl is running to escape and the teacher runs out to her and gives her food and gives her a pile of books to read, saying, "These aren't lies!" And at the very top of the pile is the Bible. And I remember, I worked on that, I did the publicity for that movie in '89. And I just remember – after I saw the movie – cringing. And they had a rescreening of it, it's been retouched, redone, about three months ago, they rescreened it. It was a made-for-TV movie, but they did it on a big screen. I remember watching it, and I remember going up to the director and saying, "You know how much that made me and most Native people cringe?" And he leaned over and said, "Me too, that was supposed to be Shakespeare!" [laughter] It was the props people who just grabbed a bunch of old books, wrapped them up, to give. And it was just a shot by itself, a hand holding a bunch of books, and the Bible was on top. And he said, "We did not put the Bible in there, I promise you. That was the props people."

Hartmut: Have you thought about why people go for the spiritual and think every *indian* has access to – or is – a guru, or is a medicine man, or if not, knows a medicine man who has initiated him or her? Why is there this need in Europe?

Drew: I don't know about Europe. Everybody is looking for direction. There is a man in the Kitigan Zibi Reserve, Canada, who every summer has a three-day seminar, he has a thing called "A Circle of All Nations." And 2,000 to 2,500 people come up and camp on his front yard for three days for workshops, sweat lodges, talking about wampum belt, all these different things. And people just know. People come up from South America. I ran into these three people from New York, various sites of New York, they came up. And they keep saying they were followers of – one was Black, two were these

White women – and they said they followed the Lakota way of life. And I just rolled my eyes.

But they are all up there looking for direction. And I don't think it is just Europeans, I think everybody is looking for direction. You know, that whole drop-out culture in the late sixties, early seventies, I think, for Germans, it's just partly because of all those reasons I've mentioned, there was this belief that Native people live like Carlos Castaneda,[104] right? And, it's like, Carlos Castaneda was a fraud – he was arrested for fraud in South America, all those different things.

But in a sense this is a very serious thing, because one of the books ... I have my next four novels thought out in my head, and one of them is going to be about an *indian* messiah, a Native messiah, who starts up in Germany. And he starts his own religion. It's going to be sort of like my take on Scientology. And then he starts to believe his own stuff, and something bad happens.

There's good fodder for that sort of thing happening in Germany, because so many people out there are looking for direction, and they think we have the passage for direction. Up in Whitehorse, from May to October, there's a non-stop flight from Whitehorse to Frankfurt.

Florentine: That is true. Germans love to go up North, watching and participating in dog sled races and these kinds of things.

Drew: They're looking for a connection with nature.

Renae: That's right, yeah.

Drew: I remember once driving through Germany, and there was this forest. And it was so interesting! There was a line down the middle, one side was deciduous, one side was coniferous. They had been planted like that and there was a line right up the middle. And I just thought, "Wow!"

Florentine: Everything's groomed.

Drew: Yeah. So I think there's a search for nature, a search for direction, a search for spirituality, and a search for identity. And for some reason, they think we're one-stop shopping. Why, I'm not sure, it just seems obvious to me.

Renae: I want to go back to something you said earlier. You said you know a lot of Native people who danced, performed, fell in love. Do they still live there?

Drew: A few. I've met them. I don't know them. It's a little funny, right, you come into town and they go, "Oh, I know other Native people, let me call them up for you." "Hi!" [laughter] "Oh, we're from the southern States, hey brother!" [laughter] So I would meet these people all over, you know? I would take them into conversation like we were supposed to connect on some ...

Renae: Some Native level.

Drew: Yeah, exactly. Bro! [laughter]

Hartmut: Do you have something that you wanted to add from your side with regard to German Indianthusiasm?

Drew: I am quietly amused by it. I saw that documentary, *If Only I Were an Indian*. Did you see that? I saw they're so wimped out. My dream some day is to get a documentary team, go over to one of these things, and have me there making snarky comments. [105]

Renae: You know they won't let you go. Do you know Kent Monkman?

Drew: Oh, yeah.

Renae: So, he wanted to do his Miss Chief Eagle Testikle at one of these camps. They would not let him. And I told him, "They're not going to let you in, especially they won't let cameras in." He said, "Just believe me, we'll try." I said, "Go ahead, try, they won't let you." Because, he wants to do the same thing, so ... anyway.

Somehow, we have to infiltrate. We have to agree – we! – that we're not going to go there in our loincloth and be one with nature and leave all our cameras and stuff all behind. That's the only way it will happen. They are so controlling of what they think Native culture is.

Drew: I know. What's that term? They think we've been corrupted by the twenty-first century, so we're "Coca-Cola Indians." Well, if you remember *Motorcycle & Sweetgrass*, me talking about the three great inventions by White people? You know, toilets, push-up bras, all these different things. But I've lost my train of thought.

Renae: About twentieth-century gadgetry, us not being able to be ...

Drew: Yes, yes, thank you. There's a production of *The Rez Sisters*[106] that was done in Peterborough, the town next to my reserve. And the local reviewer was reviewing it, and the first line of the review was: "Theatre does not come naturally to Native people" or "is not culturally indicative of Native people." And it goes on to talk about the production. And I wrote a response – I have a column in that paper – and I wrote a response to it, saying, "The porcelain toilet does not come culturally naturally to Native people, but we've mastered its intricacies." [laughter]

Hartmut: Anything else you want to add?

Drew: I have a couple of "Drew-Hayden-Taylor-in-Germany" stories that I'm going to save for you for tomorrow.

Hartmut: So, can we record that?

Drew: As long as you promise not to steal my spirit. [laughter]

Hartmut: We've already captured that.

Drew: What's left of it.

EMMA LEE WARRIOR

They want redemption somehow.

Live interview by Florentine Strzelczyk and Hartmut Lutz at Hotel Alma, University of Calgary

Hartmut: Renae Watchman is a Navajo from down south, and she always starts the interviews by asking people what their tribal affiliation is. So, I'm asking that question.

Emma: Oh. Well, I'm Peigan, from southern Alberta.

Hartmut: Well, you know that in our project that is just beginning, we're looking, on the one hand, at the German fascination with *indians*, and on the other hand at reactions by Aboriginal writers like you, who have dealt with that in their writing. And our first question is: How did you get into contact with that? How did you come up with the figure of Hilda Afflerbach,[107] or those Germans who are so enthused about *indians*? Maybe you can tell us a little about that.

Emma: Well, first of all, I thought of Adolf Hungry Wolf,[108] I guess, who has ancestors who are German. And somebody said he was Swiss, but then he married somebody from the Blood reserve, and I think his children used ... I can't remember if they used their mother's name or what. And one of the children lives on reserve. But they have Indian names, English Indian names. Well no, I think, he has a Blackfoot name. I think it means, something to do with a stone, yeah, a stone shaped like a buffalo. I think that's his Indian name ... A stone shaped like a buffalo. And yeah, that has some significance.

Well. When I grew up, I never heard about German Indianthusiasm. But then I guess, these people must research stuff like that. That's why they're smart about those things. They have knowledge about that. I should say, they are knowledgeable about things like that.

Hartmut: In those stories you also have this German character, Hilda Afflerbach.

Emma: Oh yeah, Hilda.

Hartmut: And she is very much enthused about old-time *indians*. So she doesn't see the reality much, right?

Emma: Yeah.

Hartmut: And how did you come up with her?

Emma: Hilda?

Hartmut: Hilda Afflerbach, a German girl that you were talking about, and the medicine woman.

Emma: Yes. I just fabricated her.

Hartmut: Okay. But I mean, in fabricating Hilda – you have her in a story with a medicine woman. You also have her in the story with …

Emma: Oh … with Walking Eagle?

Hartmut: Yeah, Walking Eagle. So, how did you come up with that character?

Emma: Okay, the Walking Eagle. Well, I ran away with another girl from Canada and hitchhiked down to New York. I got put into a Catholic high school, and there was this girl, a fraud. They used to send people out to other schools. So I got put into a downtown place. I went to high school there. And these other girls they got sent to Westpoint, across the river – there was an academy, Catholic. So these girls from that Good Shepherd Home, they got sent over there, to the academy. It's a Catholic school. And one of them, her name was Afflerbach, and I went, "What kind of name is that?" And she: "Oh, it's German." And so that's where I got that name.

Hartmut: Okay. And Hilda?

Emma: Hilda. I just took it because I think it must have been German.

Hartmut: Yeah, sure, sure!

Emma: Well, anyway, that [fraud] girl later confessed. She came clean and said, "Ah, my name is Carol McKenny. I ran away from my father. I made up this story [of my last name] because they couldn't find my father." Yeah, she used the name Carol Afflerbach. And, I thought, "Oh, it's a name that sticks." That stuck in my head. So that's where that name came from.

Hartmut: And what made you sort of pick that? You have two stories. Actually, when you think of "The Powwow Committee,"[109] there's another story, where it is a Blackfoot setting, and it is about Germans coming in on the reserve doing powwow dancing, or they are meeting with ...

Emma: "Powwow Committee"?

Hartmut: Yeah. "Powwow Committee."

Emma: And the elders' scene?

Hartmut: Yeah, and it's always about outsiders coming in and wanting to be *indians*.

Emma: Yes, because at that time, you know, that was what was going on. People were talking about it. And they'd say, "Oh, that German guy." You know? 'Cause we didn't know what he was. We just know he's a White guy and all that, and we think he's a German.

And [there was] D., she was always bringing people around. She hooks up with some White person, and brings them around.

Hartmut: Who?

Emma: The girl in the story, Flora, is the D. character, 'cause she's always hooking up with someone.

Hartmut: Yeah, she said she met her [Hilda] at the Stampede.

Emma: Yes. And Hilda said she wanted to go to an Indian reserve. So she brought her over there.

Hartmut: Have you experienced that? I mean, that you've been to places and there were German tourists around there?

Emma: Well, you know, I've seen Hungry Wolf. Everybody knows Hungry Wolf. And it's from that D. you know, who tells me. She always has White people at her house, some strange persons. And there was this German girl, Hilda, and she was all gaga, she wanted to see *indians*. [laughs]

Hartmut: You know, but that's something very common. A lot of Germans get very gaga and want to see *indians*, you see.

Emma: Oh yeah! And you know what happened, just recently, this year, this summer?

Hartmut: No?

Emma: I saw it in the newspaper. One time my grandson came here, he was still young. Now he's almost thirty ... he is twenty-eight or something, Joel. And he's a real good dancer, a real good dancer. He's a champion, you know. And we went to Siksika, and they were all making a big deal about these foreigners. And this one man, he's real short, he wears this little golf cap or what, with a peak, and a kind of a baggy-looking top part of it. It's all beaded, and he wears the whole thing. He's got the whole outfit. It's all white buckskin, beaded. And he's a scam.

Hartmut: He was a German?

Emma: I don't think so. I think he is related to Germans around there, you know. He may be a ... What's around Germany, anyway?

Florentine: Austria?

Emma: Maybe, maybe. Anyway. And he has his son. A very small son, and who competes in that Boy's Fancy [dance competition]. And he's real fast, you know. He's real small and very fast. But in my mind, he is not in Joel's league. But they give him the prize.

Hartmut: Oh.

Emma: And this was a few years ago, and it really upset me, and I told him so. And Joel tells us all these stories. "Oh, they came in a plane, and they hired ... they rented those big ..." There's one over there, see? [points at a big camper in the parking lot]

Hartmut: Like a Winnebago?

Emma: Yes, those big things. And they come here. And so I said, "You know what? You danced better than him. These people are suck-all into those White people. You know. And I don't like that." And so I told that boy: "You know, my grandson beat you in that dance. But it's not right that those Indians should give you the First Prize 'cause you guys just come here to have fun, just come here to make money. And these Indians, they make their outfit, and they're very poor, and this is their chance to make money. And you come all the way flying over here, and having a good time and you beat him and you just ... It's stealing! That's what it is!" And then Joel, after that, said, "Grandma, you shouldn't have talked to that fool like that!" But I said, "It's true. And you did dance better than him!" And he said, "'Cause, you know what?" I said, "What?" He said, "He gave me fifty dollars." So I said, "Good for him. He should have given you more than that!" [laughs]

Hartmut: That boy who got that, who did not "win" but got the prize: was he from Germany?

Emma: He was from Austria.

Hartmut: From Austria.

Emma: And his father, this year – I saw it in a *Blackfoot Newspaper* or something – his father got First Prize, Men's Traditional.

Hartmut: Okay.

Emma: But see, they *always* go to Siksika. And there's *something* going on there. It was in the Indian newspaper, Siksika newspaper: "These are Winners," you know? And I just recognized that name. I don't know their name, but I know it's their name. It's strange, you know, it's not a Blackfoot name. And I just knew it was them. And somebody, I told him, "Who won at Siksika?" And he said, "Oh, this guy. He is a White guy, European, and he wears a little cap." And I said, "Ahh, that's those guys."

Hartmut: But to come back to Hilda and to Adolf ...

Emma: Ah, yeah, Hilda wants an *indian* experience, religious thing, or whatever.

Hartmut: And, you know, the way you wrote that story is psychologically so deep, although you do not theorize much about psychology. But the way she reacts! I have the feeling you must have known her for a long time.

Emma: No! No, I didn't know anybody like that. But it's from D., who tells me about these people, you know? Because she's always bringing people straight to her house and ...

Hartmut: How do you feel about that? That some Germans, or some Europeans have this gaga fantasy ...

Emma: I don't know. I sort of feel amused about it, you know? And I get some positive feeling, kind of like: "It's a fan." It's *that* thing! And I didn't have any negative feeling about it. I just thought, you know, go for it, if it's a ... you know, if something feels good.

Hartmut: Have you thought about why they do that?

Emma: Ahh, no. Not really. Anyway, when I went to Germany. Oh, I thought everybody is very civilized, very nice. I didn't have any ... Especially your family, you know, they are ... Everybody was really nice to me. And I, you know, that Kerstin[110] and somebody, we went on that ride to the white cliffs. Oh no, I thought everybody was very nice.

Hartmut: And you didn't meet anything ... sort of people being enthused and "gaga" about *indians*?

Emma: Ahh, yes! Remember that man. I think he was a professor. I just remember he said, "I'm gonna go to Alberta and I'm gonna find you." [Hartmut and Emma laughing] Yeah, that's the only one. But he was enthusiastic and happy to meet me.

Hartmut: Okay.

Emma: Yeah. I find everybody real regular and normal and [humorous]. Nice people.

Hartmut: But there is also a lot of racism in Germany.

Emma: It is? I don't know. I don't think we have to worry about that, 'cause they're over there, and we're over here. [laughs]

Hartmut: So you think you got your own [racists]?

Emma: Yeah.

Hartmut: Okay. Some of your stories were published in Germany? And there was also a translation of one.[111]

Emma: Yes.

Hartmut: Having readers over in Germany, has that affected you in any way and your writing, knowing that there were people there? Has it interfered with, or confirmed your writing?

Emma: No. I'm seeing myself, I'm not a person who's aware. I don't know that much about other people. You know, just from my little real place on the earth. [Florentine and Emma laughing] I have really limited experience with foreigners. All I know is from the Hutterites. Mostly we go there to buy some eggs, and buy stuff from them. And sometimes people hire them to come to their events, like a funeral, and they cook. And it's sort of a neighbourly thing. That's the only way I know them. You know, we get along with them, Indians and Hutterites.

Hartmut: If, you know, people ask you, "Can we publish your story?," and maybe they send you a little cheque, maybe they don't, but I think some of them do: Does that influence you in any way, or do you think about that?

Emma: Well. No. I call myself a lazy person. A lazy writer, you know. Sometimes I'll write, sometimes I don't. You know, I have too many problems to write. [laughs]

Hartmut: Everyday life interferes all the time.

Emma: Yeah, it's a reserve life, I guess that's one of the big factors. I'm not in one place, I'm very transient. You know, I didn't know where I wanna be living, or how I'm going to be living. There is so much uncertainty in my life. But I would like to settle down and do some more serious writing.

Hartmut: Full-time.

Emma: Yeah. Full-time. That'd be great!

Hartmut: You haven't met any German hobbyists? Well, except for those Austrians or so, who were dancing at Siksika.

Emma: That's all, I think. I don't think I ever met any more. I get a funny feeling sometimes, at Sik-ooh-kotok, in Lethbridge. It's called "Sik-ooh-ko-tok." It's the name for Lethbridge. It means "Black Rock," because there used to be coal there. And the Indians call it Black Rock, but White people call it Lethbridge, after one of their family or somebody. But we still call it in Blackfoot "Sik-ooh-kotok." And they have a centre there, an Indian Centre, it's called "Sik-ooh-kotok," and they have powwow, and they had ... I wouldn't call them hobbyists. I don't know, they're ... Unless hobbyists includes a whole range of people. They were, you know, "Four Worlds." Did you ever hear of that?

Hartmut: Four Worlds?

Emma: Yeah. Four Worlds. I think it has to do with a belief in the world that there's four worlds. I don't know what the four worlds are. Maybe the colours of the people, eh? Grey, white, black, and red?

Hartmut: Yeah, like in some medicine wheels, the colours?

Emma: Yes. Yes. Those colours. Anyway, they had a powwow, and they were ... You know, things like that happen.

Hartmut: Were they Indigenous, some of them?

Emma: No, no. They're White.

Hartmut: There are so many non-Indigenous people, and a lot of them in Germany, who are really interested in Aboriginal religion.

Emma: We have people over there from Brocket – who are over there in Germany. But I don't know where. They married over there, yes.

Hartmut: There is quite a demand in Germany, for people to come and do ceremonies and things like that.

Emma: Yes.

Florentine: Is that what they're doing there?

Hartmut: How do you feel about that?

Emma: Well, before I just thought, woah, like, they are hipsters, like the hippies, eh? When the hippies, the hippie days were around, and people all wanted to be walking barefoot, and walking all of this crazy stuff, yeah, like a fad.

Hartmut: But you said "before," how do you feel about it now?

Emma: I don't know ... You find them every so often, there's White people who get really interested in Native stuff. They want to get into ... It doesn't really work like that. Well, I guess it does, there's two ways. One is that Indian way. And I would say in Brocket. Brocket has pretty much lost that Blackfoot. They don't have the societies like they used to when I was a little girl. But Blood reserve is stronger, and Siksika has started up. The Blood reserve has what they called The Horn Society – they have societies – and I guess they have other societies. And there's the Siksika. They started up their Horn Society a few years ago. It survived. So they have their society over there. They're starting to have the Sundance over there, and it's very new. I mean it's revived, new. But Brocket hasn't anything like that. And I don't know where these [people who are over in Germany] get all their, you know, society knowledge, and all that, because it doesn't exist in Brocket. But I guess there's ways of finding out. They go and they pick it up from ...

Hartmut: In your short story "Compatriots," one of the Aboriginal women says, "Oh yeah, I'm not into the Sundance and all that."[112]

Emma: Yeah.

Hartmut: And she said: "They're bringing it in from other nations." Some of them do Sioux Sundance, and others Cree.

Emma: Yeah, still! When there's a death, like recently, there was a family, they all started singing a Sioux song! I didn't know what they were doing, until I heard "Tatanka," you know, because it means "Great Spirit," or whatever.

Hartmut: "Wakan Tanka?"

Emma: Yeah! And they were singing, and I said, "What's going on here? I thought there's a Blackfoot death. How come these people are doing that?" And when you go into Brocket, when you come down, on the east end of the reserve, there's a coulee, and you go down, and then you drive up. Just look on that side, there's a creek that goes through there, and there are some trees. Right there, they have a Sundance lodge. And that's where they have their Sundance, those Tatanka people.

Hartmut: Is that the Sundance you refer to in the story?

Emma: No, no. The Sundance I refer to is really, like a ... people who are Bloods, you know.

Hartmut: The one in the story, the one that Helmut goes to?

Emma: The other one, the other guy who's ... What's his name? Adolf, he is Swiss, not German. He's Swiss. But they have the same interests. I think it comes from Germany, that interest.

Florentine: So, you were saying, when these people come here, and they want to learn some of the *indian* traditions, that there's a good way about it and a bad way about it. And you said, in Brocket at least, you lost some of those, your own traditions. So, what should these people do when they want to learn – these Germans?

Emma: Oh, you mean, when you are talking about those guys in Germany? Look, it has a lot to do with money, I think. Well, as I'm getting older, I think I'm getting a little wiser, and I just say, "Oh, there is a lot of foolishness in the world," you know? Good and bad. And what can you do about it? Nothing! Let things be. Leave them alone. Nothing you can do. It's not your business. It's their business. [laughs] But I've this reading ... You know that red book?[113]

Hartmut: Yeah.

Emma: Reading it really enlightened me about a lot of things about Germans. And I'm really thankful for that information, because otherwise I have this jaded look, meaning negative, eh? But I really understand it, and I have more of, I guess, you could almost call it compassion, you know, and warmth – a feeling of warmth and understanding. That's why they do it, you know? Because they went through hell. And they've pulled out of hell. You know, wherever all this hell came from. It's such a horrible thing, you know, the Holocaust and all that, that I can understand they want redemption somehow ...

Hartmut: Yeah. I think you're right on.

Emma: ... and understanding, and they're human beings like everybody else. And I don't care, because I'm trying to be an understanding old woman. I've been called "old woman" so long now that I finally accepted it. [laughing] And I just think, they're just human beings like everybody else, like us, you know? No better than anybody. I did my share of crap in this world.

Hartmut: I think that's a good conclusion.

Florentine: Yeah.

Emma: Glad to do it for you.

Hartmut: Okay.

Emma: Happy!

AFTERWORD

In their teachings, Indigenous knowledge holders and traditional educators tend to refrain from abstract didacticisms and generalizing interpretations, but rather rely on the power of stories to unfold, and respectfully give the recipients the space to arrive at their own conclusions. Our volume follows this approach and encourages readers to develop their own perspective from the accounts of those interviewed. We conclude this book by doing the same ourselves, and, again following Indigenous protocol, locate ourselves in relation to what we have heard from those we asked, and share what we have learned in the process.

Renae Watchman

I was born in Ogden, Utah, in 1974 to teen parents who were on the infamous "Indian Placement Program" established by the LDS Church. My maternal grandma, shimásání, or grams, once told me she did not even know I existed until I was six months old, when my mother returned home to the rez, to Shiprock, New Mexico, to finish her senior year of high school. My aunts and uncles have shared stories with me about my upbringing, but my clearest memories are those with my grams. My parents struggled as most teen parents on the rez do, so I was fortunate to have some stability in my grams as a young girl. As I got older, I inherited big sister duties as a mother figure to my siblings. My experience was typical perhaps of tumultuous mother–daughter relationships, yet extraordinary in that there was physical and emotional violence that I normalized. During eighth grade, I left home due to a heated physical exchange, and chose to live with my uncle Bobby Watchman for an entire year. The following year, I transferred to Navajo Academy, and I moved back home, but I did not stay. The violence continued, and one incident resulted in my having two black eyes, which I tried to hide behind sunglasses. I was a strong student who hid my home life, but this particular morning I could not hide the abuse any longer.

Instead of calling the local authorities as mandated, my then-principal as well as the guidance counsellor investigated my records to discover that I was an A student. They feared that being placed in foster care would have a negative impact on my educational opportunities. They probed me to find out if I had any options: did I have a safe place to stay during the weekends, if I stayed in the dorms during the school week? I told them I could stay at my uncle's or at another caregiver's house on weekends. They probed further, "That's fine, but what about the summer? And what about next year?" They were thinking ahead about my future, but I was frustrated with the questions and I shot back, "I don't know! Why don't you just send me to another country for the year?" I saw a light bulb go off above their heads. Navajo Academy (revamped as Navajo Preparatory School in 1991) had a brief history with hosting foreign exchange students from northern European countries, but it was, up until then, a one-way exchange. One of Navajo Academy's chemistry teachers was also a local representative of the American Scandinavian Student Exchange (ASSE) program. With the guidance of these three – principal, counsellor, and chemistry teacher – I was aided in the arduous process of applying to become a foreign exchange student. The principal asked me where I wanted to go for a year, but, as an unseasoned traveller, the answer to that question was abstruse and unreal. My principal (a non-Diné) suggested Germany, and for all I knew, he could have just as easily spun a globe and randomly used his index finger to stop it at a destination. I had no knowledge of German language or culture and, coming from the Navajo Nation, I had no reason to continue my own learning with all things German beyond this exchange year, so I was willing to leave home for another world. In total ASSE selected forty students from North America for the program. Of these forty students, I was one of two selected to receive a 95 percent stipend. The remaining 5 percent was covered by the Navajo Nation for my flight from Farmington, New Mexico, to JFK in New York.

My first direct experiences with Germans and Germany, then, were during my junior year of high school, in 1990–91. When I left "The Land of Enchantment" in July 1990, I had no preparation for the culture shock I was to endure. Thankfully, I had a loving and supportive host family with whom I still maintain contact; I was exposed to normalcy, to kindness and love through my host parents, Doris and Klaus Cantzler and their son (ten years younger than me), Clemens Cantzler. They were the stability I needed, given my own New Mexico home life of dysfunction and violence. They welcomed me in Rellingen (a suburb of Hamburg), and I learned of the wealth that German culture offered: from fresh-baked goods to recycling, to the lone, literary figure, the Apache Winnetou. Living in Germany for one year piqued my interests, as I was often asked to speak about my home and all things *indian*. I quickly realized that knowing the intricacies of Dinétah (Navajo land), and the related stories of both the land and of our culture, was not enough for Germans who already thought they knew about *indians* through their literary fiction that personified a German *indian*, in Winnetou. While I knew of some stories related to where I was from, I had to suddenly be the expert on Lakota, Apache, or Blackfeet culture (the top three Indigenous nations that are widely known in Germany). This spun me into a longing for my own home, for the landscape, for the landmarks, and for the food. Furthermore, I got the feeling of sudden awareness when I was abroad at the ripe age of sixteen, similar to that uttered by Keith Basso in his study of place-based Western Apache stories rooted in the land: "It is then we come to see that attachments to places may be nothing less than profound, and that when these attachments are threatened we may feel threatened as well" (Basso 1996, xiii). The threat I perceived was my lived experience with not knowing the full canon of Navajo oratory, which I saw as the new, contemporary norm among my peers back home on the rez. In Rellingen, I had an opportunity to learn of a culture quite different from my own, which included variances in language, lore, eats, and defeats (history). While I embraced the new experiences, I also longed for watching competitive girls' basketball games, driving long distances to see family, and just being in the once-familiar setting of northwest New Mexico. My sense of place remained intact, despite my dislocation. While I was still on my foreign exchange program, the Academy Award-winning movie *Dances with Wolves* (1990) refocused attention on *indians*. There I had an overwhelming sense of Indigenous pride; this coupled with the fact that my high school basketball team, the Lady Eagles, were on their way to the Class 2A State Championships. By June 1991, I was ready to return home.

I flew back from Germany after a one-year exchange and this life-changing experience paved a unique path for my future endeavours. I completed my senior year of high school and graduated as the 1992 valedictorian of Navajo Preparatory School. It was a great honour that I was able to bring my family together to celebrate the occasion: my dad came in from Sheep Springs, NM, extended family came from all around the Navajo Nation (Shiprock, Crownpoint, and Chinle), and my host mother flew all the way from Hamburg to Albuquerque, not expecting to drive three hours more after an international flight!

After graduation, I left the rez again for college. I enrolled in German-language classes solely to never lose contact with my host family. I had become mostly fluent in German, yet had no plans to do anything with this skill. I was a psychology major, yet because I ended up having excess German courses, I was able to double-major in German, and earned concurrent bachelor's degrees. I was encouraged to teach German to undergrads, earning my MA from Arizona State University. This venture into graduate studies encouraged me to pursue doctoral studies in the discipline of German Studies, jointly with the Graduate Program in Humanities at Stanford University.

When I was an MA student, I was enrolled in a course called "German Theatre" in which we brought Grimm's tales to the stage. One day, shortly before class was to begin, I was chatting online with my late father. I told him I had to go to class; he asked, "Which class?" and I said, "German Theatre." He said, "What's that? I envision Nazis marching ..." I froze, because it was then that I realized that busting myths was not a one-way street, and this propelled me to try to find a way to bridge my work with who I was. This journey has been life-long and I have learned that educating others (from Indianthusiasts to my own family on the Navajo Nation) about misconceptions versus what really matters in my life can never be satisfactorily completed. I sought to understand the transcultural exchange and promote mutual respect among Indigenous people and Germans.

When I lived in Germany, I was exposed to Indianthusiasm, but it did not overshadow the daily life of going to a *Gymnasium*, attending rock concerts, eating good food, dancing in discos, and building life-long relationships. I have been travelling back and forth, almost annually since 1990. Each time I return to Germany, I discover more layers to Indianthusiasm, but I was initially dismissive of Germany hobbyism, so I did not take the time to get to know them.

As my interest in the German hobbyist clubs increased, so did the need for Indianthusiasts to take the activities of all things Plains *indian* and put them into practice, via attempting to live like "real *indians*." This was not novel, as hobbyism has a long history in Germany, but what was new, was that to live like a "real *indian*," they incorporated contemporary powwow culture into their Plains fascination and instead of living on harsh reservation lands, with everyday anti-Indigenous racism, as was *really* happening in North America, Indianthusiasts pitched their tipis along the Rhine or on the greenery of Germany's rolling hills to play *indian* in what they call pre-reservation times. These hobbyist camps continue to thrive, but I have personally not been to a pre-reservation-era hobby camp. I had been invited to attend such hobbyist camps, but refused to go backwards in time, when citizens of our respective Nations have struggled historically and culturally to simply exist and matter in the present-day and age. I won't abide by their rules, which are inflexible and rigid: to wear only natural, handmade loincloths and dresses, reflective of pre-reservation romanticism. When I was invited, I was told I could not bring or use technology[1] or depict signs that I live in modernity, in other words, I would have to consciously enact my own vanishing, erasing my active presence. Why would I want to be complicit in Indigenous erasure and fiction? I choose to be a contemporary, iPhone-using, high-heel-wearing, German-speaking matriarch of the Navajo Nation.

When Hartmut was invited by members of the local Greifswald *Indianistik* to attend their Indian Week, he replied, "You won't see me in loincloth."

I am honoured that we were able to procure Cree artist Kent Monkman's *Miss Europe* (2016, acrylic on canvas, featured in the instalment *The Four Continents*). I was first introduced to Monkman's art in 2012, while giving a talk in Zurich at the Nordamerika Native Museum (NOMA). It was here that I witnessed the advent of Miss Chief Eagle Testickle in the video *Dance to Miss Chief* (2010, 4:49), which critiqued Indianthusiasm by intercutting footage of Red westerns with a fictious love affair between Miss Chief and Winnetou. Monkman's work goes beyond a critique of Indianthusiasm,[2] and his counter-gaze of colonialism, genocidal policies, and their effects on contemporary Indigeneity are deeply influential. Monkman says his art is "a form of reparation through reappropriation,"[3] Monkman has been able to capture what so many contemporary Indigenous people feel about representations, one-sided history of the nation-state, of Indigenous love and lives. *Miss Europe* is controversial and contains imagery that some Germans may find uncomfortable, yet it is my hope that the scholarly work around Indianthusiasm will be elevated beyond tired stereotypes and tropes. The cover image, *Miss Europe*, adds to the body of work on Indigenous responses to Indianthusiasm.

When people find out about Indianthusiasm for the first time, it always strikes them as new news. In 2016, for example, I was contacted by Timo Kiesel, who wanted to interview me for the then upcoming documentary *Forget Winnetou*,[4] in which director Red Haircrow wished to expose Indianthusiasm. I asked him to send me the interview questions since we could not have a face-to-face interview. I would have been happy to answer his questions, but I declined, because his questions were essentially the same ones that we asked of our own interviewees in this anthology. The documentary *Forget Winnetou! Loving in the Wrong Way* was released in 2018.

My own early work focused on the powwow phenomenon, and I tend to ignore the pre-reservation hobbyists and their mimetic Indigeneity, or what Penny calls "surrogate Indigeneity." In the Introduction, we quoted Penny, who shared a reporter's findings of one particular hobbyist, Mr. Diecke, with whom I am friends, who was "neither a social misfit nor insane. His wife was a dentist, and his compatriots included doctors, engineers, cooks, and scholars." This reminds me of the year I travelled to Prague to interview a family that was active in Indianthusiast circles, until they discovered powwows. The daughter, Karolina, was a fancy shawl dancer and was the first title holder of the Westerwald Powwow Princess.[5] Her father was a dentist in the former Czechoslovakia, now the Czech Republic. Their modest apartment building was like a living museum: full of handmade Plains (Lakota-style) crafts, regalia, and other material cultural items. The family (like many I have encountered over the past twenty-five years) was respectful, humble, and quite knowledgeable and rightly concerned about what Indigenous peoples in North America think of their lifetime hobby. Karolina was an ideal pow-wow princess, in terms that we have here in North America; at the end of her term, as she was giving up the title, she held a giveaway and in addition to the standard giveaway fare, she brought four carloads of traditional *medovnik*, a Czech cake, to share with those in attendance.

After I earned my PhD in 2007, I taught in the Transcultural German Studies Department at the University of Arizona. One course I taught was called "Minority Views of German Culture." In addition to introducing students to Afro-German, Japanese German, Jewish German, and other "minority" voices, I sought to find the voices of the 300-plus (an unverified number) Indigenous people who called Germany home. Their stories piqued my interest in this transcultural connection. I quickly discovered the few vocal Indigenous voices in Germany who wrote about Indianthusiasts and hobbyists and was introduced to several educators, artists, and performers. Over the years, I have interviewed several who strive to make their Indigenous presence in Germany known, to bust the myths that some Indianthusiasts and hobbyists perpetuate. These full-time, Indigenous residents of Germany walk the fine line between being tokenized and assuming the role of representing all things *indian*.

After living in Germany a few times during my lifetime, I too have direct experience as educator, performer, and mythbuster, while having also been a target of liminal racism. Despite my loving host family and the many (non-racist) people whom I cherish in Germany, racism does exist. It's overt only if the racists think I am from Turkey or another Eastern European country. Their racism, however, turns to sudden admiration and respect when they discover I am Diné; this is why I call it liminal racism. This in-between racism is not "less than" actual, explicit racism, but the racists project that it is. I don't mean to conflate Indianthusiasm with liminal racism; my experience in Germany is that the situation is complex. A majority of Germans love all things *indian,* but Germans still have to make room for and with non-Indigenous residents. It's not comfortable to be metaphorically patted on the head as an acceptable minority in Germany, simply because I am *indian*. After twenty-eight years, I am still torn as to how to discuss Indianthusiasm. Masquerading as Indigenous peoples (from a pre-reservation-era past, or only on weekends, dressed in meticulously designed powwow regalia) is active erasure and epistemicide. Having lived there, I know that marketing, advertisements, and the overall praise of and playing as *indians* will

not stop in my lifetime. Additionally, there are connected Indigenous people, originally from communities on Turtle Island, who now call Germany
home, full-time. Their children are registered or status and are growing up
speaking German. Out of respect for their personal lives and experiences –
which include a yearning to find Indigenous community connections in
Germany, and in some cases have found this through Indianthusiasm – I
choose not to be reactively critical. They all miss home (the communities
and nations they are from in North America), but their children and future
grandchildren, their loves and lives, are across the pond and they have established careers there. As these generations grow up alongside Indianthusiasts,
dialogue and conversations will flourish. Indigenous responses to Indianthusiasm are essential for some sort of cross-cultural understanding. In her
interview, describing the process and methodology of *Enowkinwix*ʷ and its
role in active listening with an open heart and mind, Jeannette Armstrong
said it best: "if you're not informed, you shouldn't trust your assumptions.
You shouldn't trust your own analysis. You should listen to all the data, and
allow that to accumulate, and then you will form a new assumption, and a
new understanding therefore." In seeking understanding from what my late
father told me, whose memory I hold dear, we also seek *hózhǫ́* to come to
harmony, wellness, and balance. It is in this spirit that I continue my own
learning and healing journey.

Ahéhee', thank you, for all those who've given their time and shared their
stories in this anthology.

Florentine Strzelczyk

I came to this project through a number of different paths, academic, professional, and personal, all of which have been touched by what I learned in
working on this volume. Indigenous methodologies and research approaches
have been central for me to articulate why a volume on Indianthusiasm matters to Indigenous peoples today. The Indigenous contributors to this volume
and their views on the legacies of genocide and colonialism in both Germany
and Canada have deepened my commitment to work toward decolonization
of the post-secondary institutions that have been so deeply implicated in
creating and perpetuating colonial and racialized mindsets about Indigenous
peoples. My personal background as a first-generation immigrant woman of
mixed ethnicity, my research on genocide, and my administrative work on
the university's Indigenous strategy led me to this project, and the teachings
I take from it have impressed on me that actively listening to the experiences,
histories, and viewpoints of those who have consistently been excluded from
the dominant account of history is the starting point for decolonization.

My academic work has evolved around national narratives in culture, including film and literature. I have worked on genocide, in particular the Holocaust and how this event has locked both victims and perpetrators into specific discourses and responses that have influenced how Germans view others in their midst and others in faraway places. Through one slice of my academic work on literary narratives about Germans encountering First Nations when they came to Canada in the early twentieth century, I met Hartmut Lutz and then Renae Watchman. Their research on Indianthusiasm and hobbyism and my work converged in a common interest in how cultural representations support and enforce existing ideologies that in turn perpetuate political injustice. When I embarked on this project, my initial aim was to understand better the complexities of a transatlantic dialogue that began centuries ago.

The Indigenous contributors used their German experiences to reflect on European and Canadian histories of colonialism, genocide, and contemporary identity politics, and the discussions resulted in a deeper understanding of the complex power dynamics between Indigenous people and Europeans, a topic compellingly addressed by Jace Weaver in *The Red Atlantic*. Indigenous peoples, as politicians, diplomats, labourers, slaves, performers, and travellers, brought resources and knowledge, and their accounts of what they experienced shaped world history. As "cosmopolitan agents" of transnational dialogue and exchange, they acquired knowledge about other societies that enabled them to advocate for their own sovereignty, a sovereignty that was challenged and eventually controlled by the colonial powers before and around 1800 (2014, vii–xiv). Weaver discusses German Indianthusiasm (without using this term) at the end of his book and shows how, ironically, May's fictional German depiction of *Indianer* influenced how Americans thought of Indigenous peoples (2014, 256). This volume extends this transatlantic conversation into the present.

While the concept of Indianthusiasm is steeped in colonial history and designed to fix Indigenous people in a mythical past, the volume demonstrates that this fictional concept has ironically and surprisingly opened opportunities for Indigenous artists, scholars, writers, thinkers, performers, and storytellers to challenge German narratives about Indianthusiasm through their work in Germany. Waubgeshig Rice explicitly calls himself a "mythbuster" who created educational opportunities for Germans to confront the popular fictions they hold about Indigenous peoples. Other contributors educate through satire and comedy (Drew Hayden Taylor), documentary (John Blackbird), or authentic performance (Quentin Pipestem). Ahmoo Angeconeb's approach and response to Indianthusiam is consciously hybrid and conceptual, intertwining and playing against one another medieval German notions and symbols with representations of Indigenous peoples and their symbols. His work is a bricolage, a conscious creation of a work of art from diverse media and sources; it blends styles so as to draw out the mythical pasts and political present of two cultures in conversation with each other.

Indianthusiasm has also prompted German scholars not just to understand and critique this fictional concept, but also to build strong relationships with real Indigenous peoples, bringing their concerns to the forefront of European scholarship. Hartmut is one of those well-known European scholars who have worked extensively and collaboratively with Indigenous communities. His work has prompted Indigenous peoples to pursue PhDs in Germany instead of in Canada. Jo-Ann Episkenew and Jeannette Armstrong worked with Hartmut because the German system's emphasis on original research enabled them to introduce Indigenous methodologies and approaches into their dissertations. That led to productive academic careers, empowering them to push forward Indigenous research at their institutions and to teach their supervisors as much as they learned from them. For me, these transatlantic dialogues contained a number of surprising twists that shed new light on the cosmopolitanism and agency of Indigenous artists and thinkers.

As a scholar of the Holocaust and post–Second World War memory discourses, I am aware of how a traumatic genocidal past surfaces in the present, shaping contemporary national politics, mainstream culture, public debates, and institutions such as museums, schools, and universities. I was struck by how much the German legacy of National Socialism, as one of the sources that fuelled Indianthusiasm, formed a point of reference for a number of the discussion partners to reflect on how nations go about addressing their genocidal legacies. Warren Cariou, Jo-Ann Episkenew, Jeannette Armstrong, Audrey Huntley, and others utilize their German experience to reflect deeply on the complex points of convergence and divergence in European and North American histories of appropriation, reflections that zero in on how nations confront and cover the traces of their violent pasts.

To me, one of the most delightful aspects of this volume resides in side remarks, thematic detours, casual observations, and humorous stories that a number of the discussion partners relate during the interviews. José David Saldívar, in his compelling 1991 book *The Dialectics of America*, calls for "a new trans-geographical conception of American culture, one more responsive to the hemisphere's geographical ties and political crosscurrents than to narrow national ideologies" (xi–xii). Such a transgeographical dynamic opens the long-standing lockdown between Indigenous peoples and settlers in Canada to a conversation with other voices, from other perspectives.

Jo-Ann Episkenew relates in her interview almost guiltily how good it felt to be actually liked by mainstream Germans she encountered in Germany, knowing full well that such positive attitudes stem from a problematic fascination with an idealized fictional Indigenous essence. Episkenew describes how adversarial interactions between Indigenous and non-Indigenous people play out on a daily basis in Canada, and how much emotional energy Indigenous people invest in countering the daily racism they experience. Warren Cariou tells the funny story about his family's expectations about German environmentalism and their essentially failed attempt to live up to these expectations, fully aware of the irony that German environmentalists feel a deep connection to Indigenous peoples as the original custodians of environmental protection. The transgeographical perspectives evident in every interview seemed to bring into sharper focus for the contributors the historical, economic, and structural injustices that have to be addressed in order to achieve reconciliation. To me, the side conversations about literary theory contemplated from a cultural distance (Cariou), humour (Taylor), and how people form relationships to the land (Armstrong) are central to this volume's purpose, which is to trace transatlantic connections as well as Indigenous agency, both of which continue to intervene in national dialogues across time and space.

This project has strengthened my belief that the intellectual, professional, and personal aspects of identity must all be engaged in fuelling and enacting change. Over the past seven years, I have been increasingly involved at University of Calgary in committees that address Indigenous student, faculty, and institutional issues. From an intellectual standpoint, this was the right thing to do. But it was only when I participated in community consultations and in listening circles that I began to appreciate the experiences of Indigenous peoples today. This project has solidified my commitment to listen to the truth in stories. The conversations about Indianthusiasm brought together in this volume resulted in a set of highly diverse individual viewpoints that offered critical interventions into this problematic German discourse. Along the way they also prompted me to reflect on the connection points between national histories and legacies of colonialism and genocide. It is the deeply personal, ironic, humorous, and critical accounts that bring these discourses to life and that mark the value of this book for me and hopefully also for its readers.

I am deeply grateful to all involved in this project, to my collaborators and friends, Renae Watchman and Hartmut Lutz, from whom I learned so much, and to the Indigenous artists, intellectuals, critics, and performers interviewed, whose insights and experiences have surprised, amazed, and also humbled me.

Hartmut Lutz

It was a long and challenging learning experience for me to work on this book, and I am profoundly grateful to all who contributed, especially to Florentine and Renae for their enthusiasm, friendship, commitment, and stamina. I have studied Indianthusiasm as one expression of German racism for more than four decades, but through this project, I have learned things about Germany and myself of which I had not been so aware before. All through my youth and adult life I have lived with the legacy of the Holocaust and the Second World War. Whenever I went abroad or heard others talk about Germany and Germans, I expected yet another reference to Germans frozen in time as being either racist and arrogant Nazis (e.g., as depicted on the cover of this book: two SS officers stealing the Mona Lisa) or imbecilic but jolly beer drinkers in *Lederhosen*. I would become anxious and nervous, feel hurt or defensive, sad, ashamed, and utterly helpless to undo the past. In that depression it must have slipped by my consciousness that negative reactions to my German-ness, which I experienced frequently during my travels as a younger person, had abated over time, and that today there are people out there who, though aware of our past, are recognizing that Germans do not all fit the stereotypes, and that there are even some developments in contemporary Germany which they find commendable.

Just two weeks ago while working on this book, I experienced something like an epiphany, and I said to Ruth, to whom I have been married for longer than my involvement in Native Studies, "Ich habe mir eigentlich nie verziehen Deutscher zu sein" (I never really forgave myself for being German). After reading the interviews, and after thinking more about my inability to let go of the shame, sadness, and futility, hugging a past beyond my control, I feel more inclined now to at least try to wrap all those shameful images, feelings of sadness, memories, and painfully haunting family stories into a separate mental bundle, not to throw them out, but to contain them, open for scrutiny if need be, but no longer as cancerous debris cluttering my path in old age.

All of the Indigenous scholars and artists we asked seem to be aware of how prevalent the Holocaust is in German historical consciousness, and several of them speak about our attempts to address our history without denial. Yet it was a surprise for me to hear some of the interviewees say that they themselves did not experience pronounced racism in Germany. While I am glad for those who did not encounter it, I know that racism and antisemitism are prevalent. With more than a million refugees having arrived in less than two years in Germany, including in regions where there had been practically no contact before with people from other cultures, and with the social and logistic problems all unorganized mass immigrations entail, racists and Nazis express their hatred more openly today. There have been arson attacks, and there have been murders. The asylum seekers, whom I volunteered to teach German for two years once a week in nearby Anklam (northeastern Germany), talked about the closed faces and verbal insults they encountered from Germans in the streets. Some of the Indigenous visitors who did not encounter racism were protected by the academic or hobbyist environments they moved within, or perhaps their appearance shielded them. Several of them realized also that Indianthusiasm saved them from being treated like Turkish Germans or other minorities, and they utilized it for their own benefit. Quentin Pipestem's experiences with people in Templin confirm my observation, that alas, neo-Nazism is *not* incompatible with Indianthusiasm.

In the beautiful and wide-open (by German measure) countryside where Ruth and I live, close to the Baltic Sea and the Polish border, there are numerous wind-parks (often the giant rotor blades are stopped because they are producing more energy than is needed or can be transmitted). This aspect of environmental protection seems commonplace to us. I grew up with "biological-dynamic" gardening – no chemicals touched "our" earth, and our compost would mature for four years before being recycled to fertilize – and today I follow that tradition. People in Germany habitually recycle, and kids in schools learn about environmental protection. We can buy local products, including fish and venison (if we have the money), we have toad and frog migration fences, many of us ride bicycles or walk to work, we have wide and forested "deer bridges" across some of our *Autobahns*, we drink our tap water without fear. Those things are so normal to me that I was not aware of them as anything remarkable, until Warren Cariou, Jeannette Armstrong, and others found them so.

Another thing that became clearer to me through this book project is how ethnocentric we in Germany tend to be when defining who is German. We tend to have very little awareness of, or interest in, people of German descent living outside our borders. While emigrants "abroad" may self-identify as Germans even while holding a Canadian passport, we tend not to think of them as "really" German, especially if they no longer speak the language, whereas people in Canada see them as German, and Indigenous contributors we talked to share this perception. I am not sure where our thoughtless lack of empathy with German emigrants comes from. Maybe it is a reaction against the ethnocentric approach during the Nazi period that appropriated as *Volksdeutsch* (ethnically German) any one of German origin (except for Jews and others not deemed "pure"). But it may also be quite simply that we feel left behind with our national problems by those who left, especially if they emigrated after the Second World War. Both possibilities would attest to how deeply the historical past impacts our reactions to issues of national identity. Listening to Indigenous people talk about Germans in North America is helping me see German-ness as more complexly comprehensive than before.

My perception of German Indianthusiasm is also changing. For decades, I had little but (arrogant) ridicule for *indian* hobbyists in Germany, finding them politically naive appropriators and ideologically suspicious escapists, and I was careful to deny any connections with them. After having met some of them personally as colleagues in East Germany, and especially after now hearing Indigenous knowledge holders talk about German Indianthusiasts, I do not feel so self-righteous anymore, and I understand better my own motivations and growing involvement in Indigenous Studies. Here, I humbly acknowledge and gratefully accept that my grandfather, Hermann Reinke (1882-1967), instilled in me as a child that common German fascination with *Indianer*, to which I then returned almost two decades later as a politically conscious academic with a PhD, eager to "enlighten" Germans about our own racism. My approach to Indigenous Studies came via political activism, not through ethnology or other scholarly pursuits. Leftist intellectuals in the late sixties were not exactly prone to analyze the emotional side of their activism, and I denied the empathetic connection between my own juvenile Indianthusiasm and my nascent interest in Native American Studies (and later Canadian Indigenous Studies). Several of the contributors to this book understand this connection very clearly, and they point out that German Indianthusiastic interest in Indigenous cultures from Turtle Island may be utilized to initiate the dialogic learning process, which is direly needed if we are to continue on our planet. In this context, it is encouraging that Western academia is beginning to provide platforms for First Nation, Métis, and Inuit knowledge holders to teach increasing numbers of non-Aboriginals who are ready to listen. This book, I hope, will add to this dialogue, by laying open the distortions necessarily entailed in any processes of refraction, and by adding another morsel to the construction of a transatlantic bridge of knowledge.

Thank you all for contributing to this effort.

NOTES

INTRODUCTION

1 The German text of the advertisement reads: "Segeberger Kliniken / Gesucht: Blutsbrüder und – schwestern / für unser Herzzentrum in Bad Segeberg für das Herzkathederlabor und für die Radiologie suchen wir Medizinisch-technische Radiologieassistenten (m/w) oder Medizinische Fachangestellte (m/w) / Wir sind ein fortschrittlicher Arbeitgeber und als familiengeführtes Gesundheitsunternehmen mit 1.000 Betten erfolgreich in den Bereichen Akutmedizin, Rehabilitation und Prävention in Bad Segeberg – Stadt der Karl-May-Spiele. / Weitere Informationen unter: ..."

2 At times we refrained from changing Indian to *indian* (e.g., North American Indian, Blood Indian) when referencing living Indigenous peoples. *indian* was used to signify the representation, the fiction, as conceptualized by Anishinaabe critic Gerald Vizenor: "Native names and identities are inscrutable constructions; the ironic suit [*sic*] of discoveries, histories, memories, and many clusters of stories. Native identities and the sense of self are the tricky traces of solace and heard stories; the tease of creations, an innermost brush with natural reason, precarious visions, and unbounded narcissism. The *indians* are the simulations, the derivative nouns and adjectives of dominance, and not the same set as natives, the *indigène*, or an indigenous native, in the sense of a native presence on the continent ... The *indians* are that uncertain thing of discoveries, and the absence of natives, some*thing* otherwise in the simulations of the other culture. Natives are elusive creations; the *indigène*, that real sense of presence, memories, and coincidence is borne in native stories ... native stories must tease out of the truisms of culture exclusions and the trumperies of simulations." Vizenor, *Fugitive Poses*, pp. 69–70.

3 For a discussion of the beginnings of the appropriation ("whiteshamanism") debate in the United States in the late 1960s and its beginnings in Canada in the late 1990s ("stop stealing Native stories"), see Lutz (2002, pp. 75–97).

4 www.indigenousliterarystudies.org/-indigenous-voices-award.

5 The distorted representations that non-Indigenous writers and artists have created of North American Indigenous peoples have been discussed in a range of critical studies on both sides of the Atlantic. See the bibliographical entries for Barnett; Bataille; Berkhofer; Briese; Calloway et al.; Churchill; Colin; Deloria; Feest; Fiedler; Fitz; Francis; Friar and Friar; Haible; Huhndorf; Lutz; D.B. Smith; Usbeck; and Zantop.

6 Including Absolon, Andersen and O'Brien, Archibald, Battiste and Henderson, Brandt-Castellano, Cajete, Cole, Deloria, Ermine, Kovach, Kurtz, Martin, L. Smith, S. Smith, Weber-Pillwax, Wilson, and Younging.

7   The conference, "Deutsche und Indianer/Indianer und Deutsche: Cultural Encounters across Three Centuries," turned into a volume of edited essays: Calloway et al., eds. (2002).

8   Two Two's story is captured in the 2012 documentary *Bury My Heart in Dresden* by Bettina Renner: see promo at https://www.youtube.com/watch?v=mnXIfL6Npm0. For an "insider's" account of being exhibited in Hagenbeck's Zoo and other locations in Europe, where he eventually died, see Lutz (2005).

9   Hassrick et al. (1984).

10 Reagin's essay analyzes the German Western fan community using media studies methodology and fan scholarship. While this is an insightful method, Reagin's mistakes regrettably overshadow her intended findings.

11 See for example the works by Christian Feest, Anthony Pagden, Ray Allen Billington, Daniel Francis, Pamela Kort and Max Hollein, H. Glenn Penny, and Michelle Thompson.

12 The following sources attest to the ongoing German and European Indianthusiasm: "Ich bin ein Indianer," *The Walrus*, https://thewalrus.ca/ich-bin-ein-indianer, by Adam Gilders; Red Haircrow's "Germany's Obsession with American Indians Is Touching – and Occasionally Surreal"; Haircrow's 2018 documentary, *Forget Winnetou! Loving in the Wrong Way*; Wir sind Helden's song *Wenn es passiert*; Romano's *Klaps auf den Po* https://vimeo.com/135335858; MDR, "Die Hobby Indianer," http://reportage.mdr.de/hobby indianer#2465; Mandan Indians of Taucha, http://www.mandan-taucha.de/powwow .htm; Indianermuseum, Derenburg, http://indianermuseum.jimdo.com/bilder-pictures; Fasching/Karneval parade in Derenburg, https://www.youtube.com/watch?v=YE _xSKoY8tE; Powwowthusiasts, powwow-kalendar.de; Indianerwoche, https://www.you tube.com/watch?v=uqWrgz4uNGE; Nahnda Garlow, "Indians in Russia: It's Not a Fairy Tale," *Two Row Times*, 4 August 2014, https://tworowtimes.com/columns/indians-in -russia-its-not-a-fairy-tale; "Last of the Munichans: Inside Europe's 'Indianists' subculture," by Monika Bauerlein, August 2015; http://www.motherjones.com/media/2015/07/ europeans-dressed-as-native-americans-photos; "German Indians," 1997/98, photoshow, http://robbinsbecher.com/projects/germanindians; "Dressing up as cowboys and Indians is big in Germany: Native Americans aren't amused," by Jason Overdorf, *The Sentinal.com*, 10 June 2014.

13 Philip Deloria pointed to the constructedness of "authenticity," arguing that it is a "culturally constructed category created in opposition to a perceived state of inauthenticity" (1998, p. 101).

14 Penny cites the interview in two of his works: *Kindred by Choice* (2013, p. 4), and "Not Playing Indian" (2014, p. 171).

15 Some of the papers presented at that conference were later published in a special issue of *Zeitschrift für Kanada-Studien* on "Indigenous Knowledges and Academic Discourses," edited by Kerstin Knopf (Sonderband, 2018).

16 Janssen, Gross, Knopf, Lutz, Mackenthun and Hock, Sarkowsky.

17 Dürr; von Foerster and Floyd; von Mutius; Ott.

18 See the bibliography under Taiaiake Alfred; Richard Atleo; Lisa Brooks; John Carlson; Jeff Corntassel; Jo-Ann Episkenew; Margaret Kovach; Rauna Kuokkanen; Dennis Runnels; Karla Jessen Williamson; Shawn Wilson.

19 Mr. Angeconeb preferred this spelling of Anishnaabe. Others in the book preferred the spelling Anishinaabe.

20 This academic is none other than Hartmut Lutz.

21 At the time we interviewed Taylor, he had ideas about a documentary, which has recently been released. In 2018, *Searching for Winnetou* was released by the CBC. https://www .cbc.ca/cbcdocspov/episodes/searching-for-winnetou.

22 Drew Hayden Taylor's works have received substantial critical attention from German literary scholars in Native Studies. Birgit Däwes in her foundational research on *Native*

North American Theater (2007) focuses extensively on his stories and plays, and Eva Gruber, in her study on *Humor in Contemporary Native North American Literature* (2008), also deals substantially with Taylor and especially Thomas King.

23 When the Anishinaabe residents become increasingly disillusioned with the Ojibway World project, one of the characters remarks, "I am becoming less and less enchanted with these Germans," to which another replies: "I know. Who could have thought that they could be so mean and efficient" (76). As a result of the Second World War and the Holocaust, mercilessness and efficiency have become stock ingredients in the stereotyped German mindset. Taylor's character expresses an observation that echoes a passage by the British Nobel Prize–winning novelist William Golding, who described, in the 1960s, German tourists in Stratford-upon-Avon "doing" Shakespeare's birthplace with "cheap and merciless efficiency." Lutz, *William Golding*, p. 58.

INTERVIEWS

1 The fact that historically the Ojibway (Anishinaabe) displaced the easternmost Sioux (Dakota) and drove them farther west has given rise to much intertribal bantering between Anishinaabe and Dakota people.

2 Karl May, *Winnetou*, trans. David Koblick (Pullman, WA: Washington State University Press, 1989).

3 This is a reference to a drawing Ahmoo Angeconeb gave to students in Greifswald for a book publication. The artist has repeatedly donated some of his prints and drawings as illustrations to be used in bilingual anthologies of poetry and prose by contemporary Aboriginal authors from Canada which have been published in Germany – for example, Hartmut Lutz and Osnabrück students, eds. (1993). *Four Feathers: Poems and Stories by Canadian Native Authors*; and Hartmut Lutz and Greifswald students, editors, *Heute sind wir hier / We Are Here Today: A Bilingual Collection of Contemporary Aboriginal Literature(s) from Canada*. In 1991 Ahmoo also donated a set of eight drawings to the library of the University of Osnabrück, which thanks to Dr. Sabine Meyer have been proudly displayed in the main meeting room of the Institute for British and American Studies at the University of Osnabrück since 2015. The works of Ahmoo Angeconeb have literally left an imprint on German academia.

4 Besides his individual exhibitions in Basel, Berlin, and Cologne, Angeconeb also had a joint exhibition together with fellow Anishinaabe artists Blake Debassige and Roy Thomas. The show travelled to several German cities under the title "Anishnabe Art: Ojibway Künstler aus Kanada." It was co-sponsored by Canadian governmental and private donors as well as by several German universities and the Gesellschaft für Kanada-Studien (Canadian Studies Association).

5 On its opening day, 12 September 1989, Hartmut Lutz visited the En'Owkin International School of Native Writing in Penticton, BC, and on the following day Jeannette and he had a recorded conversation that formed the first essay in the book *Contemporary Challenges: Conversations with Canadian Native Authors*, authored and edited by Hartmut Lutz, Fifth House, 1991. Hartwig Isernhagen, a renowned German scholar of North American Studies at the University of Basel, Switzerland, visited the En'Owkin Centre on 10 August 1994; there, he and Jeannette had an extended in-depth conversation on Native literatures, which was later published in Isernhagen (1999, pp. 135–83).

6 Konrad Ott, who then held the only professorial chair in environmental ethics in Germany, was Jeannette's co-supervisor for her interdisciplinary PhD in Environmental Ethics and Canadian (Native) Literature at the University of Greifwald, Germany, completed in 2010: *Constructing Indigeneity: Syilx Okanagan Oraliture and tmix^{w}centrism*.

7   The "Oka Crisis": From 11 June until 26 September 1990, the Mohawk people of Kane-satake, Quebec, blocked and then occupied their burial ground, on which the town of Oka, Quebec, wanted to extend their golf course. In an unprecedented act of Indigenous solidarity with the Mohawks, Indigenous peoples and their friends throughout Turtle Island rose in support, staging demonstrations, road blocks, prayer vigils, and multiple acts of civil disobedience. The Canadian government reacted by calling in the army, and the tense standoff lasted for months, costing the lives of two people and damaging the property and mental well-being of far too many. Jeannette Armstrong and her husband Marlowe Sam were involved in solidarity actions with the Oka resistance. For a history of the event, see York and Pindera (1991). For an "inside" film documentary, see Obom-sawin (1993).

8   "Gustafsen Lake" was a one-month stand-off (18 August–17 September) in 1995 in British Columbia during which Shuswap and other First Nations people defended the site of their (6th) Sun Dance at Gustafsen Lake against a massive RCMP paramilitary presence. There were several shoot-outs, but fortunately only one person was injured. Here again Jeannette Armstrong and her husband Marlowe Sam were involved in de-escalating the situation. For more on Marlowe Sam's argument that being a warrior is not about dying but about saving lives, see Sam (1996, pp. 11–13). In German: "Den Krieg heute aufnehmen," in Armstrong (1996, pp. 241–44).

9   Wounded Knee, on the Rosebud Reservation in South Dakota, is the site where, around Christmas 1890, the 7th US Cavalry massacred about three hundred Lakota men, women, and children. In 1973 the American Indian Movement (AIM) occupied the same site to protest the corrupt leadership of tribal chairman Dick Wilson and his goon squad on the neighbouring Pine Ridge Reservation. The siege of Wounded Knee by the FBI, vigilantes, and security forces using heavy military equipment lasted from 27 February until 8 May 1973, and led to international support for AIM. For a Native American account of the siege, see Akwesasne Notes (1974).

10 Public talk held at the University of Calgary as part of a larger series.

11 The En'Owkin School of International Writing opened on 13 September 1989, in Pent-icton, BC. It was initiated by Jeannette Armstrong, who served as its director for about a decade. It was accredited with the University of Victoria.

12 Three years after earning her DPhil at the University of Greifswald, Germany, Jeannette Armstrong was appointed Canada Research Chair in Okanagan Indigenous Knowledge and Philosophy at the University of British Columbia Okanagan, where she still teaches.

13 In 2006, Jo-Ann Episkenew was awarded her DPhil in Canadian Native Literature at the University of Greifswald, Germany, based on an excellent thesis titled "Beyond Catharsis: Truth, Reconciliation and Healing in and through Indigenous Literature." Her thesis was later published as a book under the title *Taking Back Our Spirits: Indigenous Literature, Public Policy, and Healing*. It has won several prestigious prizes. A professor in the English Department of the First Nations University of Canada, Dr. Episkenew took leave from that institution to serve as director of the Indigenous Peoples' Health Research Centre (IPHRC) at the University of Regina. Tragically, Jo-Ann Episkenew died suddenly early in 2016.

14 In the fall of 2012, in conjunction with a Killam Visiting Professorship in Native Lit-erature, the University of Calgary's (then) Department of Germanic, Slavic, and East Asian Studies, chaired by Florentine Strzelczyk, together with the university's Native Visitor Centre (director: Shawna Cunningham), hosted a series of readings and talks by prominent Aboriginal authors, engaging town and gown about Aboriginal literatures and related issues in Canada.

15 Mimicking Charlie Hill's "Hi, how are you?" skit, featured on the Richard Pryor Show in 1977 https://www.youtube.com/watch?v=545t5SvcyDo.

16 *Powwow* is still distributed by Moving Images; the documentary *Indianer* is viewable online on YouTube.

17 The magazine was published by Carol Quattro Levine and was called *Nativevue*.

18 Briese (2005).

19 *Volkshochschulen* (literally: peoples' high schools) are a type of open university educational institution common in Germany; they offer courses, entire programs, and workshops on a broad variety of areas independent of the prior qualifications of its attendants.

20 Translated by Olaf Nollmeyer.

21 Métis is not a tribal affiliation. To maintain consistency throughout the book, we did not put quotes around tribal affilitation, but it is notable here, and in Episkenew's interview, that this question elicited grimaces and humour from them.

22 Robinson (2000).

23 Wolfgang Klooss, Professor Emeritus of Angophone Literatures at the University of Trier, the partner institution of the University of Manitoba, is co-founder of the Canadian Studies Association in Germany and one of Germany's foremost Canadianists, honoured by a Canadian Governor General's Award. After a PhD in postcolonial African Literature, Klooss wrote his *Habilitationsschrift* (post-doctoral thesis required of German career academics wishing to qualify for a university professorship) on Métis history and the portrayal of Louis Riel and Métis people in Canadian anglophone (and francophone) literature. To meet Kiel University's (then) requirements, he wrote and published his *Habilitationsschrift* in German, so that this unsurpassed source is unfortunately unavailable and practically unknown in Canada: *Geschichte und Mythos in der Literatur Kanadas: Die englischsprachige Métis und Riel-Rezeption* (1989).

24 See Lutz (2014).

25 Lutz and Greifswald students (2005).

26 Berlin is actually home to the largest Turkish community outside of Turkey.

27 For example, Warren Cariou, *Lake of the Prairies: A Story of Belonging* (Doubleday Canada, 2002).

28 Cariou and McArthur (2009b).

29 "Prora" is the name of a small Baltic seaside resort on the island of Rügen, where during the Nazi era between 1936–1939, a gigantic, five-storey edifice was erected that stretches 4.5 kilometres along the beach in a prime location. Originally designed as part of the Nazi government's "Kraft durch Freude" (strength through joy) recreational program aimed at low-income German Nazi families, the monstrous building was never fully completed. After the war the Russians tried and failed to blow up the structure, and it was eventually used for army barracks in the GDR. After reunification and decades of decay with agonizing ideological debates about its future, including many abortive attempts to find a proper use for it – memorials, museums, recreational facilities – it is now gradually being converted into what it was originally designed for – thousands of apartments right by the beach. These will be interspersed with museums and facilities that hopefully will not erase or deny its shameful history.

30 When visiting Auschwitz, Warren Cariou was shocked to find a building named "Canada." His experiences are reflected in his essay "Going to Canada" (2009a).

31 Hartmut would like to thank his former colleague Dr. Anette Brauer of Greifswald University for sharing her experiences with and thoughts and research on East German Indianistik groups with him.

32 After having been directed to studies by Lewis H. Morgan by his friend and collaborator Karl Marx, Friedrich Engels wrote in *Der Ursprung der Familie, des Privateigentums und des Staats* (The Origin of the Family, Private Property and the State, an enraptured chapter (pp. 96–111) about the Seneca and their constitution, which he described as "primitive

communist," that is, pre-capitalist and pre-industrial. For a brief discussion of how Engels was torn between the Eurocentric structural racism of his time and his almost romantic enthusiasm for Haudenosaunee liberty, egalitarianism, and sisterhood, see Lutz (2002, pp. 77–79).

33 There are several villages along the Baltic and North Sea coasts called "Wiek" or "Wyk," including one right next to Greifswald spelled "Wieck," with which Warren Cariou is familiar.

34 Attending classes wasn't a requirement in this program, except for taking part in and presenting at a "Doktorandenkolloquium" (colloquium for PhD students) once a term and staying in touch with the supervisor throughout the years it took to research and write the thesis.

35 While researching and writing her *Magister* (master's thesis) on Aboriginal women and film in Canada, Kerstin Knopf won a scholarship from the German Academic Research Service that allowed her to spend six months in 1986 at the Saskatchewan Indian Federated College, to which she returned in 1998 for research on her PhD project. The recipient of numerous fellowships and research awards, Kerstin Knopf has since published a number of books in Indigenous Studies, including *Decolonizing the Lens of Power: Indigenous Films in North America* (2008), *Aboriginal Canada Revisited* (2008), and *North America in the 21st Century* (2011). In accordance with the traditional German career requirements for university professors, she did her "Habilitation" – her second PhD – in another field, which resulted in *The Female Canadian Gothic: Nineteenth-Century Women's Literature at the Interface between Romance and Horror* (2012). She has also published research in other areas, such as environmental, North American, women's, film, and postcolonial studies. She now holds the professorship in Postcolonial Literary and Cultural Studies at the University of Bremen, Germany.

36 Jo-Ann Episkenew's doctoral thesis, "Beyond Catharsis: Truth, Reconciliation, and Healing In and Through Indigenous Literature," came out in book form under the title *Taking Back our Spirits: Indigenous Literature, Public Policy, and Healing*, and won two prestigious awards in Canada: the Saskatchewan Book Award for Scholarly Writing (2009) and the Saskatchewan Book Award for First People's Writing (2010).

37 Before coming to Germany for the first time, Jo-Ann Episkenew shared that her relatives were very wary of neo-Nazi skinheads, especially in eastern Germany.

38 The badges were of right-wing slogans in English. Jo-Ann realized that Nazi symbols were commodified.

39 Jo-Ann Episkenew was an invited speaker at the 32nd annual conference of the German Association for Canadian Studies (Gesellschaft für Kanada-Studien) in Grainau, Bavaria, held 25–27 February 2011. The conference topic was "Rethinking Post/Colonialism." She spoke about "Neo-colonial Canada: Colonizing Indigenous Imaginations."

40 In the 1990s, several students from the University of Osnabrück won exchange scholarships to study at the Saskatchewan Indian Federated College (SIFC) in Regina, Saskatchewan.

41 Dr. Bernard Selinger was, for many years, head of the English Department at SIFC.

42 Paskievich (1995).

43 Coleman (2005).

44 Hartmut Lutz was a guest professor at the Saskatchewan Indian Federated College (SIFC), now the First Nations University of Canada, from April 1990 to March 1991.

45 This is a reference to the Canadian Forces station at Iserlohn-Hemer, about 25 kilometres from Hagen, West Germany.

46 Chrystos is one of the best-known contemporary Indigenous poets in North America and one of the most radical activists on behalf of Indigenous women. While networking

internationally with feminists and lesbians of colour worldwide, she also has an active profile as a Native reader and speaker in Canada and the United States. Among her numerous books of poetry, with Press Gang publishers in Vancouver, are *Not Vanishing* (1988), *Dream On* (1991), and *In Her I Am* (1993).

47 Chrystos came to Germany for a reading tour in 1997. That same year, Audrey Huntley translated and edited a selection of short prose and poetry by Chrystos under the title *Wilder Reis* (Wild Rice). She published this book with the prestigious Orlanda Frauenverlag in Berlin, a publisher instrumental in disseminating works by multicultural lesbian, transgender, and feminist authors in German translation.

48 Huntley (1996).

49 Chrystos (1997, pp. 148–51).

50 Armstrong (1997); Lutz, "Nachwort" (1997); Sam, "Den Krieg heute aufnehmen" (1997).

51 Chrystos, *Wilder Reis*.

52 Lorde (1993)

53 Armstrong, "I Study Rocks / Ich betrachte Steine," in Lutz et. al., eds. (1993, pp. 46–53).

54 Armstrong (2009).

55 Black Elk ([1932]1972). While this "as-told-to" autobiography contains Black Elk's famous vision (pp. 19–39), his second book gives an account of Oglala Lakota religious practice: Black Elk ([1953]1971). For a study of how Lakota spirituality is appropriated, exploited, and marketed by New Age practitioners in Austria, Switzerland, and Germany, see Briese (2005).

56 Eva Gruber's comprehensive study, *Humor in Contemporary Native North American Literature: Reimagining Nativeness,* Camden House, 2008, based on her PhD thesis that was successfully defended at the University of Konstanz in Germany, discusses many of Thomas King's works.

57 Karl May travelled to the United States in 1908.

58 Paskievich (1995).

59 King discusses "dead *indians*" in his book *The Inconvenient Indian.*

60 At the time this interview was recorded, Thomas King was visiting Calgary as part of a cross-continental reading tour for this new book.

61 Lutz (2003a).

62 Watchman (2005).

63 Thomas King's novel *Truth and Bright Water* (Harper Flamingo), came out in 1999, and on the back cover blurb it states that the author "is of Cherokee and Greek descent." Blurbs on the covers of earlier books stated that his heritage was Cherokee, Greek, and German.

64 The Dunkers (*Tunker*), or German Baptists, are a Protestant group founded in Germany after the Thirty Years' War (1618–48). Persecuted like the Amish and Mennonite, many of them fled to America.

65 David T. McNab is married to Ute Lischke, a German-born professor of German Literature and Film Studies, Canadian First Nations, and Native American Literature at Wilfrid Laurier University in Waterloo, Ontario.

66 In the Haldimand Grant of 25 October 1784, the Six Nations were granted in perpetuity the territory "Six Miles deep from each side of the River beginning at Lake Erie and extending in the proportion to the Head of Said River, which Them and Their Posterity are to enjoy forever." The Bear (later the Grand) River was included in the Haldimand Grant of 1784. Today the Six Nations Reserve near Brantford, Ontario, comprises only a small fraction of the original Haldimand Grant, which had been set aside for the loyalist Six Nations [Iroquois / Haudenosaunee] under the Mohawk chief Joseph Brant. Six Nations had lost their territories in the United States after having fought for the British

against the rebels during the American Revolution, and had to seek exile in Upper Canada to escape Washington's wrath.

67   The Haudenosaunee or Iroquois Confederacy, bonded by "The Great Law of Peace," were originally founded by the (listed from east to west) Mohawk, Oneida, Onondaga, Cayuga, and Seneca; the Tuscarora joined them in the early eighteenth century, thus forming the Six Nations.

68   Cumberland House, on the South Saskatchewan River in northeastern Saskatchewan, was a very early Hudson's Bay Company trading post and is now adjacent to the Cree First Nation Reserve by that name – ancestral Cree and Métis territory.

69   The prominent Canadian playwright, poet, and university professor Daniel David Moses, FRCS, is a Delaware who grew up on and is registered at the Six Nations Reserve on the Grand River.

70   The famous Two Row Wampum – a belt woven of beads made of dark (purple) and white wampum shells – marks a 1613 treaty between Dutch colonists and the Haudenosaunee or Iroquois Confederacy. The two dark parallel stripes running the total length of the wampum signify the two separate but equal nations travelling each in their own vessel/ canoe, the Dutch and the Haudenosaunee, moving alongside each other in peace and mutual respect, not interfering with the affairs of the other but respecting each other's independence and sovereignty.

71   McNab is being ironic here, implying that by marrying Indigenous people, Germans are transgressing the non-interference implied in the Two Row Wampum.

72   Lischke and McNab, eds. (2005, pp. 283–304).

73   Just a few days prior to this interview, Hartmut Lutz had been talking on the phone with Neil Diamond in the hope of doing an interview with him for this book, but the filmmaker was just on his way to the former Yugoslavia to film locations used in the DEFA *Indianerfilme* with Gojko Mitic, whom he was hoping to interview for a film based on him.

74   In "signing his/her own health" (*sich selbst gesund schreiben*), a patient, without the doctor's consent, declares herself or himself healthy and fit again. Here it means that Germans, not wanting to acknowledge their involvement in Nazism and the Holocaust, will absolve themselves and declare themselves guilt-free, regardless of international opinion.

75   Lischke and McNab (2005).

76   Louise Erdrich is one of the most prominent Native American authors today. In several of her many novels she addresses her Anishinaabe and German ancestry – for example, in *Love Medicine* (1984, 2009), *The Beet Queen* (2006), *The Master Butcher's Singing Club* (2005), and *The Antelope Wife* (2012).

77   Renae Watchman calls them Powwowthusiasts.

78   A long-term Canadianist, educator, and literary scholar, Professor Emeritus Dr. Albert-Reiner Glaap was the most influential academic in Germany specializing in Canadian theatre. He introduced Indigenous playwrights to German academia, inviting some of them to Germany for performances and speaking tours – for example, Yvette Nolan, Tomson Highway, and Drew Hayden Taylor.

79   Drew Hayden Taylor's *Toronto at Dreamer's Rock and Education Is Our Right: Two One-Act Plays* (1990) was edited in 1995 for use in German high schools by Albert-Reiner Glaap in his TAGS-series (Theme Author Genre Similarity).

80   Taylor, ed. (2008).

81   Taylor, *The Berlin Blues*.

82   Taylor (2006).

83   Playing on the German beer-drinking stereotype, the name "Birgit" is readily misunderstood and mispronounced as "beer gut" in *The Berlin Blues*.

84 Birgit Däwes, a professor at the University of Flensburg since 2015, has taught Indigenous literatures at the Universities of Mainz in Germany and Vienna in Austria. She is a leading expert in Europe on North American Indigenous literatures. In 2007, based on her extensive PhD thesis, she published the most substantial existing study of contemporary Native drama, including works by both American and Canadian Aboriginal playwrights: Birgit Däwes, *Native American Theatre in a Global Age.*

85 This is a reference to what Drew Hayden Taylor wrote about in the introduction, "Pretty Like a White Boy," to his 1996 collection of essays, *Funny, You Don't Look Like One: Observations from a Blue-Eyed Ojibway*: "I've spent too many years explaining who and what I am repeatedly, so as of this moment, I officially secede from both races. I plan to start my own separate nation. Because I am half Ojibway, and half Caucasian, we will be called the Occasions. And of course, since I am founding the new nation, I will be a Special Occasion" (14).

86 In August 1911, Ishi, "the last Yahi," came out of hiding from settler contact in Oroville, northern California. Near starvation, he had to give up his solitary self-concealment. He entered modern life in urban San Francisco, where he spent his remaining years until March 1916 as a curator in the Museum of Anthropology on the University of California campus, employed by anthropologist A.L. Kroeber. See Kroeber (1961); and Heizer and Kroeber, eds. (1979).

87 A student of the pioneering American anthropologist Franz Boas, A.L. Kroeber became a university professor and museum director in San Francisco and wrote the first standard *Handbook of the Indians of California* (New York: Dover, n.d.), which was first published by the Smithsonian Institution in 1925. His second wife, Theodora, later wrote books about Ishi (see above). Their daughter Ursula K. Le Guin became one of America's foremost science fiction writers and is notable for sensitively addressing issues of intercultural relations in her novels.

88 Henck 2014, pp. 212–27.

89 Taylor (1996).

90 Taylor (1998).

91 British playwright Willy Russel's two-act play *Educating Rita* (1980) is very popular as a school text in English-language classes in German high schools, and quite a number of school editions and interpretative guides are available.

92 An award-winning one-act play by Russell, which premiered in Liverpool in 1998.

93 After his military successes in the American Civil War, General George Armstrong Custer tried to make a name for himself as an "Indian fighter," but it was not until his utter defeat and death at the Little Big Horn River (Montana) on 25 June 1876, when he and his 7th Cavalry were wiped out by the joint forces of the Lakota, Cheyenne, Assiniboine, and their allies, into whose huge camp he had foolishly charged, that his name became associated with (Native) American history.

94 Sitting Bull (Tatanka Yotanka, 1831?–1890), the Hunkpapa Lakota holy man, and Crazy Horse (Tashunka Witco, 1842?–1877), the Oglala-Brulé Lakota strategist, were both involved in the destruction of Custer's force. Today they are probably the best known and most revered Lakota historical personalities.

95 In my analysis of *indians* in American popular culture and literature and German popular culture and children's literature, the Apache and the Sioux were statistically the most frequently mentioned nations, and among American and German schoolchildren sampled, they were listed as the best-known "Indian tribes" on both sides of the Atlantic. See Lutz (1985, pp. 451, 462).

96 Chamberlin (2004).

97 Taylor (2006).

98 Taylor (2011).

99 Taylor (2002).

100 Taylor (1991).

101 King (2005, pp. 169–86).

102 *Coyote. Indianische Gegenwart: Entwicklungen, Hintergründe, Engagment* is a magazine published by the organization: Aktionsgruppe Indianer & Menschenrechte, e.V. (http://www.aktionsgruppe.de/).

103 Probably the first German writer to deal with the homoerotic appeal of Karl May's novels was the immensely creative and somewhat eccentric German author Arno Schmidt, whose painstakingly detailed, erudite, and satirically funny book *Sitara und der Weg dorthin* (1969) is a veritable mock-psychoanalysis – or psycho-anal-ysis – of May's oeuvre. Schmidt pokes fun at May's moral contortions and, at the same time, at conventional literary scholarship and Freudian theories.

104 Carlos Castaneda was an American anthropologist who in the sixties claimed in his books to have been initiated by a Yaqui spiritual guide named Juan. His books were, at first, widely read and accepted, not only in hippie and New Age circles, but also by academics (e.g., Jack D. Forbes); others, though, rejected him as a fraud. Since Castaneda never produced evidence to substantiate the experiences he described in his books, he gradually declined in popularity and is now generally seen to be what skeptics had regarded him as from the very start.

105 Drew Hayden Taylor did go to Germany eventually with a film crew to shoot a film about Karl May's legacy and German Indianthusiasm. During this trip in the summer of 2017 he also visited the open-air Karl May performance at Bad Segeberg in northern Germany, which left him almost stunned by its professionalism and unabashed stereotyping. The result of his visit is a funny yet respectful documentary, which aired in Canada on CBC: *Looking for Winnetou* (2017).

106 Highway (1988).

107 In her most anthologized short story, "Compatriots" (1987), Emma Lee Warrior has a fictitious German character, a student by the name of Hilda Afflerbach, who is visiting the Peigan Reserve in Alberta. While there she encounters Aboriginal people who do not fit her stereotypical notions about *Indianer*, but she also meets one character, Helmut Walking Eagle, who is of German origin but has turned into a "traditional *indian*" and is ostensibly living a lifestyle that meets Hilda's romantic expectations. In a later, unpublished short story (which has since disappeared), Warrior has Hilda meet a Cree medicine woman who exploits her naive Indianthusiasm. In a more recent short story, "The Powwow Committee" (2003), Warrior deals with the question of whether a Blackfoot reservation should admit non-Aboriginal competitors from Europe, especially Germans, to their annual powwow.

108 Adolf Hungry Wolf is a German man, Adolph Gutöhrlein (born in 1944) who has immersed himself in First Nations culture and adopted the surname Hungry Wolf. He is married to Beverly Hungry Wolf, née Little Bear, from the Blood Indian Reserve in Alberta. Both have published on First Nations culture, experience, and history.

109 Warrior (2003, pp. 201–16).

110 Dr. Kerstin Knopf was then an assistant professor at the University of Greifswald and is now a professor at the University of Bremen. After the conference that Emma Lee Warrior attended, we went on a day excursion to the island of Rügen and its famous white cliffs.

111 Warrior (2009, pp. 182–89).

112 "'I can't wait to go to the sun-dance! Do you go to them often?' Hilda asked Lucy.

  'No, I never have. I don't know much about them,' Lucy said.

  'But why? Don't you believe in it? It's your culture!' Hilda's face showed concern.

'Well, they never had sun-dances here; in my whole life there's never been a sun-dance here.

'No, I don't care to go. It's mostly those mixed-up people who are in it. You see, Indian religion just came back here on the reserve a little while ago, and there are different groups who all quarrel over which ways to practise it. Some use Sioux ways, and others use Cree. It's just a big mess,' she said, shaking her head.

Hilda looked at Lucy, and Lucy got the feeling she was telling her things she didn't want to hear."

(Warrior [1998]).

113 The hardcover version of *Germans and Indians* has a bright-red cloth binding. The book also contains Warrior's famous "Compatriots" (pp. 15–23). See Calloway, Gemünden, and Zantop, eds. (2002).

Afterword

1 Things are shifting. A simple Google search will expose many of these rules being broken by journalists, writers, and filmmakers, who have either infiltrated these *indian* villages and camps or have been granted permission to use their technology in them.

2 See for example, Monkman's changing exhibit *The Atelier* (2011) and *Two Kindred Spirits* (2012).

3 Andrew Nunes, "Kent Monkman's Massive Renaissance-style Paintings Upend Colonial Narratives," *Vice*, 6 April 2017: https://www.vice.com/en_us/article/ezwepp/ kent-monkman-massive-renaissance-style-paintings-colonial-narratives.

4 http://www.forgetwinnetou.com.

5 See Watchman, "Afterword," in Mackay and Stirrup, eds., *Tribal Fantasies* (2013, pp. 211–25).

BIBLIOGRAPHY

Absolon, Kathleen E. 2011. *Kaandossiwin: How We Come to Know.* Fernwood Books.

Akwesasne Notes. 1974. *Voices from Wounded Knee, 1973, in the Words of the Participants.* Akwesasne Notes.

Alfred, Taiaiake, and Jeff Corntassel. 2005. "Being Indigenous: Resurgences against Contemporary Colonialism." *Government & Opposition* 40, no. 4, pp. 597–614.

Andersen, Chris, and Jean M. O'Brien. 2017. *Sources and Methods in Indigenous Studies.* Routledge.

Angeconeb, Ahmoo. 1987. *Ahneesheenahpay Still Life.* Thunder Bay Art Gallery.

———. 2001. *The healing and returning home series.* Thunder Bay Art Gallery, 10 August to 23 September.

Archibald, Jo-anne. 2001. Editorial: "Sharing Aboriginal Knowledge and Aboriginal Ways of Knowing." *Canadian Journal of Native Education* 25, no. 1, pp. 1–5.

———. 2008. *Indigenous Storywork: Educating the Heart, Mind, Body, and Spirit.* UBC Press.

Armstrong, Jeannette. 1985. *Slash.* Theytus Books.

———. 1997. *Slash.* trans. Audrey Huntley. "Nachwort" by Hartmut Lutz. Unrast Verlag.

———. 2009. *Constructing Indigeneity: Syilx Okanagan Oraliture and tmixʷcentrism.* PhD diss., University of Greifswald. http://ub-ed.ub.uni-greifswald.de/opus/volltexte/2012/1322.

Ashcroft, Bill, Gareth Griffiths, and Helen Tiffin. 1989. *The Empire Writes Back: Theory and Practice in Post-Colonial Literatures.* Routledge.

Atleo, Richard (Umeek). 2004. *Tsawalk: A Nuu-chah-nulth Worldview.* UBC Press.

———. 2011. *Principles of Tsawalk: An Indigenous Approach to Global Crisis.* UBC Press.

Barnett, Louise K. 1975. *The Ignoble Savage: American Literary Racism 1790–1890.* Greenwood Press.

Basso, Keith. 1996, *Wisdom Sits in Places: Landscape and Language among the Western Apache.* University of New Mexico Press.

Bataille, Gretchen M., and Charles L. P. Silet, eds. 1980. *The Pretend Indians: Images of Native Americans in the Movies.* Iowa State University Press.

Battiste, Marie, and James Henderson Youngblood. 2000. *Protecting Indigenous Knowledge and Heritage.* Purich Publishing.

Berkhofer, Robert F. 1978. *The White Man's Indian.* Random House.

Billington, Ray Allen. 1981. *Land of Savagery – Land of Promise: The European Image of the American Frontier in the Nineteenth Century.* University of Oklahoma Press.

Blackbird, John, dir. 2005. *Powwow*. First Nations Films.

Black Elk. 1932. *Black Elk Speaks: Being the Life Story of a Holy Man of the Oglala Sioux,* as told through John G. Neihardt. Washington Square Press, 1972.

——. 1953. *The Sacred Pipe: Black Elk's Account of the Seven Rites of the Oglala Sioux,* recorded and edited by John Epes Brown. Penguin Books, 1971.

Brandt-Castellano, Marlene. 2004. "Ethics of Aboriginal Research." *Journal of Aboriginal Health* 1, no. 2, pp. 98–114.

Briese, Marco. 2005. *Kolumbus' letzter Raubzug: Die Opferung der Lakota. Soziale und politische Folgen der Indianerrezeption des New Age.* Mediengruppe König.

Brooks, Lisa. 2008. *The Common Pot: The Recovery of Native Space in the Northeast.* University of Minnesota Press.

Buendía, Edward. 2003. "Fashioning Research Stories: The Metaphoric and Narrative Structure of Writing Research about Race." *Interrogating Racism in Qualitative Research Methodology* 195, pp. 49–69.

Cajete, Gregory. 1995. *Native Science: Natural Laws of Interdependence.* Clear Light Publishers.

Calloway, Colin G., Gerd Gemünden, and Susanne Zantop, eds. 2002. *Germans and Indians: Fantasies, Encounters, Projections.* University of Nebraska Press.

Cariou, Warren. 2002. *Lake of the Prairies: A Story of Belonging.* Doubleday Canada.

——. "Going to Canada." 2009a. *Across Cultures / Across Borders: Canadian Aboriginal and Native American Literature,* edited by Paul DePasquale and Renate Eigenbrod. Broadview Press, pp. 17–24.

Cariou, Warren, and Neil McArthur, dirs. 2009b. *Land of Oil and Water* and *Overburden.* Documentary films. Winnipeg Film Group,

Carlson, John. 2018. "Manoomin Is Not Wild Rice: An Anishinaabeg Treaty." *Indigenous Knowledges and Academic Discourses,* edited by Kerstin Knopf. *Zeitschrift für Kanada-Studien* 38, no. 1, pp. 37–65.

Castellano, Marlene Brant. 2004. "Ethics of Aboriginal Research." *Journal of Aboriginal Health.* University of Toronto 1, no. 1, pp. 98–114.

Chamberlin, J. Edward. 2004. *If This Is Your Land, Where Are Your Stories? Finding Common Ground.* Alfred A. Knopf.

Chrystos. 1988. *Not Vanishing.* Press Gang Publishers.

——. 1991. *Dream On.* Press Gang Publishers.

——. 1993. *In Her I Am.* Press Gang Publishers.

——. 1997. *Wilder Reis.* Transl. Audrey Huntley. Orlanda Frauenverlag.

Churchill, Ward. 2001. *Fantasies of the Master Race: Literature, Cinema, and the Colonization of American Indians.* City Lights.

Cole, Peter. 2002. "Aboriginalizing Methodology: Considering the Canoe." *International Journal of Qualitative Studies in Education* 15, no. 4, pp. 447–59.

Coleman, Daniel. 2005. *In Bed with the Word: Reading, Spirituality, and Cultural Politics.* University of Alberta Press.

Colin, Susi. 1988. *Das Bild des Indianers im 16. Jahrhundert.* Idstein. Schulz-Kirchner Verlag.

Cornell, George L. 1985. "The Influence of Native Americans on Modern Conservationists." *Environmental Review* 9, no. 2, pp. 104–17.

Corntassel, Jeff. 2012. "Re-envisioning Resurgence: Indigenous Pathways to Decolonization and Sustainable Self-Determination." *Decolonization: Indigeneity, Education & Society* 1, no. 1, pp. 86–101.

Däwes, Birgit. 2007. *Native North American Theater in the Global Age: Sites of Identity Construction and Transdifference*. American Studies Ser. 147, Universitätsverlag Winter.

Deloria, Vine, Jr. 1969. *Custer Died for Your Sins. An Indian Manifesto*. Macmillan.

———. 1973. *We Talk – You Listen: New Tribes, New Turf*. Delta Books.

Deloria, Philip. 1998. *Playing Indian*. Yale University Press.

———. 2004. *Indians in Unexpected Places*. University Press of Kansas.

Drawson, Alexandra S., Elaine Toombs, and Christopher J. Mushquash. 2017. "Indigenous Research Methods: A Systematic Review." *International Indigenous Policy Journal* 8, no. 2, pp. 1–27.

Dürr, Hans-Peter, ed. 2012. *Physik und Transzendenz: Die großen Physiker unserer Zeit über ihre Begegnung mit dem Wunderbaren*. Driediger Verlag.

Engels, Friedrich. 1971. *Der Ursprung der Familie, des Privateigentums und des Staats* (1884). Dietz Verlag.

Episkenew, Jo-Ann. 2006. "Beyond Catharsis: Truth, Conciliation, and Healing In and Through Indigenous Literature." Diss. phil. U Greifswald.

———. 2009. *Taking Back Our Spirits: Indigenous Literature, Public Policy, and Healing*. University of Manitoba Press.

Erdrich, Louise. 1984/2009. *Love Medicine*. Holt, Rinehart, and Winston.

———. 1986. *The Beet Queen*. Holt, Rinehart, and Winston.

———. 2005. *The Master Butcher's Singing Club*. HarperCollins.

———. 2012. *The Antelope Wife*. Harper Perennial.

Ermine, Willie. 2000. "Aboriginal Epistemology." Marie Battiste and J. Barman (Eds.). *First Nation Education in Canada. The Circle Unfolds*. UBC Press, pp. 101–11.

———. 2007. "The Ethical Space of Engagement." *Indigenous Law Journal* 6, no. 1, pp. 193–203.

Feest, Christian, ed. 1989. *Indians and Europe: An Interdisciplinary Collection of Essays*. University of Nebraska Press.

Fiedler, Leslie. 1968. *The Return of the Vanishing American*. New York: Stein and Day.

Fitz, Karsten, ed. 2001. *Visual Representations of Native Americans: Transnational Contexts and Perspectives*. Regensburger Arbeiten zur Anglistik und Amerikanistik 43. Lang.

Foerster, Heinz von, and Christiane Floyd. 2004. "Systemik oder: Zusammenhänge sehen." *Die andere Intelligenz: Wie wir morgen denken werden*, edited by Bernhard von Mutius. Klett-Kotta, pp. 57–74.

Francis, Daniel. 1992. *The Imaginary Indian: The Image of the Indian in Canadian Culture*. Arsenal Pulp Press.

Friar, Ralph, and Natasha Friar. 1972. *The Only Good Indian: The Hollywood Gospel*. Drama Book Specialists/Publishers.

Gasyuk, Lisa. 2016. "Personal Myth of Joseph Beuys: Between Social and Spiritual." *Usisio* 24, July.

Gaudry, Adam, and Danielle Lorenz. 2018. "Indigenization as Inclusion, Reconciliation, and Decolonization: Navigating the Different Visions for Indigenizing the Canadian Academy." *AlterNative: An International Journal of Indigenous Peoples* 4, no. 3, pp. 218–27.

Gemünden, Gerd. 2002. "Between Karl May and Karl Marx: The DEFA Indianerfilme." *Germans and Indians: Fantasies, Encounters, Projections*, edited by Colin G. Calloway et al., pp. 243–56. University of Nebraska Press.

Gross, Konrad. 2011. "Traditional Ecological Knowledge and the Image of the Green Aboriginal." *North America in the 21st Century: Tribal, Local, and Global – Festschrift für Hartmut Lutz,* edited by Kerstin Knopf. Wissenschaftlicher Verlag Trier, pp. 131–44.

Gruber, Eva. 2008. *Humor in Contemporary Native North American Literature: Reimagining Nativeness.* Camden House.

Haible, Barbara. 1998. *Indianer im Dienste der NS-Ideologie: Untersuchungen zur Funktion von Jugendbüchern über nordamerikanische Indianer im Nationalsozialismus.* Verlag Dr. Kovač.

Haircrow, Red. 2013. "Germany's Obsession with American Indians Is Touching – And Occasionally Surreal." *Indian Country Today,* 24 March. https://indian countrymedianetwork.com/news/indigenous-peoples/germanys-obsession-with -american-indians-is-touchingand-occasionally-surreal.

Haircrow, Red, director. 2018. *Forget Winnetou! Loving in the Wrong Way.* Documentary.

Hassrick. Peter H., et al. 1981. *Buffalo Bill and the Wild West.* Brooklyn Museum.

Heizer, Robert F., and Theodora Kroeber, eds. 1979. *Ishi The Last Yahi: A Documentary History.* University of California Press.

Henck, Maryann . 2014. "Identity Joyriding with the Trickster in Drew Hayden Taylor's *Motorcycles & Sweetgrass.*" *Fake Identity? The Impostor in North American Culture,* edited by Caroline Rosenthal and Stefanie Schäfer. Campus Verlag, pp. 212–27.

Highway, Tomson. 1988. *The Rez Sisters.* Fifth House, 1988.

Holley, Linda. 2007. *Tipis, Tepees, Tipis: History and Design of the Cloth Tipi.* Gibbs Smith.

Huhndorf, Shari. 2001. *Going Native: Indians in the American Cultural Imagination.* Cornell University Press.

Huntley, Audrey. 1996. *Widerstand schreiben! Entkolonialisierungsprozesse im Schreiben indigener kanadischer Frauen.* Unrast Verlag.

Isernhagen, Hartwig. 1999. *Momaday, Vizenor, Armstrong: Conversations on American Indian Writing.* University of Oklahoma Press.

Janssen, Jessica. 2018. "L'autohistoire amérindienne: une method pour conciliar les saviors autochthones et le discours scientifique (de l'histoire) au Québec." *Indigeneous Knowledges and Academic Discourses,* edited by Kerstin Knopf. Thematic Issue. *Zeitschrift für Kanada-Studien* 38, no. 1, pp. 156–75.

Keeshig-Tobias. Lenore. 1990. "Stop Stealing Native Stories." *Globe and Mail,* January 26.

Keh, Andrew. 2018. "Tomahawk Chops and Native American Mascots: In Europe, teams don't see a problem." *New York Times,* online edition, May 7, https://www.nytimes .com/2018/05/07/sports/native-american-mascots-europe.html.

King, Thomas. 1991. "Thomas King" (interview). *Contemporary Challenges: Conversations with Canadian Native Authors,* edited by Hartmut Lutz. Fifth House, pp. 107–16.

———. 1999. *Truth and Bright Water.* Harper Flamingo Canada.

———. 2005. "Performing Native Humour: The Dead Dog Café Comedy Hour." In *Me Funny,* comp. and ed. Drew Hayden Taylor. Douglas & McIntyre, pp. 169–86.

———. 2012. *The Inconvenient Indian: A Curious Account of Native People in North America.* Random House/Doubleday Canada.

Klooss, Wolfgang. 1989. *Geschichte und Mythos in der Literatur Kanadas: Die englischsprachige Métis und Riel-Rezeption.* Carl Winter Universitätsverlag.

Klotz, Marcia. 2005. "The Weimar Republic: A Postcolonial State in a Still-Colonial World." In *Germany's Colonial Pasts,* edited by Eric Ames et al. University of Nebraska Press, pp. 135–47.

Knopf, Kerstin. 2008a. *Decolonizing the Lens of Power: Indigenous Films in North America.* Rodopi.

———. 2012. *The Female Canadian Gothic: Nineteenth-Century Women's Literature at the Interface between Romance and Horror.* Habilitationsschrift. Greifswald University.

———. 2015. "The Turn Toward the Indigenous Knowledge Systems and Practices in the Academy." *Amerikastudien/American Studies* 60, nos. 2–3, pp. 293–329.

Knopf. Kerstin, ed. 2008b. *Aboriginal Canada Revisited.* University of Ottawa Press.

———. 2011. *North America in the 21st Century.* Festschrift für Hartmut Lutz. Wissenschaftlicher Verlag Trier.

———, ed. 2018. *Indigenous Knowledges and Academic Discourses.* Thematic Issue. *Zeitschrift für Kanada-Studien* 67, no. 1.

Kort, Pamela, and Max Hollein, eds. 2006. *I Like Amerika: Fiktionen des Wilden Westens.* Schirn Kunsthalle Frankfurt. Pretel Verlag.

Kovach, Margaret. 2009. *Indigenous Methodologies: Characteristics, Conversations, and Contexts.* University of Toronto Press.

———. 2019. "Conversational Method in Indigenous Research." *Special Issue: Celebrating 15 Years of Wisdom. First Peoples Child & Family Review* 14, no. 1, pp. 123–36.

Kroeber, Theodora. 1961. *Ishi in Two Worlds: A Biography of the Last Wild Indian in North America.* Foreword by Lewis Gannett. University of California Press.

Kuokkanen, Rauna. 2007. *Reshaping the University: Responsibility, Indigenous Epistemes, and the Logic of the Gift.* UBC Press.

Kurtz, Donna L.M. 2013. "Indigenous Methodologies: Traversing Indigenous and Western Worldviews in Research." *AlterNative: An International Journal of Indigenous Peoples* 9, no. 3, pp. 217–29.

Lischke, Ute, and David T. McNab, eds. 2005. *Walking a Tightrope: Aboriginal People and Their Representations.* Wilfrid Laurier University Press.

Lorde, Audre. 1993. *Poetry Is Not a Luxury / Lyrik ist kein Luxus,* ed. and trans. Sigrid Markmann and Petra Oerke. *OBEMA*-Sonderband. Druck- & Verlagscooperative.

Lutz, Hartmut. 1975. *William Goldings Prosawerk im Lichte der Analytischen Psychologie Carl Gustav Jungs und der Psychoanalyse Sigmund Freuds.* Wissenschaftliche Verlagsgesellschaft Athenaion.

———. 1985. *"Indianer" und "Native Americans": Zur sozial- und literarhistorischen Vermittlung eines Stereotyps.* Georg Olms Verlag.

———. 1997. "Nachwort." In *Slash* by Jeannette Armstrong, trans. Audrey Huntley. Unrast Verlag, pp. 231–39.

———. 2002. *Approaches: Essays in Native North American Studies and Literatures.* Wissner.

———. 2003a. "German Indianthusiasm: A Socially Constructed German National(ist) Myth." *Germans and Indians: Fantasies, Encounters, Projections,* edited by Colin G. Calloway et al. University of Nebraska Press, 2003, pp. 167–84.

———. 2003b. "'Okay, I'll be their annual Indian for next summer' – Thoughts on the Marketing of a Canadian Indian Icon in Germany." *Imaginary (Re-)Locations: Tradition, Modernity, and the Market in Contemporary Native American Literature and Culture,* edited by Helmbrecht Breinig. Stauffenburg Verlag, pp. 217–45.

———. 2014. "'Writing Back,' 'Writing Home,' and 'Writing Beyond?': Native Literature in Canada Today." *Despite Harper: International Perceptions of Canadian Literature and Culture*, edited by Weronika Suchacka et al. Verlag Dr. Kovač, pp. 153–61.

———. 2015. *Contemporary Achievements: Contextualizing Canadian Aboriginal Literatures*. Wissner Verlag.

———: 2018. "'They Talk, We Listen': Indigenous Knowledges and Western Discourse." *Indigenous Knowledges and Academic Discourses*, edited by Kerstin Knopf, Thematic Issue. *Zeitschrift für Kanada-Studien* 67, no. 1, pp. 66–88.

Lutz, Hartmut, author and ed. 1991. *Contemporary Challenges: Conversations with Canadian Native Authors*. Fifth House.

Lutz, Hartmut, and Osnabrück students, trans. and eds. 1992. *Four Feathers: Poems and Stories by Canadian Native Authors / Vier Federn: Gedichte und Geschichten kanadischer Indianer/innen und Métis*. Illustrations by Ahmoo Angeconeb. *OBEMA* (Osnabrück Bilingual Editions of Minority Authors) no. 7. Druck- und Verlagscooperative, 1993, 2nd ed.

Lutz, Hartmut, and Greifswald students, trans. and eds. 2005. *The Diary of Abraham Ulrikab: Text and Context*. Foreword by Alootook Ipellie. Photos by Hans-Ludwig Blohm. University of Ottawa Press.

———. 2009. *Heute sind wir hier / We Are Here today: A Bilingual Collection of Contemporary Aboriginal Literature(s) from Canada*. Illustrations by Ahmoo Angeconeb and Bob Boyer, vdL-Verlag.

Mackenthun, Gesa, and Klaus Hock. 2012. "Introduction: Entangled Knowledge, Scientific Discourse, and Cultural Difference." In *Entangled Knowledge: Scientific Discourses and Cultural Difference*, edited by Klaus Hock and Gesa Machenthun. Waxmann, pp. 7–27.

Marten, Karen, and Booran Mirraboopa. 2009. "Ways of Knowing, Being, and Doing: A Theoretical Framework and Methods for Indigenous and Indigenist Re-search." *Journal of Australian Studies* 27, no. 76 (2003), pp. 203–14.

May, Karl. 1989. *Winnetou*, trans. David Koblick. Washington State University Press.

Medicine, Bea, and Liucija Basauskas. 1999. *Seeking the Spirit: Plains Indians in Russia*. Documentary Educational Resources.

Mitscherlich, Alexander, and Margarete Mitscherlich. 1967. *Die Unfähigkeit zu trauern. Grundlagen kollektiven Verhaltens*. R. Piper & Co.

Mutius, Bernhard von. 2008. "Die andere Intelligenz oder: Muster die verbinden. Eine Skizze." In *Die andere Intelligenz: Wie wir morgen denken werden*, edited by Bernhard von Mutius. Klett-Cotta, pp. 12–41.

Obomsawin, Alanis, dir. 1993. *Kanehsatake: 270 Years of Resistance*. National Film Board of Canada.

Ott, Konrad. 2011. "Beyond Beauty." In *North America in the 21st Century: Tribal, Local, Global*, edited by Kerstin Knopf. Festschrift für Hartmut Lutz. Wissenschaftlicher Verlag Trier, pp. 119–29.

Pagden, Anthony. 1998. *European Encounters with the New World*. Yale University Press.

Paskievich, John, dir. 1995. *If Only I Were an Indian*. National Film Board of Canada.

Penny, Glen H. 2006. "Elusive Authenticity: The Quest for the Authentic Indian in German Public Culture." *Comparative Studies in Society and History* 48, no. 4, pp. 798–818.

———. 2013. *Kindred by Choice: Germans and American Indians since 1800*. University of North Carolina Press.

———. 2014. "Not Playing Indian: Surrogate Indigeneity and the German Hobbyist Scene." In *Performing Indigeneity: Global Histories and Contemporary Experiences*, edited by Laura R. Graham and H. Glenn Penny. University of Nebraska Press, pp. 169–205.

Peyer, Bernd. 1997. *The Tutor'd Mind: Indian Missionary-writers in Antebellum America*. University of Massachusetts Press.

Reagin, Nancy. 2012. "Dances with Worlds: Karl May, 'Indian' hobbyists, and German fans of the American West since 1912." *Participation: Journal of Audience & Reception Studies* 13, no. 1, pp. 553–83.

Renner, Bettina. 2012. *Bury My Heart in Dresden*. Deckert.

Robinson, Eden. 2000. *Monkey Beach*. Alfred A. Knopf / Random House of Canada,

Runnels, Dennis. 2001. "The past is right before us." Personal information given to Hartmut Lutz. Dartmouth College, Hanover, New Hampshire, September.

Saldívar, José David. 1991. *The Dialectics of Our America: Genealogy, Cultural Critique, and Literary History*. Duke University Press.

Sam, Marlowe. 1996. "Taking on the War Today." In *Standing Ground: Strength and Solidarity amidst Dissolving Borders: Gathering VII*, edited by Kateri Akiwenzie-Damm and Jeannette Armstrong. Theytus Books, pp. 11–13.

———. 1996. "Den Krieg heute aufnehmen." In *Slash*, by Jeannette Armstrong, trans. Audrey Huntley. Unrast Verlag. pp. 241–44.

Sarkowsky, Katja. 2018. "'This is why I'm remembering': Narrative Agency and Autobiographical Knowledge in Maria Campbell's *Halfbreed* and Joy Harjo's *Crazy Brave*." In *Indigenous Knowledges and Academic Discourses*, edited by Kerstin Knopf, Thematic Issue, *Zeitschrift für Kanada-Studien* 38, no. 1, pp. 176–96.

Schmidt, Arno. 1969. *Sitara und der Weg dorthin: Eine Studie über Wesen, Werk & Wirkung Karl Mays*. Fischer Bücherei.

Sieg, Katrin. 2002a. *Ethnic Drag*. University of Michigan Press.

———. 2002b. "Indian Impersonation as Historical Surrogation." In *Germans and Indians: Fantasies, Encounters, Projections*, ed. Colin G. Calloway et al. University of Nebraska Press, pp. 217–42.

Smith, Donald B. 2014. *Mississauga Portraits: Ojibwe Voices from Nineteenth-Century Canada*. University of Toronto Press.

Smith, Graham Hingangaroa, and Linda Tuhiwai Smith. 2018. "Doing Indigenous Work: Decolonizing and Transforming the Academy." In *Handbook of Indigenous Education*, January, pp. 1–27.

Smith, Linda Tuhiwai. 2012. *Decolonizing Methodologies: Research and Indigenous Peoples*. Zed Books, 2nd ed.

Strzelczyk, Florentine. 2014. "'Fight against Manitou' – German Identity and Ilse Schreiber's Canada Novels." In *Sophie Discovers America: German-Speaking Women Write the New World*, edited by Michelle James and Rob McFarland. Camden House, pp. 347–70.

———. 2012. "Vom Osten in den Westen: Fiktionale Raumstörungen in Ilse Schreibers Kanadaromanen." In *Störungen im Raum – Raum der Störungen*, edited by Carsten Gansel and Pawel Zimniak. Universitätsverlag Winter, pp. 197–220.

Taylor, Drew Hayden. 1990. *Toronto at Dreamer's Rock and Education Is Our Right: Two One-Act Plays/* Fifth House Publishers.

———. 1991. *The Bootlegger Blues*. Fifth House.

———. 1995. *Toronto at Dreamer's Rock: Handreichungen für den Unterricht*, ed. Albert-Reiner Glaap. TAGS: Theme Author Genre Similarity. Cornelsen.

———. 1996. *Funny, You Don't Look Like One: Observations from a Blue-Eyed Ojibway*. Theytus Books.

———. 1998. *Only Drunks and Indians Tell the Truth*. Introduction by Lee Maracle. Talonbooks.

———. 2002. *Buz'Gem Blues*. Talon Books.

———. 2006. *In a World Created by a Drunken God*. Talonbooks.

———. 2007. *The Berlin Blues*. Talonbooks.

———. 2011a. *Motorcycles and Sweetgrass*. Vintage Canada/Random House.

———. 2011b. *God and the Indian*. Talonbooks.

Taylor, Drew Hayden, comp. and ed. 2005. *Me Funny*. Douglas & McIntyre.

Taylor, Drew Hayden, ed. 2008. *Me Sexy: An Exploration of Native Sex and Sexuality*. Douglas and McIntyre.

Taylor, Drew Hayden, dir. 2018. *Searching for Winnetou*. CBC Documentary.

Thompson, Michelle. 2018. *Imagined Stories: Repercussions of (Re)telling Fiction as Fact: An Anthropological Study of Transatlantic Reactions to German Indianthusiasm*. CreateSpace.

Turner Strong, Pauline. "Cultural Appropriation and the Crafting of Racialized Selves in American Youth Organizations: Toward an Ethnographic Approach." *Cultural Studies – Critical Methodologies* 9, no. 2, pp. 197–213.

Turner Strong, Pauline, and Laurie Posner. 2010. "Selves in Play: Sports, Scouts, and American Cultural Citizenship." *International Review for the Sociology of Sport* 45, no. 3, pp. 390–409.

Usbeck, Frank. 2015. *Fellow Tribesmen: The Image of Native Americans, National Identity and Nazi Ideology in Germany*. Berghahn Books.

Vizenor, Gerald. 1998. *Fugitive Poses: Native American Indian Scenes of Absence and Presence*. University of Nebraska Press.

Warrior, Emma Lee. 1998. "Compatriots." *Canadian Fiction Magazine* 60, 1987, pp. 129–137. Also in *All My Relations: An Anthology of Contemporary Canadian Fiction*, edited by Thomas King. McClelland and Stewart, 1990, pp. 48–59. Also in *Anthology of Canadian Native Literature in English*, edited by Daniel David Moses and Terry Goldie, Oxford University Press, 2005, pp. 170–77. Also in *Fremdsprachenunterricht. Zeitschrift für das Lehren und Lernen fremder Sprachen* 42/51, no. 2, pp. 91–94.

———. 2003. "The Powwow Committee." In *Imaginary (Re-)Locations: Tradition, Modernity, and the Market in Contemporary Native American Literature and Culture*, edited by Helmbrecht Breinig. Stauffenburg Verlag, pp. 201–16.

———. 2009. "Magic/Magie," In *We Are Here Today / Heute sind wir hier: A Bilingual Collection of Contemporary Aboriginal Literature(s) from Canada / Eine zweisprachige Sammlung zeitgenössischer indigener Literatur(en) aus Kanada*. Trans. and ed. Hartmut Lutz and Greifswald students, vdL-Verlag, pp. 182–89.

Watchman, Renae. 2005. "Powwow Overseas: The German Experience." In *Powwow*, edited by Clyde Ellis et al. University of Nebraska Press, pp. 241–57.

———. 2013. "Afterword." In *Tribal Fantasies: Native Americans in the European Imaginary, 1900-2010*, edited by James Mackay and David Stirrup. Palgrave Macmillan, pp. 211–25.

Weaver, Jace. 2014. *The Red Atlantic: American Indigenes and the Making of the Modern World, 1000-1927*. University of North Carolina Press.

Weber-Pillwax, Cora. 2001. "What Is Indigenous Research?" *Canadian Journal of Native Education* 25, no. 2, pp. 166–74.

Williamson, Karla Jessen. 2000. "Celestial and Social Families of the Inuit." In *Expressions in Canadian Native Studies,* edited by Ron F. Laliberte et al. University of Saskatchewan Extension Press, pp. 125–44.

Wilson, Shawn. 2001. "What Is an Indigenous Research Methodology?" *Journal of Native Education* 25, no. 2, pp. 175–79.

———. 2008. *Research Is Ceremony: Indigenous Research Methods.* Fernwood.

Wolfe, Alexander. 1988. *Earth Elder Stories: The Pinayzitt Path.* Fifth House, 1988.

York, Geoffrey, and Loreen Pindera. 1991. *People of the Pines: The Warriors and the Legacy of Oka.* Little, Brown.

Younging, Gregory. 2018. *Elements of Indigenous Style: A Guide for Writing by and about Indigenous Peoples.* Brush Education.

Zantop, Susanne. 1997. *Colonial Fantasies: Conquest, Family, and Nations in Pre-Colonial Germany, 1770–1870.* Duke University Press.

Žižek, Slavoj. 1993. *Tarrying with the Negative.* Duke University Press.

INDEX

Aboriginal: ancestry, 76, 163; artist, 38; culture, 64, 91, 167; journalism, 167–68; literature, 45, 47, 79, 80, 98, 107; looks, 81, 99, 106, 109, 120, 164, 176, 177; man, 104; performers, 109–10, 146, 150, 151, 153, 187, 197; perspective, 46; regalia, 90; responses, 9; tradition, 37; spirituality, 113, 200; stereotypes, 75; Studies, 54, 104; as victim, 95; woman, 43, 201; writers, 78–79, 80, 81, 87, 194; writings, 45, 47, 95. *See also* Indigenous; Native

Abraham (Ulrikab), 82

Adams, Howard, 123

AIM (American Indian Movement), 123

Alexie, Sherman, 184–85

Algonquin, 140, 141, 142

Alison. *See* Calder

Anette. *See* Brauer

Angeconeb, Ahmoo Allen, 25, **35–42**, 214–15, 223n3–4

Anishinaabe (*also* Anishnabe, Anishnaabe), 14, 25, 28, 30, 35–36, 38–41, 92, 162, 167, 173, 221n2, 223n1

anthropocentrism, 10, 24

antisemitism, 28, 109, 120, 121, 217

Apache, 4, 13, 15, 182, 208, 209, 229n95

appropriation: as commodification, 119, 129, 197; cultural, 4, 6, 18, 24, 28, 31, 89–90, 116, 117, 118; history of, 12, 215; and hobbyism, 5, 19, 219; of land, 107; as respect, 4; reverse, 38, 211; as silencing, 5; of spirituality, 24, 221n3, 227n55; of voice, 95

Armstrong, Jeannette: **43–56**, 90, 218; on Indigeneity, 11; on listening, 26, 46, 50–51, 54, 213; literary works, 46, 121; PhD research, 20–24, 42, 43–44, 47, 52, 53, 98, 215

Ashcroft, Bill, 24

Assiniboine, Anita, 152, 160

Association for Canadian Studies in the German Speaking Countries. *See* GKS

Auschwitz, 9, 88–89, 225n30

Australia, 100, 122, 177, 181

Austria, 20, 24, 151, 152, 197, 198, 200

authenticity, 16, 128, 159, 222n13

Bad Segeberg (site of Karl May festival), 3, 4, 221n1, 230n105

Banks, Dennis, 123

Basso, Keith, 209

Belgium, 4, 132, 163, 165

Beuys, Joseph, 25, 42

Blackbird, John, 9, 10, 17, 26, **57–73**, 112, 124, 214

Black Elk, 126, 227n55

Blackfoot, 16, 29, 134, 150, 194, 196, 198, 200, 201, 209

Blood, 16, 129, 137, 190, 194, 201, 202

blood-brotherhood, 3, 4

Boy Scout Movement, 17, 18

Boyer, Bob, 25

Brauer, Anette, 94, 107, 108, 112

Briese, Marco, 15, 65

Britain/British, 4, 48, 140, 182, 184, 227–28n66

Bryant, Ed, 152

Buffalo Bill, 14, 151

Books in the Indigenous Studies Series
Published by Wilfrid Laurier University Press

Blockades and Resistance: Studies in Actions of Peace and the Temagami Blockades of 1988–89 / Bruce W. Hodgins, Ute Lischke, and David T. McNab, editors / 2003 / xi + 276 pp. / illus. / ISBN 0-88920-381-4

Indian Country: Essays on Contemporary Native Culture / Gail Guthrie Valaskakis / 2005 / x + 293 pp. / illus. / ISBN 0-88920-479-9

Walking a Tightrope: Aboriginal People and Their Representations / Ute Lischke and David T. McNab, editors / 2005 / xix + 377 pp. / illus. / ISBN 978-0-88920-484-3

The Long Journey of a Forgotten People: Métis Identities and Family Histories / Ute Lischke and David T. McNab, editors / 2007 / viii + 386 pp. / illus. / ISBN 978-0-88920-523-9

Words of the Huron / John L. Steckley / 2007 / xvii + 259 pp. / ISBN 978-0-88920-516-1

Essential Song: Three Decades of Northern Cree Music / Lynn Whidden / 2007 / xvi + 176 pp. / illus., musical examples, audio CD / ISBN 978-0-88920-459-1

From the Iron House: Imprisonment in First Nations Writing / Deena Rymhs / 2008 / ix + 147 pp. / ISBN 978-1-55458-021-7

Lines Drawn upon the Water: First Nations and the Great Lakes Borders and Borderlands / Karl S. Hele, editor / 2008 / xxiii + 351 pp. / illus. / ISBN 978-1-55458-004-0

Troubling Tricksters: Revisioning Critical Conversations / Linda M. Morra and Deanna Reder, editors / 2009 / xii+ 336 pp. / illus. / ISBN 978-1-55458-181-8

Aboriginal Peoples in Canadian Cities: Transformations and Continuities / Heather A. Howard and Craig Proulx, editors / 2011 / viii + 256 pp. / illus. / ISBN 978-1-055458-260-0

Bridging Two Peoples: Chief Peter E. Jones, 1843–1909 / Allan Sherwin / 2012 / xxiv + 246 pp. / illus. / ISBN 978-1-55458-633-2

The Nature of Empires and the Empires of Nature: Indigenous Peoples and the Great Lakes Environment / Karl S. Hele, editor / 2013 / xxii + 350 / illus. / ISBN 978-1-55458-328-7

The Eighteenth-Century Wyandot: A Clan-Based Study / John L. Steckley / 2014 / x + 306 pp. / ISBN 978-1-55458-956-2

Indigenous Poetics in Canada / Neal McLeod, editor / 2014 / xii + 404 pp. / ISBN 978-1-55458-982-1

Literary Land Claims: The "Indian Land Question" from Pontiac's War to Attawapiskat / Margery Fee / 2015 / x + 318 pp. / illus. / ISBN 978-1-77112-119-4

Arts of Engagement: Taking Aesthetic Action In and Beyond Canada's Truth and Reconciliation Commission / Dylan Robinson and Keavy Martin, editors / 2016 / viii + 376 pp. / illus. / ISBN 978-1-77112-169-9

Learn, Teach, Challenge: Approaching Indigenous Literature / Deanna Reder and Linda M. Morra, editors / 2016 / xii + 580 pp. / ISBN 978-1-77112-185-9

Violence Against Indigenous Women: Literature, Activism, Resistance / Allison Hargreaves / 2017 / xv + 282 pp. / ISBN 978-1-77112-239-9

Read, Listen, Tell: Indigenous Stories from Turtle Island / Sophie McCall, Deanna Reder, David Gaertner, and Gabrielle L'Hirondlle Hill, editors / 2017 / xviii + 390 pp. / ISBN 978-1-77112-300-6

The Homing Place: Indigenous and Settler Literary Legacies of the Atlantic / Rachel Bryant / 2017 / xiv + 244 / ISBN 978-1-77112-286-3

Why Indigenous Literatures Matter / Daniel Heath Justice / 2017 / xxii + 284 / ISBN 978-1-77112-176-7

Activating the Heart: Storytelling, Knowledge Sharing, and Relationship / Julia Christensen, Christopher Cox, and Lisa Szabo-Jones, editors / 2018 / xvii + 210 pp. / ISBN 978-1-77112-219-1

Indianthusiasm: Indigenous Responses / Hartmut Lutz, Florentine Strzelczyk, and Renae Watchman, editors / 2019 / x + 252 / ISBN 978-1-77112-399-0